THE INVALIDATING EFFECTS OF FORCE, FEAR, AND FRAUD UPON THE CANONICAL NOVITIATE

A Historical Conspectus
And a Commentary

The Catholic University of America
Canon Law Studies
No. 311

The Invalidating Effects of Force, Fear, and Fraud Upon the Canonical Novitiate

A Historical Conspectus and a Commentary

A DISSERTATION

SUBMITTED TO THE FACULTY OF THE SCHOOL OF CANON LAW OF THE CATHOLIC UNIVERSITY OF AMERICA IN PARTIAL FULFILLMENT OF THE REQUIREMENTS FOR THE DEGREE OF DOCTOR OF CANON LAW

BY

JAMES VICTOR BROWN, O.R.S.A.

Priest of the Province of St. Augustine

The Catholic University of America Press
Washington, D. C.
1951

IMPRIMI POTEST:

Angelus Almarcegui, O.R.S.A.
Prior Provincialis

Omahae, die 1 decembris 1950.

NIHIL OBSTAT:

Hieronymus D. Hannan, A.M., LL.B., S.T.D., J.C.D.
Censor Deputatus

Washingtonii, die 30 januarii 1951.

IMPRIMATUR:

Eugenius F. Vallely, V.G., LL.D.
Administrator Kansanopolitanensis in Kansas

Kansanopolitanae in Kansas, die 8 februarii 1951.

Murray & Heister
Washington, D. C.

Printed by
Times and News Publishing Co
Gettysburg, Pa., U.S.A.

TO MY MOTHER AND FATHER

TABLE OF CONTENTS

TABLE OF CONTENTS (Continued)

PART II

Canonical Commentary

TABLE OF CONTENTS (Continued)

TABLE OF CONTENTS (Continued)

FOREWORD

Ever since the first followers of Our Saviour heard His divine challenge to follow Him in perfection, Christian men and women of each succeeding generation, moved by a thoughtful and constant will and the sustaining help of divine grace, have sought to serve God more perfectly through the practice of the evangelical counsels in the religious state. As Christ Himself presented the acceptance of the duties and obligations of the state of perfection as being of the nature of a counsel and not of a command, so too has the Church shown a constant solicitude, both in its teachings and legislation, that those who embrace the religious state do so as complete masters of their choice.

Freedom of will and full deliberation are demanded for every legal transaction involving the transfer of rights and the acceptance of obligations. The more important the obligations, the more sacred the transaction, so much the greater in proportion must be the liberty of choice and freedom of action of those who embrace them. Since few transactions approach in meaning and in importance the act of entry or acceptance into the religious state, which aims ultimately at binding the human will to the Divine Will, reason alone suggests that no individual should be bound by the obligations of the religious life unless he freely and spontaneously desires to accept them. Hence the Church, in order to surround this choice of the faithful when entering religion with the fullest possible liberty, refuses to sanction as valid a canonical novitiate, entered upon in preparation for the religious profession, whenever consent given to its inception, either on the part of a candidate or on the part of the admitting superior, represents the product of the agencies of force, fear, or fraud.

The present Code of Canon Law, for the first time in general ecclesiastical legislation, extends the invalidating effects of physical violence, grave fear, and deceit to the act of entering the canonical novitiate, as well as to the profession of religious vows. Formerly the law attached to the use of these agencies the effect of invalidity only when they were employed for inducing the consent given to the religious profession itself, and, indeed, that of solemn vows. Hence, in sketching the historical evolution of the diriment impediment of force, fear, and fraud, as it is stated in canon 542, 1°, of the present Code, one must of necessity fall back for the most part upon the sources and theories upon which the legal doctrine concerning the invalidity of the religious profession was formulated, since the present law has in effect likewise made this doctrine applicable to the act of entering the novitiate in the same manner as it was formerly applied to the profession itself.

Finally, it must be observed, the canonical norms which regulate the invalidity of the act of embracing religion under the influence of fraud or duress are identical with those which regulate the invalidity of other juridical acts performed under the influence of these same agencies, especially the contract of matrimony. Closely related, indeed, are the doctrine governing the effects of these influences upon consent given to the marriage contract and the doctrine governing their effects upon entry into religion; this is readily apparent from the fact that canonical writers have constantly referred to the act of entering religion as a type of spiritual matrimony, which is begun by entry into the novitiate, ratified by the religious profession, and consummated through the perfect fulfillment of the rule and the constitutions of the institute embraced. It is little to be wondered at, therefore, that much of the doctrine advanced in this present study has been derived from canonical theory concerning the validity of the contract of matrimony.

Some effort has been made throughout the Commentary to show the legislation of the present Code of Canon Law as the synthesis and the improvement of preceding legislation. An attempt has likewise been made to treat of the practical application of the norms governing the effects of duress and deceit upon this act with relation to particular cases which are either not explicitly touched upon by the common law or which are disputed among authors.

The writer wishes to express his gratitude to the Rev. Gabriel Salinas, O.R.S.A., former Provincial, for the opportunity to pursue advanced studies in Canon Law, and to the Very Rev. Angelus Almarcegui, O.R.S.A., present Provincial of the (American) Province of St. Augustine of the Recollect Augustinian Fathers, for allowing him to continue. He likewise wishes to thank the Faculty of the School of Canon Law of The Catholic University of America for their guidance and direction, the Augustinian Fathers of the Augustinian College, Washington, D. C., for their kind suggestions and assistance, and all others who have in any way, by interest or by active aid, contributed to the preparation of this dissertation.

PART I

Historical Conspectus

CHAPTER I

The Effects of Coercion on Entry Into the Religious State From the Beginning to the Twelfth Century

There is perhaps no practice in the history of the Church which seems more alien to the modern mind than the custom of consecrating children to God's service while they were still in infancy, and of establishing thereby an absolute and perpetual bond between the child and the monastic life. And yet, this custom, in which the element of coercion could so readily be present, continued through almost eight centuries of the Church's history as a legitimately recognized custom, and thence down to the time of the Council of Trent as an abuse. Since the custom of child oblation gave rise to most of the documentary evidence concerning the legal effects of coercion on the act of embracing the religious state during these earlier centuries, the canonical evolution of this impediment shall be sketched upon the framework of the historical evolution of this custom from its inception until the twelfth century.

ARTICLE I. EARLY CHRISTIAN PRACTICE AND THE MONASTIC RULES

A. *Early Background*

The custom of consecrating children to God's service while still in infancy stems, it seems, from the ancient practice in vogue among the Israelites, by whom this act was regarded as one of the greatest piety. The First Book of Kings relates how Samuel, a child of three years, was consecrated by his mother, Anna, to the service of God, and, from the words which she used in this act, it seems that she meant to bind her child's will to God's service during his entire lifetime.[1] During all the centuries the custom of child oblation continued in vogue, its proponents constantly referred to this Old Testament incident both as a prototype and as a scriptural foundation for it.

[1] I Kings, I, 11, 22, 28.

But not only was the high regard which the early Christians entertained for the Old Testament Scriptures responsible for the mentality which gave rise to this custom, for the ancient legal institute of the *patria potestas* of Roman Law, whereby the male head of the family possessed complete power over his offspring of both life and death, also played a major rôle in its development, as is evidenced through the frequent references made to it by those who supported the oblature during all the years it remained in effect. If this Roman concept of parental power did not have a direct influence upon the origin of the Christian custom, at least it formed a definite background for its development.[2]

Side by side with this strange custom, however, the fundamental principle that those who assumed the obligations of the religious state must do so with complete freedom and deliberation was firmly established from the beginning. The Fathers of the Church in their writings constantly insisted upon this point.[3]

B. *The Monastic Rules*

1. The Rule of St. Pachomius

Although St. Anthony of Egypt (251-356) is traditionally hailed as the "Father of Christian Monks," nothing that resembled organized monasticism existed among his eremitical followers in the early fourth century.[4] Strictly considered, monasticism as a cenobitic type of the religious life had its inception in the monasteries founded by St. Pachomius (ca. 292-346) in southern Egypt on the Nile about the year 318. For it was in these monasteries that the common life as it is now known took its form under the monastic "Rule" which St. Pachomius wrote for his followers in Coptic in the year 315.

---

[2] Benedictus XIV, *De Synodo Dioecesana* (4 voll., Mechliniae, 1842), lib. IV, cap. III, nn. 2, 3.

[3] Cf., e.g., S. Hieronymus, *Epistola XXII* (ad Eustochium) . . . *de Custodia Virginitatis*—apud Migne, *Patrologiae Cursus Completus, Series Latina* (221 voll., Parisiis, 1844-1864), XXII, 407 (hereafter cited *MPL*). S. Ambrosius, *Liber Primus de Virginibus*, c. 2—*MPL*, XVI, 206.

[4] Butler, *Benedictine Monachism* (London: Longmans, Green and Co., 1919), p. 12.

In the forty-ninth chapter of this "Rule," St. Pachomius laid down the provisions under which new members were to be admitted into his monasteries. The outline which he there presented is remarkable for the manner in which it respected and protected the complete liberty of those who sought entry into the monastic state. If anyone came to the door of the monastery to seek entry, he was to be left standing there for several days in order that there might thus be tested the spirit with which he came. During that time he was to be taught the Lord's Prayer and the Psalms, while his previous life was subjected to a thorough investigation for the purpose of ascertaining whether he had committed some crime from which he fled, or if he were a slave. Only after this procedure had been complied with, and he was found apt for a life of prayer and willing to leave the world, was it permitted to receive him.[5]

It is apparent from these observations that St. Pachomius was most solicitous lest those who entered his monasteries do so without full deliberation and complete liberty of choice. The influence of these simple provisions of the Pachomian Rule upon the future monastic discipline on this point can scarcely be overexaggerated. Most of the later Rules, as a matter of fact, are so closely modeled upon these provisions of St. Pachomius that at times they even revert to his phraseology.

2. The Rule of St. Basil

St. Basil (330-379), Archbishop of Caesarea in Cappadocia, in about the year 360 drew up two monastic rules for the monks under his care. Both of these rules, commonly referred to as the "Longer Rule" and the "Shorter Rule," contained provisions for the manner in which candidates were to be received into his monasteries. For the most part, these closely follow the ones laid down by St. Pachomius. There was to be the same testing of the spirit, the same investigation of morals, and a period of probation during which the candidate could be accepted or rejected.[6]

---

[5] Martène, *S. Eusebii Hieronymi Translatio Latina Regulae Sancti Pachomii—MPL,* XXIII, 61-86.

[6] *Regulae Fusius Tractatae,* Interrogatio X—Migne, *Patrologiae Cursus Completus, Series Graeca* (161 voll., Parisiis, 1857-1866), XXXI, 943 (hereafter cited *MPG*).

But, over and above these provisions for the admission of adult novices, St. Basil introduced an innovation into his monastic arrangement which sharply departed from that of St. Pachomius, and which was to have a far-reaching influence upon the future history of coercion in the act of embracing the religious life. He thought it right that candidates be received not only after they had reached full maturity, but even from their tenderest years, especially if they had been offered to the monastery by their parents. In support of his view upon this question he quoted the words of Christ, "Suffer little children to come unto me,"[7] and alluded to St. Paul's praise of those who had been educated in the service of God from their youth.[8] It does not seem to have been the intention of St. Basil, however, that these children be bound to the monastic state for life. For, although he spoke of their admission as being a profession, he later stated that once they had reached an age when they were capable of acting with full knowledge and liberty they were to ratify their former action.[9] Hence, although he admitted the principle of child oblation, he understood this in a qualified sense, i.e., that the child oblate should be free to accept or reject the monastic state once he had attained the full use of reason.

3. The Rule of St. Benedict

No piece of monastic legislation wielded a more preponderant influence in shaping the monastic ideals of the Western Church from the eighth to the twelfth centuries than the Rule of St. Benedict of Nursia (ca. 480-550/553), composed on Monte Cassino in the year 529. It was upon the statutes of this Rule that almost all the legislation in the particular councils of the West based their canons on the monastic life.[10]

St. Benedict provided for the admission of both adult novices and

---

[7] Mark, X, 14.

[8] *Regulae Fusius Tractatae,* Interrogatio XV—*MPG,* XXXI, 951.

[9] *Ibidem,* col. 955.

[10] Cf., e.g., Autun (670), can. 15—Mansi, *Sacrorum Conciliorum Nova et Amplissima Collectio* (53 voll. in 60, Parisiis, Leipzig, Arnhem, 1901-1927), XI, 124 (hereafter cited Mansi); Augsburg (743), can. 7—Mansi, XII, 367; Mainz (813), can. 11—Mansi, XIV, 68; Rheims (813), can. 9—Mansi, XIV, 68; Chalon-sur-Saone (813), can. 22—Mansi, XIV, 98.

child oblates into his monasteries. His norms for the reception of adult novices were patterned closely after those already adopted in the earlier monastic rules of both the Eastern and the Western Church, especially that of St. Pachomius.[11] New candidates were not to be granted entrance easily, but rather they were first to be tried through humiliation, and then, if they were found worthy, they were first to be admitted to the guest house of the monastery, and thence into the novitiate. They were to remain under probation for one entire year, with ample time for meditation upon the step they were about to take. During this time the Rule was to be read to the candidate on three occasions, "ut sciat ad quod ingreditur."[12] Hence, St. Benedict, as St. Pachomius, showed himself most solicitous that those who entered his monasteries in an adult age could do so as complete masters of their choice.

When St. Benedict came to treat of the reception of child oblates into his monasteries, however, he took an entirely different view of this custom than that held by any of his predecessors. To him, the act of solemn oblation made by the parents when offering a child to the monastery was not merely a provisional, but a valid and final, profession which needed no subsequent ratification on the part of the child to bind him to the monastic obligations for his entire lifetime.[13] Hildemar (fl. 850), in his commentary on this section of the Benedictine Rule, stated that the solemn ceremony of oblation, so minutely described in the fifty-ninth chapter, bound the child to the three vows of stability, conversion of manners, and obedience, in the same manner as those who made a solemn religious profession at a mature age.[14]

How such a practice could be reconciled with the principle so staunchly defended by all the founders of the monastic life, namely,

---

[11] Cf. *Concordia Regularum Patrum—MPL,* CIII, 702-1380.

[12] Butler, *Sancti Benedicti Regula Monasteriorum* (2. ed., Friburgi Brisgoviae: Herder, 1927), c. LVIII.

[13] Butler, *ibidem,* c. LIX; Deroux, *Les Origines de l'Oblature Bénédictine* (Vienne, 1927), p. 13; Huonder, "Oblati—Oblatae," *Kirchenlexikon* (2. ed., 12 voll. et Index, Freiburg im Breisgau: Herder, 1882-1903), IX, 620; Delatte, *A Commentary on the Rule of St. Benedict* (New York: Benziger, 1921), p. 407.

[14] Schroll, *Benedictine Monasticism as Reflected in the Warnefrid-Hildemar Commentaries on the Rule* (New York: Columbia University Press, 1941), p. 77.

that those who took upon themselves the obligations of this state should do so with complete liberty, is difficult to explain. Yet it was this concept of the juridic binding force of the oblature which remained in vogue during all the following centuries in which Benedictine monasticism flourished so widely throughout the whole of Western Christendom. And it was this portion of the Benedictine monastic rule that set into motion a current of juridic thought upon this point which was to be evidenced in nearly all the legislation produced by the particular councils of the West down to the end of the twelfth century.

ARTICLE II. LEGISLATION FROM ST. BENEDICT TO GRATIAN

The general tenor of the legislation of the Western Church from St. Benedict to Gratian indicates that, although the Benedictine concept of the oblature quite generally prevailed, there was a lack of defined and uniform thought on the actual extent of the obligations this profession, made by the parents themselves as proxies, placed upon the child. Although for the most part the documentary evidence of the councils held in this period reproduced and in a sense crystallized the Benedictine concept of the oblature, there were times when there was a noticeable tendency to revert to the Basilian requirement of subsequent ratification in an apparent attempt to reconcile this practice with the liberty of the child.

A. *Early Papal Letters*

Only one letter of the early Popes dealing with forced entry into the religious state is still extant. Pope Leo I (440-461), in writing to the Bishop of Narbonne in 458 or 459, decided a case in which a young lady had freely elected to enter religion and had later left to marry. The Pontiff charged her to return to the obligations of her vows which she had embraced "*proprio arbitrio et voluntate . . . non coacta . . . sed spontaneo judicio.*"[15] Although it is true

[15] C. 1, C. 20, q. 1 and c. 1, C. 20, q. 3—Jaffé, *Regesta Pontificum Romanorum ab condita Ecclesia ad annum post Christum natum* MCXCVIII (2. ed., correctam et auctam auspiciis Gulielmi Wattenbach curaverunt S. Loewenfeld, F. Kaltenbrunner, P. Ewald, 2 voll., Lipsiae, 1885-1888), n. 544 (hereafter cited Jaffé).

that this early decision did not directly state that forced entry into the religious state produced no obligations, from the Pontiff's insistence upon the fact that the obligations in the case were freely assumed it seems that this was clearly his mind.

B. *Councils of the Sixth and Seventh Centuries*

Five particular councils held during the sixth and seventh centuries took up the question of the child oblate. Two of these were of French origin, three were held in Spain. Of the two French Councils, the one that was held at Orleans (V) in 549 in its nineteenth canon clearly demanded that children offered to the monastic life in infancy needed subsequently to ratify their oblature on attaining a mature age.[16] But the I Council of Mâcon, held in 583, again reverted to the Benedictine concept of the oblature, and excommunicated those who later left the monastery to marry after having been offered there by their parents.[17] However, the texts of this latter Council might also be understood as referring to those children who made a profession merely at the request of their parents.

Of the Spanish councils, the IV Council of Toledo, held in 633, formulated a canon in which the juridic concept of the Benedictine oblature was so clearly and concisely stated that it served as a model for all the legislation defending this practice in the remaining centuries of its existence. The forty-ninth canon of this Council read:

> *Monachum aut paterna devotio aut propria professio fecit; quidquid horum fuerit aligatum tenebit. Proinde his ad mundum reverti intercludimus aditum, et omnes ad saeculum interdicimus regressum.*[18]

Both the child oblate and the freely professed adult were placed on the same juridical basis; both oblation and profession constituted the individual a true monk with equal obligations of a perpetual

[16] Can. 19—*Monumenta Germaniae Historica, Legum Sectio III, Concilia* (2 voll. in 4, ed. Maassen, Werminghoff, Bastgen, Hannoverae-Lipsiae, 1893-1924), I, p. 107, n. 19 (hereafter cited *MGH*).

[17] Cann. 12, 19—Mansi, IX, 935.

[18] C. 3, C. 20, q. 1—Bruns, *Canones Apostolorum et Conciliorum Saeculorum IV-VII* (2 voll., Berolini, 1839), I, 235 (hereafter cited Bruns).

nature; under pain of excommunication it was prohibited for either of these to leave the monastery.[19] The VI Council of Toledo (638) reaffirmed this legislation, and pronounced excommunication upon anyone who dared desert the monastic state once he had been freely professed in the monastery or offered there.[20] And the X Council of Toledo in 656, while approving the oblature, restricted the right of parents to determine the wills of their children to those who had not reached their tenth or twelfth year.[21] Thus the Spanish Councils of the sixth and seventh centuries adopted the Benedictine concept of the oblature in its most severe form.

C. *Carolingian Legislation*

Due to the fact that the Germanic concept of paternal power over their offspring differed so widely from the Roman *patria potestas,* the Carolingian legislation on the binding force of the oblature was considerably more mild than that of the previous generation. Although the Germanic nations recognized a certain paternal power over their offspring, it in no way approached the Roman concept whereby the child was merely an object possessed by the father (*la chose de père*).[22] Because of this background, the Carolingian capitularies, although admitting the legitimacy of the custom of child oblation,[23] affirmed that such children were to have complete freedom of choice in accepting or rejecting the monastic life once they had reached maturity.[24]

This more mild view of the oblature was likewise reflected in the eighty capitularies drawn up and adopted by the abbots of the Frankish kingdom who met with Benedict of Aniane (+ 821) at Aix-la-Chapelle in 817 for the purpose of establishing a uniform

[19] Can. 50—Mansi, X, 631.

[20] Can. 6—Bruns, I, 235.

[21] Can. 6—Bruns, I, 301. The age limit set by this Council varies among the different manuscripts. Some set it at ten years, others at fourteen. Cf. McLaughlin, *Le trés ancien droit monastique de l'Occident* (Vienne-Parisiis: A. Picard, 1935), p. 66, note 7.

[22] Deroux, *Les Origines de l'Oblature Bénédictine,* pp. 21-25.

[23] *MGH, Legum Sectio II, Capitularia Regum Francorum* (2 toms in 5 voll., ed. A. Boretius et V. Krause, Hannoverae, 1883-1897), I, n. 42, p. 119.

[24] *Ibidem,* n. 43, p. 122.

monastic discipline throughout the entire kingdom. For this gathering, in an attempt to reconcile the custom of the oblature with the personal liberty needed for contracting the perpetual obligations of the monastic state, permitted the oblates to confirm their oblature once they had attained the proper age.[25] From the wording of the provisions they later adopted, it seems that they meant to grant the child complete liberty in placing this subsequent ratification, although some authors are of the opinion that this subsequent confirmation was meant only to strengthen the original act of oblation.[26] The more mild view seems confirmed through the fact that the Council of Mainz (813) four years before this meeting had decreed: *"Nullus tondeatur, nisi in legitima aetate et spontanea voluntate,"*[27] and allowed one year in which anyone forced into the monastic state could appeal to the Pope or the ordinary to release him from his obligations.[28]

Perhaps no incident had a more profound influence in perpetuating the custom of child oblation than a decision of the Council of Mainz in 829 in which a Saxon monk, Gottschalk by name, was permitted to leave the monastery at Fulda where he had been offered as a child. The Abbot of Fulda, and later Archbishop of Mainz, Rabanus Maurus (+ 856), was incensed at this decision and appealed to Louis the Pious to repeal it by writing his defense *par excellence* of the custom, the *"Liber de Oblatione Puerorum contra eos qui repugnant institutis B. P. Benedicti."*[29] Replete with quotations from Scripture and the Fathers in praise of this practice, the main point of its argument was that all men were slaves in Christ and that therefore those who were attacking the oblature were in reality denying a species of that slavery to which they themselves were subjected. He attempted to draw a parallel between the right of the parents to bind their child's will in baptism, and their right to bind them to the monastic state. He assailed those who attacked the custom as *"institutores novorum dogmatum,"* and at-

[25] Can. 36—*MGH, ibidem,* I, n. 170, p. 346.

[26] Cf. Leclercq, "Oblat," *Dictionnaire d'Archéologie Chrétienne et de Liturgie* (Parisiis: Letouzey et Ané, 1907-), XII, 1857-1877, especially 1861-1862.

[27] C. 1, X, *de regularibus et transeuntibus ad religionem,* III, 31.

[28] C. 2, X, *de regularibus et transeuntibus ad religionem,* III, 31.

[29] *MPL,* CVII, 419-440.

tributed their objections to a lack of faith and the spirit of the world.[30]

From the general tenor of this work it seems that its author considered the custom as near to a dogma of the faith. It had the immediate effect of having the decision of Mainz revoked, and the more lasting influence of having the subsequent conciliar legislation revert to the former strict views on the oblature. For the Council of Worms in 868 again stated in clear and precise terms that it considered the bond placed upon the child in its oblature as perpetual and absolute in nature. It decreed, "*Si pater vel mater filium filiamque intra septa monasterii in infantiae annis sub regulari tradiderit disciplina, non liceat eis, postquam ad pubertatis pervenerint annos, egredi, et matrimonio copulari*"[31] and "*non licet eis susceptum habitum umquam deferre; sed . . . in religionis cultu habituque velint nolint, permanere cogantur.*"[32] And the Council of Tribur (895) stated that one who had been offered to the monastery by his parents, and had begun to read and chant in church, could not return to the world, and if he did so, he was to be forced to return to the monastery.[33] It seems from the phraseology employed in this text that the Council regarded the voluntary participation in choral duties as establishing a presumption of consent. A later canon of this same Council appears to confirm this view, since it was again stated that those who had attained puberty enjoyed complete liberty in their choice of their state in life.[34]

D. *Roman Legislation of the Eighth and Ninth Centuries*

The only mention in Roman legislation of the custom of child oblation in the eighth century is contained in a letter of Pope Gregory II (715-731) addressed to St. Boniface, legate to Germany, in 726.[35] The case mentioned in this letter concerned a monk, Winfrid by name, who, though he had been offered to a monastery by his parents in infancy, left the religious life to enter matrimony. The

[30] *MPL,* CVII, 429.
[31] Can. 22—Mansi, XV, 873.
[32] C. 2, C. 20, q. 1—Jaffé, n. 2174.
[33] C. 6, C. 20, q. 1—Mansi, XVIII, 144.
[34] C. 2, C. 20, q. 2—Mansi, XVIII, 144.
[35] C. 2, C. 20, q. 1—Jaffé, n. 2147.

Pontiff declared that anyone who had been offered in this manner to the religious life while still in infancy could not leave it for the sake of entering marriage.

During the ninth century, a Roman Synod held under Eugene II (824-827) in 826 decreed that, just as anyone who freely elected to enter religion could not later leave the cloister to return to the world, so those who had been forced to enter against their will could not be forced to remain, except in just punishment for some crime.[36] This decree became of importance in the future teachings of the glossators, since it demonstrated that it was then considered permissible to force another into the monastery for certain criminal offenses.[37]

A very clear case of coercion that invalidated the forced entry of a nine-year old child is to be found in a letter of Pope Nicholas I (858-867), addressed to the bishops of the Kingdom of Louis II.[38] The case concerned a child, Lambert by name, who had been forced into a monastery by his father, a former soldier turned cleric. Although the father testified that he had intended by his action to make Lambert a true monk and to bind him to the religious state permanently, Pope Nicholas responded that if it was ascertained that the child had in reality been forced to enter against his will, he was not to be obliged to remain, and all his heredity lost through his father's action was to be restored to him. Although this case played a major rôle in the development of the doctrine of the later glossators, it had little immediate effect upon the legislation of this period, as is evidenced by the fact that the year following its issuance the stringent views of the Council of Worms (868) were adopted.

ARTICLE III. THE *Decretum Gratiani* AND THE DECRETAL COLLECTIONS

A. *The Decretum Gratiani*

Most of the legislation of the preceding ages concerning the entrance of both children and adults into the religious state was gathered together by Gratian in *Causa XIX* and *Causa XX* of the

[36] C. 9, C. 20, q. 1—Mansi, XIV, 1008.

[37] *Glossa Ordinaria* ad c. 9, C. 20, q. 1, s. v. *offensionis*.

[38] C. 4, C. 20, q. 3—Jaffé, n. 2835.

Decretum (ca. 1140).[39] But the fact that this legislation appears there in no way changed the weight or scope of its legal value; rather, each canon retained the particular force and extension which it had in its original source.[40] However, by casting this legislation of the previous centuries into a systematic form, Gratian presented the legal elements upon which he and future jurists could work out the theory of the law therein contained. He himself showed his own mind on the various points in the law both in his selection of materials and their arrangement as well as through his efforts to reconcile the apparent opposition of the legal texts by means of his insertions in the form of a *dictum* between the canons.

Although Gratian's mind is somewhat difficult to analyze, in view of his somewhat involved line of argumentation, it seems that his doctrine upon this issue may be summed up in two main points. First, he affirmed that a child offered to the monastery in infancy was bound thereby to the religious life permanently and could not depart from it. Through a series of propositions and objections based upon the confused mass of juridical texts of the preceding centuries, he finally arrived at the conclusion: "*Ex his auctoritatibus colligitur, quod paterna professio pueros tenet obligatos, nec licebit eis a proposito discedere, quod paterna devotione in puerilibus annis susceperint.*"[41]

Secondly, he asserted that parents could not determine the wills of their children to the monastic life once they had attained the use of reason (or at least after they were nine years of age), unless the child himself were willing. If they acted contrary to the law on this point, the child was not bound by their action, and he could freely leave the monastery if he desired to do so at the age of puberty.[42]

Concerning the freedom with which adults needed to act in embracing the religious state, he declared that the paternal power over

[39] The *Decretum Gratiani*, originally entitled *Concordia Discordantium Canonum*, will be cited from the *Corpus Iuris Canonici* (editio Lipsiensis secunda post Aemilii Ludovici Richter curas . . . instruxit Aemilius Friedberg, 2 voll., Lipsiae, 1879-1881, ed. anastatice repetita, Lipsiae: Tauchnitz, 1928).

[40] Van Hove, *Commentarium Lovaniense in Codicem Iuris Canonici*, Vol. I, Tom. I, *Prolegomena ad Codicem Iuris Canonici* (2. ed., Mechliniae-Romae: H. Dessain, 1945), p. 346 (hereafter cited *Prolegomena*).

[41] *Dictum* after c. 7, C. 20, q. 1. Also cf. *dictum* before c. 2, C. 20, q. 1.

[42] *Dictum* before c. 4, C. 20, q. 3.

the child's will ceased after he had attained the age of puberty, and that therefore anyone who desired to embrace the religious life after attaining puberty was to be left entirely free in his choice.[43] If coercion was exerted upon another to force him into the religious state, his entrance was rendered invalid by its use, and consequently no obligations arose from it.[44] "*Cum dicitur propositum monachi proprio arbitrio et voluntate susceptum,*" he concluded, "*intelligitur, quod si propria voluntate susceptum non fuerit, observari non cogitur.*" Thus, though Gratian seems to have admitted the binding force of the oblature, he respected the complete liberty of the adult aspirant to the religious state.

B. *The Early Decretists*

In the period immediately following the appearance of the *Decretum Gratiani,* the controversy over the binding force of the oblature continued among the jurists. Rufinus (+ 1190), in his famous work, the *Summa Decretorum,* which was written between 1157 and 1159, testified that the authors in his day continued to dispute the exact nature of the bond placed upon a child through this practice. Many thought, he said, that the act of oblation on the part of the parents established a perpetual and absolute bond between the child and the monastic life, even though the child could later object to his oblature. Others, however, were of the opinion that child oblates were not bound permanently to the religious state unless they themselves later ratified their oblature upon attaining the age of puberty. He himself was undecided on the question and did not wish to attempt a solution, merely remarking that "whether these think correctly or not, we leave to the judgment of our betters."[45]

Once a child had attained the use of reason (*doli capax*), however, he clearly stated the principle that such children, if forced to accept the monastic obligations, were in no way bound thereby unless later, through their own free will, they assumed them, or ratified their parents' former action. Hence, although the oblature

---

[43] *Dictum* after c. 9, C. 20, q. 1.

[44] *Dictum* before c. 9, C. 20, q. 1.

[45] Rufinus, *Die Summa Decretorum* (ed. H. Singer, Paterborn, 1902), ad C. XX, q. 1.

continued in effect during this period, in this last observation of Rufinus one may already see the grain of that juridic theory which was to gain ground eventually and to prepare the way for the entire revocation of the practice.

C. *Decretal Legislation*

As there was a rapid development in the law on other points of legislation following the *Decretum Gratiani,* so too the decisions of the Roman Pontiffs began to treat more frequently of the liberty with which both children and adults were to be allowed to embrace the religious state. One of the first of these decisions was that of Alexander III (1159-1181), found in a letter addressed to the Bishop of Beauvais in 1159 or 1160. The case concerned a child monk who had received the habit of the monastery at Ressons-sur-Matz before his fourteenth birthday anniversary, and who later left the monastery to return to the world. The Pope responded that if it were established that the child in question had not been offered by his parents, or that he had made his profession before the completion of his fourteenth year, then by virtue of his pontifical authority the child was to be freed of all obligations which perhaps had arisen from such a profession. But, if the child had been offered to the monastery by his parents, or had made his profession after the completion of fourteen years, he was to remain in the monastery or to transfer to another of his choice.[46]

A decretal letter of Pope Clement III (1187-1191) seems to indicate that this Pontiff considered the strict discipline of the IV Council of Toledo (633) as still governing the juridic effects of the oblature in his day.[47] Thomassinus (1619-1695) interpreted the decision as favoring that view.[48] But if one examines the text of the decision carefully, then it seems that the Pontiff, though he cited the Council of Toledo, understood its canon as meaning that child oblates were to ratify their profession after reaching puberty. This

[46] C. 8, *de regularibus et transeuntibus ad religionem,* III, 31—Jaffé, n. 13854.

[47] C. 12, X, *de regularibus et transeuntibus ad religionem,* III, 31.

[48] *Vetus et Nova Ecclesiae Disciplina circa Beneficia et Beneficiarios* (ed. postrema, cum Parisiensi accuratissime collata, 10 voll., Magontiaci, 1787), pars I, lib. I, c. 56, n. 13.

view seems substantiated by the fact that this same Pontiff permitted the oblates at the Monastery of Marmoutier to confirm their oblation at puberty or to return to the world.[49]

The final and decisive legal stroke whereby there was destroyed all the juridic binding force which the oblature obtained in the centuries of its existence was rendered in a decision reached by Pope Celestine III (1191-1198), which found its way both into the *Compilatio Secunda* and the Decretals of Gregory IX.[50] The case concerned a child who had been offered to a monastery by his father together with all his earthly possessions. Later, finding the monastic discipline too difficult, he deserted the monastery and demanded the return of his possessions. The case, after having been tried in the diocesan tribunal, was appealed to Rome. Pope Celestine responded that a child so offered was to be considered as having complete freedom, once he had attained the age of puberty, to accept or to reject the monastic habit, and if he did reject it, then all his possessions were to be returned to him. Thus, child oblates were granted complete liberty of choice, once they had attained puberty, of accepting or rejecting the monastic obligations placed upon them by their parents.

Although this general legislation, little by little, began to prevail over the old custom which had been so solidly entrenched through many years of practice, it alone did not procure the defeat of the practice. The many abuses which had already existed in the previous centuries, though not in so great a degree, began to spring up around this practice, and many protests began to be heard for its complete suppression in fact as well as in law.[51] It continued, however, even as an abuse down to the time of the Council of Trent.

D. *The Glossators*

Since the decision of Celestine III determining the fate of child oblates was already contained in the *Compilatio Secunda,* prepared by John of Wales in 1210, and was thus received into the schools, its contents were quite commonly known to the glossators writing

---

[49] Deroux, *Les Origines de l'Oblature Bénédictine,* p. 36.

[50] C. 14, X, *de regularibus et transeuntibus ad religionem,* III, 31; (C. 5, *Comp. II, h. t.,* III, 18)—Jaffé, n. 17683.

[51] Deroux, *Les Origines de l'Oblature Bénédictine,* p. 44.

after its appearance. As a result of this fact, the later glosses on the *Decretum Gratiani* around the stringent canons concerning the oblature often do not reflect the true meaning of the text in its original sense, but rather, in attempting to bring these canons into conformity with the new legislation, the glossators read into them meanings which they clearly never had. Bartholomew of Brescia (+ 1258) further corrected these glosses when he prepared the final redaction of the *Glossa ordinaria* on the *Decretum* about 1240 to 1246, adding parallel passages from the Decretals of Gregory IX, which had become universal law by the bull "*Rex Pacificus*" of 1234. And hence, after this series of manipulations, the *Glossa ordinaria* on *Causa XX* of Gratian's *Decretum* is for the most part accommodated.

1. The nature of the oblature

The *Glossa ordinaria* on the canons of *Causa XX* in the *Decretum* present an interesting study of the manner in which the glossators sometimes accommodated the texts of the *Decretum* to agree with their own views. First, they observed that it was from the letter of Pope Gregory II that those who held that the oblature was sufficient to constitute a child a true monk derived their erroneous views. For this text, if correctly understood, did not mean to state that the oblature alone sufficed, but that subsequent ratification was necessary before a perpetual bond was created between the child and the monastic life.[52] Obviously, this was not the true meaning imparted by this text.

Furthermore, they noted, the decision of the IV Council of Toledo, if correctly understood, really meant that paternal devotion made a child a monk occasionally, that is to say, sometimes the child confirmed the paternal will out of his own free choice.[53] And hence this decision was to be read: "*Monachum aut paterna devotio* [*et filii professio spontanea, professio supple*] *aut propria professio* [*per se*] *fecit.*"[54]

The doctrine held by some authors to the effect that, if parents could bind their child's will in baptism, so could they likewise bind

---

[52] *Glossa ordinaria* ad c. 2, C. 20, q. 1, s. v. *devitamus.*

[53] *Glossa ordinaria* ad c. 12, X, *de regularibus et transeuntibus ad religionem.* III, 31, s. v. *paterna devotio.*

[54] *Glossa ordinaria* ad c. 3, C. 20, q. 1, s. v. *devotio et professio.*

them to a state of perfection, was also attacked. For children were bound through their baptism only because of the sacramental character, but such a character was not present in a profession made for them by their parents.[55] Hence, they concluded, although the oblature was not condemned, it was totally lacking in any juridic binding force.

2. The free choice of the religious state

The principle which had always been well established in legal thought, even during all the years the oblature continued in vogue, namely, that those who embraced the religious state in adulthood had to do so with complete freedom of choice, was constantly referred to by the glossators in all their observations concerning entry into religion. They made frequent use of the text from the letter of Nicholas I that "there is nothing good except that which is freely willed,"[56] and paraphrased it to explain that no action is worthy of eternal remuneration unless it is freely and voluntarily chosen.[57] No one should be bound to the religious life if he was unwilling, "because God does not wish a forced servitude" and "that which one does not desire, one easily contemns."[58] Christ elected only voluntary soldiers, while the devil gathered to himself those forced into his service (through their misdeeds). And, finally, they frequently declared *"res est consilii et non praecepti"* and therefore the religious life had to be freely chosen.[59]

The only reason for which one could tolerate a just coercion that sought to enforce anyone's entry into religion obtained when the person was guilty of perpetrating some criminal offense. It seems, however, that the glossators did not mean that such individuals were forced to take monastic vows; rather, it seems that they were sent to the monastery only for the sake of doing penance.[60]

---

[55] *Glossa ordinaria* ad c. 4, C. 20, q. 1, s. v. *ablactatum.*

[56] C. 4, C. 20, q. 1: "Nullum quippe bonum nisi voluntarium."

[57] *Glossa ordinaria* ad c. 4, C. 20, q. 3, s. v. *nullum . . . bonum.*

[58] Hostiensis, *Summa Aurea* (Venetiis, 1570), ad c. 1, X, *de regularibus et transeuntibus ad religionem,* III, 31, n. 4.

[59] *Glossa ordinaria* ad c. 2, X, *de his quae vi metusve causa fiunt,* I, 40.

[60] *Glossa ordinaria* ad c. 9, C. 20, q. 1, s. v. *offensionis.*

CHAPTER II

The Invalidating Effects of Force, Fear, and Fraud on the Act of Entering Religion According to the Glossators

Decretal legislation and the medieval glossators not only developed to a high degree the positive qualities with which the act of embracing religion was to be vested, namely, its complete spontaneity and deliberativeness, but they likewise discussed at length the legal doctrine concerning the extent to which coercion or deception when used to extort consent to this act vitiated these essential characteristics. The following paragraphs do not present an exhaustive study of the effects of force, fear and fraud as they were treated by the glossators, but rather represent simply a summary of this doctrine in so far as it came into play when the Decretists and Decretalists discussed the effects of duress and fraud upon the act of entering religion.

ARTICLE I. THE EFFECTS OF FORCE AND FEAR UPON THE PROFESSION

A. *The General Theory*

That the medieval jurists were capable of working out so complete a juridical theory concerning the effects of physical coercion and moral restraint upon the validity of juridical acts was due to a great extent to the fact that Bernard of Pavia (+ 1213), shortly after 1191, had gathered together a group of decretal letters of the various Pontiffs dealing with this subject and had assembled them together under the title "*de his quae vi metusve causa fiunt*" in his *Compilatio Prima.*[1] For it was around the canons of this title, as they found their way through the various decretal collections, that the medieval glossators wove their legal doctrines concerning the effects of duress and physical compulsion upon the

[1] This title in his work was taken from the second book of Justinian's Code, title 19. The word *fiunt* was substituted for *gesta sunt.*

various juridical acts mentioned therein. Later, six of these original canons, together with one new decretal, were selected for the official collection of Gregory IX in 1234.

It was through one of these decretals, already contained in the *Compilatio Prima,* that the Roman legal theory was adopted into the canonical doctrine. For in a decretal letter of Pope Alexander III, written to the Bishop of Worcester between 1159 and 1161, this Pontiff, in deciding a case in which a certain cleric had been deprived of his benefice through the use of unjust coercion, declared that the renunciation of a benefice performed under duress was without juridical effect, and in order to substantiate his decision he appealed to the dictum of the Roman praetor: "*quae metu et vi fiunt, debent in irritum revocari.*"[2] Taking the lead from this decision as clearly pointing to the legitimacy of accepting the Roman legal theory, the canonists assimilated without any change, and constantly repeated with scrupulous fidelity in their writings, the ancient Roman juridical notions of *vis* and *metus* as likewise being the canonical concepts of these legal elements,[3] and applied them to juridical acts in the same manner as that in which the ancient Roman jurists were wont to apply them to contracts.

Force was thus defined: *vis autem est maioris rei impetus, qui repelli non potest,*[4] or that external propulsion which exerts so overpowering an influence upon its victim as to exclude any voluntary action on his part when placing a certain act. And fear was described as follows: *metus est instantis vel futuri periculi causa mentis trepidatio,*[5] or that trepidation of will which made its victim give a reluctant though active co-operation to the action placed by him.

Vis, or force, so obviously excluded consent that the act result-

---

[2] C. 2, X, *de his quae vi metusve causa fiunt,* I, 40 (C. 2, *Comp. I, h. t.,* I, 31)—Jaffé, n. 14131. The words used by the Pontiff were misquoted from D. (4.2) 1, which in reality reads: "*Quod vi metusve causa gestum erit, ratum non habeo.*"

[3] Kuttner, *Kanonistische Schuldlehre von Gratian bis auf die Dekretalen Gregors IX,* Studi e Testi, n. 64 (Città del Vaticano: Biblioteca Apostolica Vaticana, 1935), p. 301 (hereafter cited *Kanonistische Schuldlehre*).

[4] D. (4.2) 2.

[5] D. (4.2) 1.

ing from it was considered as merely a passive, physical reaction to it. But before fear could give rise to juridical action it was postulated that the fear be grave,[6] that it arise from an outside agent,[7] that it be tainted with a note of injustice,[8] and that there exist a causal relationship between its use and the act which was placed.[9] Acts placed under such duress were not considered as *ipso iure* null and void, but rather they were rendered liable to rescission upon a petition submitted to competent authority.[10] To this general rule, however, a number of specific acts, which were considered as demanding a special spontaneity of will, were commonly held to be exceptions, in so far as they were considered to be *ipso iure* null and void, by the very fact that they had been placed under duress.[11] Among these acts the glossators invariably listed that of embracing the religious state.

B. *The Effect of Duress on the Act of Entering Religion*

Two of the seven decretals which appear in the fortieth title of the Decretals of Gregory IX treat specifically of the legal effects of force and fear upon the act of embracing the religious state. Both had appeared in previous collections and were chosen here, it seems, because of the clarity with which they presented all the juridical elements involved in coercion used to induce consent to this act.

The first case presented was contained in a decretal letter of Pope Alexander III, addressed to the Bishop of Huesca, Spain,

[6] D. (4.2) 1: "metum autem non vani hominis, sed qui merito et in homine constantissimo cadat. . . ."

[7] D. (4.2) 14: ". . . sufficit enim hoc docere metum sibi illatum. . . ."

[8] D. (4.2) 3: "Sed vim accipimus . . . quae adversus bonos mores fiat, non eam quam magistratus recte intulit. . . ."

[9] D. (4.2) 3.

[10] *Glossa ordinaria* ad c. 2, X, *de his quae vi metusve causa fiunt,* I, 40, s. v. *coactus;* Hostiensis, *Summa Aurea,* s. t. *de his quae vi metusve causa fiunt,* n. 6; Joannes Andreae, *In Sex Decretalium Libros Novella Commentaria* (6 voll. in 5, Venetiis, 1581), ad c. 2, X, *de his quae vi metusve causa fiunt,* I, 40; Panormitanus, *Commentaria in Quinque Libros Decretalium* (5 voll. in 7, Venetiis, 1588), ad c. 2, X, *de his quae vi metusve causa fiunt,* I, 40 (hereafter these works will be cited *Novella* and *Commentaria,* respectively).

[11] Cf. *Glossa ordinaria, continuationes,* ante tit. 40, *de his quae vi metusve causa fiunt.*

and the Prior of Santa Maria in Saragossa.[12] A certain powerful nobleman, suspecting his wife of immoral conduct, ordered one of his henchmen to take her to a forest to kill her. The soldier, moved to compassion at the moment before executing the sentence, offered to spare the unfortunate individual provided she would enter a monastery of nuns. Fearing for her life, the woman readily consented to his proposal. Her husband, however, hearing of how his will had been thwarted, took two bishops to the monastery immediately to impose the veil upon his wife.

Although the bishops did not know of the preceding incident, they suspected the woman's intentions for entering the cloister, since she was so young and had a small child. They therefore questioned her about her intentions, and she informed them that she had entered the cloister solely because of fear for her life and that she intended to leave it on the first opportunity offered her. In spite of her testimony, however, one of the bishops, fearing lest the husband's wrath fall upon him likewise, solemnly imposed the habit upon her.

Later, after the husband's death, the woman left the monastery and remarried, whereupon the bishop of the diocese excommunicated her for deserting her profession. The case was then appealed to Rome, where the Pontiff responded that the excommunication was to be lifted immediately provided the parties were willing to abide by his decision. He then ordered the bishop to proceed in the case and, if it was legitimately proved that the woman had not entered through fear of death or, even if she had entered under duress, that she had given consent freely after her husband's death, she was to be obliged to return to the monastery under pain of ecclesiastical censure.

The second decretal letter dealing with coercion applied to the act of entering religion dealt with both the elements of fear and fraud. The case, contained in a letter of Innocent III (1198-1216) addressed to the Bishops of Marseilles and Agde, concerned a certain college of canons who, wishing to observe the Cistercian Rule, entered a monastery of that Order and transferred to it their collegiate church. Later, repenting of their action, they

[12] C. 1, X, *de his quae vi metusve causa fiunt,* I, 40 (c. 2, *Comp. I, h. t.,* I, 30)—Jaffé, n. 14041.

charged the Cistercians as having induced them to enter through the use of duress and fraud. The Pontiff, however, responded that they were bound to remain in the monastery in spite of their protests, since the fear which they alleged was neither the fear of death nor of bodily harm, and could not therefore be accounted as sufficient to move a *vir constans.* And neither was the deceit which they adduced sufficient to free them, since it was due more to their own foolishness than to any fraudulent machinations on the part of the Cistercians that they had been led to enter.[13]

The first of these decretals was by far the more important in the formation of the canonical doctrine concerning forced entry into religion, since it was held to be the outstanding case in which all the elements which might be had in a forced profession were clearly outlined. In view of the fact that this case, together with the second cited, gave such clear indications of the various elements required by reason of the Roman theory on forced acts, the glossators show a surprising unanimity in their views upon the effects of coercion on the act of entering the religious state. The following paragraphs present a summary of their doctrine on these various points.

1. The origin of the fear

The first annotation which they made upon the text of the decision of Alexander III was that the *metus* in the case was both *illatus ab extrinsico* and *praesens,* as demanded by the Roman sources,[14] i.e., it arose from outside the victim and precisely from a threat actually and expressly formulated by another.[15] They further observed that the threat was considered as present not

---

[13] C. 6, X, *de his quae vi metusve causa fiunt,* I, 40 (c. 3, *Comp. III, h. t.,* I, 23)—Potthast, *Regesta Pontificum Romanorum inde ab anno Post Christum Natum MCXCVIII ad annum MCCCIV* (2 voll., Berolini, 1874-1875), n. 733 (hereafter cited Potthast).

[14] Cf. D. (4.2) 9; also Azo, *Summa Codicis* (Venetiis, 1530), lib. II, *de his quae vi metusve gesta sunt,* rubrica 20, n. 3.

[15] *Glossa ordinaria* ad c. 1, X, *de his quae vi metusve causa fiunt,* I, 40, s. v. *evaginato gladio;* Joannes Andreae, *Novella,* ad c. 1, X, *de his quae vi metusve causa fiunt,* I, 40, s. v. *evaginato gladio;* Panormitanus, *Commentaria,* ad tit. *de his quae vi metusve causa fiunt,* n. 1.

only when the aggressor actually threatened the application of the evil, but also all the time the victim remained in such a condition that she could not deliver herself from the power of the aggressor.[16]

2. The degree of the fear

Secondly, they observed that whereas the fear mentioned in the decretal of Innocent III was declared insufficient for the reason that it did not exist in a degree which would move a *vir constans,* the fear mentioned in the decretal of Alexander III was one of those fears which was considered as falling under this Roman norm,[17] namely, the fear of death. Hence they concluded that only that degree of fear which when employed in other acts was sufficient to open the way for legal regress sufficed also for annulling an entry into the religious state.[18] But in evaluating the degree of fear which fell under the Roman norm of that which would move a *vir constans,* the glossators adhered to the rigorous standard of *metus mortis vel cruciatus corporis,* as authentically postulated by Innocent III in his decretal, and adopted a wholly objective view of the fear which called for invoking against it some penal legal sanction. And, even when they extended the limits of this rigorous Roman norm by making it embrace other specific evils not mentioned in the Roman sources, they always evaluated those evils in the light of this criterion, so that in reality the fear of death or of bodily torments continued to be the standard by which various fears were judged with relation to their juridical relevance from the beginning down through the last of the glossators.[19]

---

[16] *Glossa ordinaria, ibidem,* s. v. *postmodum;* Joannes Andreae, *ibidem,* s. v. *ratum;* Panormitanus, *ibidem,* n. 2.

[17] Cf. D (4.2) 3, 4, 5, 6, 7, 8, 9.

[18] *Glossa ordinaria,* casus ad c. 6, X, *de his quae vi metusve causa fiunt,* I, 40; Hostiensis, *Commentaria in Quinque Libros Decretalium* (5 voll. in 3, Venetiis, 1581), ad c. 1, X, *de his quae vi metusve causa fiunt,* I, 40, s. v. *evaginato gladio* (hereafter cited *Commentaria*); Joannes Andreae, *Novella,* ad c. 6, X, *de his quae vi metusve causa fiunt,* I, 40, s. v. *fatuitatem.*

[19] Cf. *Glossa ordinaria* ad c. 1, C. 15, q. 6; Hostiensis, *loc. cit.;* Joannes Andreae, *loc. cit.;* Panormitanus, *Commentaria,* c. 6, X, *de his quae vi metusve causa fiunt,* I, 40: ". . . non fuit talis . . . cum non contineat metum mortis, vel corporis cruciatum."

Among the evils which they considered as qualified to fall under the degree affecting a *vir constans,* they listed imprisonment, slavery, *stuprum,* flogging, and unjust excommunication. These were summarized in the verse of Vincentius (+ ca. 1240),

> *Excusare metus hos posse puta, quia nescis: Stupri sive status, verberis atque necis,*[20]

which was placed in the *Glossa ordinaria* by Bernard of Parma (+ 1266)[21] and thus found its way down through the later glossators.

Although Bernard of Pavia (+ 1213)[22] and St. Raymond of Pennafort (ca. 1180-1275)[23] seemed to admit the possibility of explaining the objective norm of the degree affecting a *vir constans* by taking into account the particular circumstances of the person against whom the evil was threatened, this does not mean that they in any way admitted the relevancy of *metus relative gravis* in the sense it is held today. Rather, they considered the sole hypothesis that fear which might be objectively grave for other men might be subjectively slight for a particular person in view of his personal characteristics. Outside of this observation, the only degree of fear which they considered as sufficient to invalidate entry into religion was that which was objectively and absolutely grave.

3. The manner of infliction

Thirdly, the glossators emphasized that even though there may have been a *culpa praecedens* on the part of the one making a religious profession, duress exerted upon this act nevertheless invalidated it.[24] Although the glossators spoke at times of fear being

---

[20] Vincentius, *Glossa* ad c. 1, *Comp. I, de his quae vi metusve causa fiunt,* I, 30 (quoted from Kuttner, *Kanonistische Schuldlehre,* p. 312).

[21] *Glossa ordinaria, casus* ad c. 2, X, *de his quae vi metusve causa fiunt,* I, 40.

[22] *Summa Decretalium,* Tit., *de his quae vi metusve causa fiunt,* I, 30 (cited from Kuttner, *Kanonistische Schuldlehre,* p. 311).

[23] *Summa Juris Canonici* (Veronae, 1744), lib. IV, t. 4, p. 506.

[24] *Glossa ordinaria, casus* ad c. 2, X, *de his quae vi metusve causa fiunt,* I, 40: "Ab ista doctrina sive generalitate, excipiuntur casus, in quibus fallit, etiam si culpa sua incidisset in metum . . . et in voto; quia votum per metum factum non tenet."

exerted justly to force one into a monastery, they usually qualified their statements by adding the phrase "*ad agendam poenitentiam.*"[25] Two cases do occur in the decretals, however, in which a woman could be justly forced to enter a monastery, and in one of these at least, it seems, she was forced to make a profession there.

The first of these was that in which a woman had given consent to her husband to enter religion. Under the law at that time it was always understood that if a wife gave consent to her husband to enter religion, she automatically bound herself thereby either to enter religion also, or else to make a vow of perpetual chastity in the world. If, however, after having consented to her husband's entry, she refused to comply with the law in this regard, but lived unchastely in the world, it was then permitted to force her to enter religion, even against her will.[26]

The other instance was that of a woman whom the husband refused to receive back when she had been guilty of committing adultery. Whenever such a case did occur, the judge before whom the case was tried could force the unhappy creature to do penance in a monastery even for her entire lifetime.[27] But, outside these two cases, all coercion was generally considered as unjust when used for influencing consent to the act of embracing the religious state.

C. *The Effect of Duress on the Reception of the Habit*

Although Hostiensis (+ 1271)[28] and Joannes Andreae (+ 1348)[29] made a distinction between the degree of fear needed to invalidate a religious profession and the degree of fear needed to invalidate the act of taking the habit, it must be noted that these authors were here not speaking of entry into the novitiate, but rather of tacit profession as it was then legally recognized. This is clearly evident from the fact that they considered the reception

---

[25] Cf. *Glossa ordinaria, casus* ad D. 81, c. 8; *Glossa ordinaria* ad c. 9, C. 20, q. 1, s. v. *offensionis.*

[26] C. 18, X, *de conversione conjugatorum,* III, 32—Potthast, n. 7812.

[27] C. 19, X, *de conversione conjugatorum,* III, 32—Potthast, n. 8652.

[28] *Commentaria,* ad c. 1, X, *de his quae vi metusve causa fiunt,* I, 40, s. v. *aut.*

[29] *Novella,* ad c. 1, X, *de his quae vi metusve causa fiunt,* I, 40, s. v. *aut.*

of the habit as creating a presumption not that vows would be taken, but that vows had in fact been taken.

Hence, in reality, they were merely drawing a distinction between that degree of fear needed to invalidate an express profession and a tacit one. Whereas in the former case they demanded that the fear be grave according to the accepted norm in other juridical acts, in the latter they admitted that any degree of fear whatsoever vitiated consent.[30] The reason which they adduced for this distinction was that in the express profession one openly declares his will to assume the obligations, and hence one must stand by one's expressed will unless it can be demonstrated that one was in reality under grave duress. In the tacit profession, however, only a presumption of consent was established by the assumption of the habit, a presumption which could easily yield to whatever truth existed to the contrary.

ARTICLE II. THE EFFECTS OF FRAUD UPON THE ENTRY INTO RELIGION

Because of a systematic grouping of the texts containing the pertinent legal elements, the medieval glossators were able to present a complete and systematic theory concerning the invalidating effects of duress upon the act of entering religion. This, however, was not the case when they came to consider this same act performed under the influence of fraud. For the decretal collections do not contain a title "*de dolo malo*" in which the pertinent texts are grouped; rather the cases in which the element of deceit is found are scattered throughout the various other titles in the collections.

The theory evolved by the glossators concerning the effect of fraud upon this act was most unique, differing sharply both from the canonical theory concerning *metus* in this act as well as the Roman theory concerning *dolus* in contracts. This unique theory is now known as *dolus in spiritualibus,* of which the following paragraphs are a brief summary.[31]

---

[30] Hostiensis, *loc. cit.;* Joannes Andreae, *ibidem,* s. v. *ratum.*

[31] For a more detailed and complete evolution of this theory, the reader is referred to Fransen, *Le dol dans la conclusion des actes juridiques,* dissertationes ad gradum magistri in Facultate Theologica vel in Facultate Juris Canonici consequendum conscriptae, series II, n. 37 (Gembloux: Duculot, 1946), pp. 108-143.

A. *The Textual Basis for the Theory*

The whole theory concerning the effect of *dolus* upon the act of embracing the religious state took its rise from a canon already contained in the *Decretum Gratiani,* the canon *Constituit,* which Gratian attributed to the Council of Mainz, held in 813, but which in reality was a quotation from the seventh canon of the Council of Chalon-sur-Saone, held in that same year.[32] A careful reading of the text of this canon makes it apparent that the Council was not attempting to draw any fine distinctions in formulating it; rather, it was merely a practical solution to an abuse which was apparently rampant at that time. The canon was directed towards the punishment of certain bishops and abbots who, by means of trickery, were enticing certain unlettered persons into the monastic life so as to obtain thereby their inheritance in the place of the rightful heirs. In an attempt to put down this abuse, the Council decreed that whenever such individuals had been enticed into the religious state through fraud, although they were bound to remain in the monastery, their worldly goods were to be restored to their legitimate heirs. In reality, the second provision, namely, that the material goods of such individuals were not to accrue to the monastery, seems to be the main issue in the decision. The words used in the text, however, clearly indicate that it was a case of true fraud—*circumveniendo . . . illecti . . . vanis promissionibus vel quibuslibet machinationibus persuasi*—and yet, in spite of the use of such deception the religious profession of those affected by it was declared to be validly made and binding.

---

[32] C. 5, C. 20, q. 3: "Constituit sane sacer iste conventus ut episcopi sive abbates, qui, non in fructum animarum, sed in avaritiam et turpe lucrum inhiantes, quoslibet homines (inlectos) circumveniendo totonderunt, et res eorum tali persuasione (non solum acceperunt, sed potius) subripuerunt, penitentiae canonicae (sive regulari) utpote turpis lucri sectatores subiaceant. Hi vero qui (variis promissionibus) inlecti (vel quibuslibet machinationibus persuasi, mentis inopes effecti, rerum suarum domini esse nescientes) comam deposuerunt, in eo, quod ceperunt, perseverare cogantur. Res (namque quae ab inlectis et negligentibus datae, ab avaris et cupidis non solum acceptae, sed et raptae noscuntur) heredibus reddantur."—*MGH, Leges Sectio III, Concilia,* II, part I, p. 274. (The portions of the text in parenthesis do not appear in the *Decretum Gratiani.*)

In reality, this text was the main basis for the theory *dolus in spiritualibus*. Other cases, however, contained in the later decretal collections, furnished the glossators with an opportunity to evolve their unique theory further. The first of these cases has been treated in the preceding article, since it contained both the elements of fear and fraud, namely, the decision of Innocent III whereby the professions made by a certain college of canons were declared to be valid in spite of their protests of fraud.[83] The fact that the Pontiff, in deciding the case, had attributed the alleged fraud to the foolishness (*fatuitas*) of those who alleged its use, played an important rôle in the future doctrine of the canonists, as will be seen below.

The second decretal of Innocent III to which the glossators appealed for support of their arguments was in reality not a case of fraud, but rather one of subjective error. A certain woman, because she thought her husband was afflicted with leprosy, fled from him before the consummation of the marriage and entered a monastery. The Pontiff declared in his decision that the erroneous judgment which gave rise to the woman's action had no effect upon her profession and that she was therefore obliged to observe the obligations assumed thereby.[84]

Finally, a very important textual basis for the theory was found in a decretal letter of Pope Gregory IX in which fraud was alleged, but proved insufficient to invalidate the profession.[85] The case concerned a certain individual who gave away all his possessions to the Church, and then entered a certain hospital to serve the poor, because he had been promised that he would be permitted to lead an easy life therein. Later, finding that this was not the case, he declared that his consent had been extorted through fraud when he had renounced his worldly goods. The Pontiff, however, responded that it seemed clearly evident that he had consented freely when he had placed this act, and therefore it was to be considered as validly placed and binding. Although the case did not directly affect the invalidity of entry into the religious state because of fraud, it furnished the glossators with some founda-

[83] C. 6, X, *de his quae vi metusve causa fiunt,* I, 40. Cf. above, pp. 23-24.
[84] C. 14, X, *de conversione conjugatorum,* III, 32—Potthast, n. 2651.
[85] C. 2, X, *de conversione conjugatorum,* III, 32—Potthast, n. 9653.

tion upon which to speculate as to whether the *fatuitas* of the individual concerned was not the real cause for the papal decision, as it had been in the case of the college of canons referred to above. In reality, however, it seems that the case was one in which fraud was alleged as a subterfuge to free the individual concerned of obligations validly assumed.

B. *The Theory of Dolus in Spiritualibus*

It was upon the very fragile textual basis reproduced above that the medieval theory of *dolus in spiritualibus* took its rise. The essence of this unique theory may be summed up in the following line of argumentation. According to Roman legal theory,[36] as well as canonical doctrine,[37] whenever a juridical act or contract was placed or entered upon under the preponderant influence of fraud, it was either *ipso iure* null and void, or at least juridically defective and therefore liable to rescission upon request. But, according to the text of the canon *Constituit* of the *Decretum Gratiani,* even though fraud represented the preponderant reason why an individual embraced the religious state, this act was declared to be validly placed. Therefore, this act was to be considered as an exception to the general theory concerning the effects of fraud upon juridical acts in so far as it was declared to be neither invalid nor liable to rescission when placed under the determining influence of fraud. Once this primary conclusion had been deduced from the text of the canon *Constituit* by the first of the glossators, it was accepted by all the later Decretists and Decretalists as a foregone conclusion which they, through their arguments, tried to confirm and explain. Two distinct lines of argumentation are clearly discernible in the writings of the glossators; both were based upon Roman legal theory.

1. The theory of *Dolus Bonus*

The first argument developed by the glossators was based upon the distinction which the Roman sources drew between the effects

[36] D. (4.3) 1.

[37] *Glossa ordinaria* ad c. 3, X, *de emptione et venditione,* III, 17, s. v. *deceptione.*

of fraud used to derive some unfair advantage of another and that used for a good end. In the former case fraud was referred to as *dolus malus,* in the latter as *dolus bonus.* The Roman praetor, in penalizing fraud when used for inducing consent to a juridical act, declared explicitly that only that fraud which qualified as *dolus malus* according to the above made distinction fell within his edict.[38] Taking cognizance of this fact, the glossators proceeded to develop the following argument to explain the apparent antinomy between the text of the canon *Constituit* and Roman legal theory.

According to the explicit dictum of the praetor, they said, fraud was made punishable with invalidity before the law only in so far as its use inflicted an injury upon the one against whom it was employed. But, whenever fraud was used to induce one to embrace the religious state, then the injury that was postulated was lacking, for the one who was led to take this step through deception was in reality in a better state than he was before its use: his salvation was made more easily attainable and secure through the vows of the religious state. Hence, in reality, fraud when used to induce consent to this act always redounded to the good of the individual against whom it is employed. The reason therefore why fraud did not invalidate this act lay in the fact that fraud when used to induce another to assume the state of perfection was not *dolus malus*, but always *dolus bonus*. This line of reasoning was advanced by St. Raymond of Pennafort (ca. 1180-1275)[39] by Hostiensis (+ 1271),[40] and by Guido de Baysio (+ 1313),[41] and seems to have been the preferred doctrine in the *Glossa ordinaria* as well.[42]

2. The theory of mutual compensation

Along with the theory of *dolus bonus*, St. Raymond of Pennafort also presented another argument which was based upon the

[38] Cf. D. (4.3) 1; D. (4.3) 7; D. (4.3) 15.

[39] *Summa Juris Canonici,* lib. I, t. 8, p. 6.

[40] *Commentaria,* ad c. 20, X, *de conversione conjugatorum,* III, 32, in fin.

[41] *Rosarium seu in Decretorum Volumen Commentaria* (Venetiis, 1577), ad c. 5, C. 20, q. 3, s. v. *perserverare.* (Hereafter cited *Rosarium.*)

[42] *Glossa ordinaria,* ad c. 20, X, *de conversione conjugatorum,* III, 32, s. v. *spes.*

lack of proper conditions demanded by the law before *dolus* qualified for invalidating an act, namely, the absence of blame on the part of the victim of fraud.[43] This solution was the only one admitted by Innocent IV (1243-1254)[44] and Joannes Andreae,[45] and it was presented by Hostiensis as a complementary argument alongside that which utilized the concept of *dolus bonus.*[46]

The argument upon which this theory is based may be summed up as follows. No one has a right to profit before the law because of blame on his part. But, whenever an individual is induced to consent to an act, not only because fraud has been employed by another, but also because of lack of proper prudence on his part, he himself is not without fault in placing that act. Hence, whenever the victim of fraud allows himself to be deceived because of a lack of prudence on his part he has no right to claim redress before the law. For, while the one who perpetrated the fraud merits punishment for his misdeed, it does not seem equitable that the victim of his deceit receive any benefit in the face of his own foolishness. Hence, the *dolus* of the one was canceled out by the *fatuitas* of the other.

This solution had a considerable advantage over the first one presented in that it made the validity of the profession depend upon the quality of the *dolus* inflicted on the one hand and the prudence which the victim of the fraud used to ward it off on the other. If the *dolus* employed was of such a nature as to deceive a most prudent man, there was no presumption of any lack of prudence on the part of the subject, and the profession was therefore invalid.[47] But if, objectively taken, it was not of such a quality, it was presumed that the subject had likewise been at fault, and

---

[43] *Summa Juris Canonici,* lib. I, t. 8, p. 16, casus 3.

[44] *Apparatus . . . super Decretalium Libros,* ad c. 6, X, *de his quae vi metusve causa fiunt,* I, 40, s. v. *ad fatuitatem* (cited from Fransen, *Le dol dan la conclusion des actes juridiques,* p. 118, note 1).

[45] *Novella,* ad c. 6, X, *de his quae vi metusve causa fiunt,* I, 40, s. v., *ad fatuitatem.*

[46] *Commentaria,* ad c. 6, X, *de his quae vi metusve causa fiunt,* I, 40, s. v.. *ad fatuitatem.*

[47] Hostiensis, *loc cit.;* Joannes Andreae, *loc. cit.*

therefore he had to suffer that which was caused by his own *fatuitas* as much as by the *dolus* of the aggressor.

C. *Final Evolution*

Towards the end of the period of the glossators, through the influence of Panormitanus (1386-1453), a solution began to take its rise which was eventually to reach the heart of the matter. Panormitanus separated the effects of error and fraud, and distinguished between that which was essential and that which was accidental in the contract of the religious profession. He likewise distinguished between the effects of error and of fraud in the internal and the external forums.

His opinion took its rise from the question: "*Quid si secularis videt monasterium dissolutum, et intrat, sed postea monasterium reformetur*? He solved this question by saying that the obligations which such an individual placed upon himself were not to be determined by his subjective intention in embracing that particular rule; rather, the only point which mattered was whether or not he had acted with prudence in assuming them. If he had acted through a lack of prudence, he was bound to observe the rule of that institute, not as it was observed in that particular monastery, but as it was observed in the institute in general. In the external forum the subjective error did not determine the obligations which such an individual assumed, but only the rule itself of the institute into which he entered. But in the internal forum, since a vow was a voluntary promise made to God, the extent of the obligations which such an individual assumed depended upon the extent to which he had actually intended to oblige himself in assuming them.[48] Herein is to be found the solution which was eventually adopted in the external forum as well through the writings of the canonists and moralists of the sixteenth century. However, the theory of *dolus in spiritualibus* remained the only recognized juridical theory concerning the use of fraud in the act of embracing religion up until the time of the Council of Trent.

---

[48] *Commentaria,* ad 9, X, *de regularibus et transeuntibus ad religionem,* III, 31, nn. 4, 5.

CHAPTER III

The Effects of Force, Fear, and Fraud Upon the Novitiate From the Council of Trent to the Present Code

ARTICLE I. TRIDENTINE AND POST-TRIDENTINE LEGISLATION

The general and ecumenical Council of Trent, convoked by Paul III (1534-1549) on May 22, 1542, for the purpose of restoring "to its purity and splendor the doctrine of the Catholic faith and to bring back to a better mode of life morals which had deviated from ancient usage," dedicated itself through its twenty-five sessions, held at various intervals between 1545 and 1563, to drafting salutary remedies against the corrupters of dogma as well as against the insidious abuses in the moral order then rife in the Church. Almost every phase of Christian dogma and life was touched upon in the decrees which were the result of this Council.[1]

It was in the twenty-fifth and final session, held on December 3 and 4, 1563, that the Fathers of the Council took up the question of drafting its decree for the reformation of the monastic discipline of the Church. In order to facilitate the work of the Council, the schemata or drafts of the suggested legislation were drawn up beforehand and presented to the general assembly for discussion on November 20, 1563. One of these dealt with the reformation of the discipline of regulars; the other, with the discipline of nuns.[2]

[1] Cf. Bulla Indictionis Sacrosancti Oecumenici Concilii Tridentini sub Paulo III Pont. Max., *Initio nostri,* 22 maii 1543—Schroeder, *Canons and Decrees of the Council of Trent, Text, Translation and Commentary* (St. Louis-London: B. Herder and Co., 1941), pp. 281-289 (hereafter cited *Council of Trent*).

[2] *Decretum de reformatione regularium exhibitum examinandum . . . die 20 nov. 1563,* apud *Concilii Tridentini Diariorum, Actorum, Epistularum, Tractatuum, Nova Collectio* (13 voll., Friburgi Brisgoviae: Herder, 1901-), Vol. IX, *Pars Sexta Actorum* (collegit, illustravit, edidit Stephanus Ehses, 1924), col. 1038 (hereafter cited *Collectio*). Cf. also, *Decretum de reformatione monialium, exhibitum examinandum . . . die 20 nov. 1563,* apud Ehses, *Collectio,* col. 1040.

Both of these two drafts, as well as the final decree adopted, were meant only for those religious institutes whose members took solemn vows, though they were extended to embrace institutes of simple vows as well through the constant practice and decisions of the Sacred Congregations.[3] After a preliminary reading and discussion, it was decided to unite these two proposed decrees and to treat of the matter they contained under one general heading. This was realized in the final decree, the *Decretum de regularibus et monialibus*, adopted and promulgated on December 4, 1563.[4]

Both of the two schemata presented, as well as the final decree adopted, contained provisions for the first general law setting up one complete year of novitate as a necessary requisite for valid religious profession in institutes of both men and women. They likewise contained provisions against forcing individuals to enter the religious novitiate. The Fathers of the Council framed three chapters which treated specifically of the effects of coercion upon the act of embracing the religious state, though none of these declared the invalidity of the novitiate when entered upon under these same influences.

The first of these three chapters, the seventeenth of the *Decretum de regularibus et monialibus*, ordained that "if a girl more than twelve years of age wishes to take the habit, neither shall she nor any other at a later period make profession, until the bishop, or, if he be absent or hindered, his vicar or someone delegated by them at their expense, has carefully examined the wish of the virgin, *whether she has been forced or enticed, or knows what she is doing*; and if her will is found to be pious *and free* . . . she shall be permitted freely to make profession."[5]

In the following chapter, the eighteenth, the Council laid down the juridical penalties which were to be applied to those who in any way whatsoever coerced a woman to enter religion. It excommunicated "all persons, of whatever character or rank they may

---

[3] Cf. Wernz, *Ius Decretalium ad Usum Praelectionum in Scholis Textus Canonici sive Iuris Decretalium* (6 voll. in 10, Romae-Prati, 1898-1914), III, n. 644 (hereafter cited *Ius Decretalium*).

[4] Cf. Schroeder, *Council of Trent*, pp. 485-489.

[5] Sess. XXV, *de regularibus*, c. 17. (Translation is that of Schroeder, *Council of Trent*, p. 228; italics are those of the writer.)

be, whether clerics or laics, seculars or regulars, and with whatever dignity invested, who shall, *except in the cases permitted by law,* in any way force any virgin or widow, or any other woman whatsoever, *to enter a monastery* against her will or *to take the habit* of any religious order *or to make profession.*" Those likewise fell under this excommunication who, "knowing that she does not enter the monastery or receive the habit or make profession voluntarily, shall in any way take part in that act by their presence, consent, or authority."[6]

The Council also provided that those individuals who alleged the invalidity of their profession because of force or fear "or something similar" should not be heard unless they presented their petition within five years of their profession. Thus, the Council indicated that it recognized the former jurisprudence concerning the invaliding influence of force and fear upon this act, but it is noteworthy that it made no mention of the effect of fraud upon it, unless the phrase "or something else" may be construed to have implied this.[7]

Suarez (1548-1617), in commenting upon these decrees of the Council, noted that they imposed three distinct censures for three distinct delicts, namely, forced entrance into the monastery, forced acceptance of the habit, and forced profession. He also noted that the Council inflicted these penalties only when women were forced to perform these acts, since it recognized that they were more easily and more often forced into religion than men were. Hence, it wished to throw up this bulwark of penalties about this act to assure them of their complete liberty in performing it. In so doing the Council was aiming only at a common danger, and in no way meant to minimize the complete liberty with which young men must likewise enter the monastery. It was just as sinful, he asserted, to coerce a young man to enter religion as it was to coerce a girl to do so.[8]

He likewise pointed out that the Council qualified its pro-

---

[6] Sess. XXV, *de regularibus,* c. 18. (Translation is that of Schroeder, *Council of Trent,* pp. 228-229; italics are those of the writer.)

[7] Sess. XXV, *de regularibus,* c. 19.

[8] Suarez, *Opera Omnia* (ed. nova a Carolo Berton, 28 voll., Parisiis, 1856-1878), tr. VII, *De religione,* lib. 5, c. 8, nn. 2-4—Vol. XV, 330-331.

nouncement with the phrase "except in those cases mentioned in the law." He thought that the Council was referring here to the two cases mentioned in the decretal legislation in the Decretals of Gregory IX, namely, the case in which a husband refused to receive a wife who had committed adultery, and that in which one spouse had freely given consent to the other to enter religion and then refused to make a private vow of chastity or to enter a monastery and, in fact, lived unchastely in the world. Following Suarez, almost all the authors cited these two cases as the only ones contained in the law in which a person could be forced into the religious state.[9]

Pirhing (1606-1679) pointed out that the wife was bound to enter under the circumstances of the second case, since by the very fact that she had given her consent to her husband to enter religion, she obligated herself either to enter likewise or else to preserve her chastity in the world, inasmuch as it was only under this condition that the Church permitted the entry of one of the spouses.[10] Schmalzgrueber (1663-1735) noted that even in this case she could be bound only disjunctively, namely, either to live chastely or to enter religion.[11] Later authors were of the opinion that even in this instance she could be forced to enter a monastery, but that she could not be forced either to take the religious habit or to make a profession.[12]

After the Council of Trent, as before it, most of the legislation concerning the act of embracing religion spoke more of the quali-

---

[9] Pirhing, *Jus Canonicum Nova Methodo Explicatum, Omnibus Capitulis Titulorum* (4 voll., Dilingae, 1722), lib. III, tit. 32, nn. 14, 15; Schmalzgrueber, *Ius Ecclesiasticum Universum* (5 voll. in 12, Romae, 1843-1845), lib. III, tit. 32, nn. 173, 174, 175; Reiffenstuel, *Ius Canonicum Universum* (5 voll. in 7, Parisiis, 1864-1870), lib. III, tit. 32, n. 19; Bouix, *Tractatus de Jure Regularium* (5 tom. in 2 voll., Parisiis, 1857), I, 37; Piatus, *Praelectiones Juris Regularis ad Usum Fratrum Minorum Ordinis S. Francisci Capuccinorum* (3 voll., Parisiis, 1888-1891), I, 37 (hereafter these works will be cited respectively *Jus Canonicum; Ius Ecclesiasticum; Ius Canonicum; De Jure Regularium; Praelectiones Juris Regularis*).

[10] Pirhing, *loc. cit.*

[11] Schmalzgrueber, *loc. cit.*

[12] Piatus, *Praelectiones Juris Regularis,* I, 38; Victorius ab Appeltern, *Compendium Praelectionum Juris Regularis* (editio altera et emendata. Parisiis-Tornaci, 1913), p. 23.

ties with which this act had to be vested, namely, its complete freedom and spontaneity, than of the various forms of coercion which perhaps might be used to induce consent to it. Pius V (1566-1572) in his Constitution *Etsi mendicantium* of May 16, 1567, took note of the fact that some bishops, in carrying out the prescripts of the Council of Trent concerning the interrogation which had to precede the acceptance of girls into religion, had been unduly burdening some aspirants and delaying their acceptance. He demanded that they perform this task within fifteen days, and ascertain only *"an scilicet coactae, vel seductae fuerint."*[13] In his Constitution *Conditae a Christo* of December 8, 1900, Leo XIII (1878-1903) declared this provision of the Council of Trent mandatory in the same manner for institutes of simple vows as well.[14]

Although a similar interrogation was not prescribed by the general law of the Church for institutes of men, the Constitution of Clement VIII (1592-1605) *Cum ad regularem,* of March 19, 1603, urged that the superiors of these institutes in admitting novices diligently investigate with what "spirit, mind, and will" they sought entrance into the monastery, and whether they were embracing religion solely for the sake of a more perfect life or only out of levity or inordinate emotion.[15]

ARTICLE II. THE EFFECT OF FORCE AND FEAR UPON THE NOVITIATE

Only a few authors after the Council of Trent even discussed the validity of entrance into the novitiate under the influence of force and fear. Pirhing[16] and Sanchez (1559-1610)[17] pointed out

[13] *Codicis Iuris Canonici Fontes,* cura Emi Petri Card. Gasparri editi (9 voll., Romae-postea Civitate Vaticana: Typis Polyglottis Vaticanis, 1923-1939), (Voll. VII, VIII, IX, ed. cura et studio Emi Iustiniani Card. Serédi), n. 121 (hereafter cited *Fontes*).

[14] *Fontes,* n. 644.

[15] *Fontes,* n. 189.

[16] *Jus Canonicum,* lib. I, tit. 40, n. 43; lib. III, tit. 31, n. 121: "Notandum quarto: tametsi coactio per vim aut metum, irritam reddit professionem, ut dictum, non tamen ingressum in religionem, probationis causa; quia haec nullo jure reperitur irritata, sicut professio coacte facta; quia alias, si haec valida esset, indissolubilis foret, nec injuria facta reparari posset; secus est de

that, although the law clearly declared that a religious profession when made through grave force and fear was automatically null and void, it contained no provision declaring that a like duress would invalidate the novitiate. They explained this fact by the absence of the same weighty reason for declaring the novitiate invalid as was present in the case of the profession; once a profession had been made validly, it could not be dissolved, whereas the novice was free to leave at any time during the period of his probation. Thus, even though the novice could suffer injury through the use of duress, the injury was easily reparable.

Furthermore, they argued, the purpose of the year of probation was to provide the aspirant with an opportunity to experience the austerities of the monastic life. But one who was forced into the novitiate could not be held to have experienced these austerities any less rigorously than one who had entered freely. In fact, he would probably feel their rigor more deeply than if he had freely assumed them.

Suarez, on the contrary, held that the invalidating effects of grave fear likewise extended to entry into the novitiate. He argued that one must embrace this state of preparation for the profession with full liberty and proper dispositions. Hence, it could well happen that a forced entry into the novitiate would invalidate the entry into religion as well as a forced profession. He held this theory, however, in a restricted sense, for he admitted that, if the grave fear ceased at any time during the year of probation, and the novice in fact ratified his former act, the novitiate made under such circumstances sufficed for a valid profession.[18]

Although most other authors passed over the invalidity of the novitiate under such circumstances, Wernz (1842-1914) observed that perhaps, because of the liberty which the aspirant should enjoy, the view of Suarez might be admitted. He also pointed to the

---

novitiatu, ex quo egredi licet. . . . Infertur tamen gravis injuria etiam ei, qui ad ingrediendum religionem cogitur: ideoque Concilium Trident., Sess. 25, c. 18, *de reg.*, excommunicat omnes illos, qui quamcumque mulierem invitam cogunt ad ingrediendum. . . ."

[17] *Disputatio de Sancto Matrimonii Sacramento* (3 voll., Antverpiae, 1607), lib. VII, Dis. XXXVII, n. 51.

[18] Suarez, tr. VII, *De religione*, lib. 5, c. 8, n. 8—*Opera Omnia*, XV, 333.

provisions of the Council of Trent with regard to the interrogation to be conducted by the bishop as demonstrating how desirous the Church was that this act should be fully spontaneous.[19]

ARTICLE III. THE EFFECT OF FRAUD UPON ENTRY INTO RELIGION

It is to the great credit of Suarez that he, through a more equitable application of canonical and psychological principles, was able to attack and disentangle the erroneous theory of *dolus in spiritualibus,* which theory had continued in vogue after the time of the Council of Trent until the late sixteenth century. This author, after presenting a summary of the medieval doctrine, rejected it entirely and then proceeded to demonstrate how it had been developed through an erroneous understanding of the texts upon which it was based.

First, he said, the canon *Constituit,* which furnished the real origin of the theory, did not apodictically demonstrate that a religious profession was valid in spite of the use of fraud in inducing consent to it, although he admitted that the text did present some difficulty. To explain the action of the Council in binding those individuals to the monastery who had been duped into entering it, he declared that the canon was in reality not directed against those who had merely made a religious profession, but rather against those who had likewise received the clerical tonsure and sacred orders. The reason, therefore, why they were bound to remain in spite of the fact that they had been tricked into entering was that their ordination had imprinted an indelible character from which they could not be released.[20]

Attacking the theory of mutual compensation, he declared that the real cause for the nullifying effect of fraud upon an act did not lie so much in the injury which such deceit occasioned to its victim, but rather in the fact that fraud caused the will of its victim to give only a defective consent. The primary effect of fraud was an accidential or substantial misrepresentation of the object to be willed, so as to create ignorance or error in the mind

---

[19] Wernz, *Ius Decretalium,* III, n. 628.

[20] Suarez, tr. VII, *De religione,* lib. 6, c. 5, n. 6—*Opera Omnia,* XV, 415.

of the one who is to will it. But, since *nihil volitum nisi praecognitum,* the victim of deceit cannot be said to will that part of the object or act obscured from him through fraud. Hence, consent given under the influence of fraud was effective only to that degree to which the object of consent was clearly known to the victim of the deceit. The things which were obscured from him were either entirely involuntary or at least non-voluntary.[21]

Applying this doctrine to entry into religion, he distinguished between accidental fraud and substantial fraud. If the error induced through deceit concerned such things as the perpetuity of the bond of profession or the loss of one's property through it, or even if it concerned the austerities of the particular institute which the individual embraced, it was to be considered as substantial fraud. If it concerned other details of minor moment, the fraud was accidental.[22] If an individual had been tricked into embracing the religious state through a substantial misrepresentation of it, the consent given by him in view of the fraud was directed to an object different from the reality, and therefore his profession was such in name only and not in fact, since in making it he excluded the substance of the act from his consent. If, however, the deception was only accidental, it did not invalidate the profession, since under it the object was sufficiently known that the subject was enabled to give true consent.[23]

Attacking the theory of the glossators as built upon the principle of *dolus bonus,* he pointed out the fallacy of this argument likewise. It was not correct, he said, to hold that those who had been deceived into entering religion received a greater good in consequence of fraud than they had possessed before. The religious life was a better state only when it was freely accepted, and so long as an individual continued to be deceived totally, he was rendered incapable of placing a true act of consent towards it. Hence, the whole question of the invalidity of the religious profession did not revolve around the nature of the state embraced,

---

[21] Suarez, tr. VII, *De religione,* lib. 6, c. 5, n. 4—*Opera Omnia,* XV, 414.

[22] Suarez, *ibidem,* n. 5.

[23] Suarez, *ibidem,* n. 6—*Opera Omnia,* XV, 415.

but simply on whether or not the consent as given to it was furnished validly.[24]

Although this doctrine was developed by Suarez primarily with regard to the religious profession itself, he also noted that it was applicable to the novitiate in the same manner as he applied the doctrine concerning force and fear. Entry into the novitiate could likewise be invalid if the deceit employed concerned the substantial qualities of the religious state. The invalidity of entry into the novitiate, however, was without effect upon the subsequent profession as long as the deception ceased at some time before the profession was made. For, in his view, the novitiate made under such circumstances sufficed to fulfil the law of probation as required for a valid profession, as long, namely, as the novice ratified his former act of acceptance after the deceit had ceased.[25]

All the canonical writers following Suarez accepted his doctrine in its entirety and constantly repeated his arguments down to the time of the present Code of Canon Law, with the sole exception of Fagnanus (1598-1678), who continued to adhere to the medieval theory of *dolus in spiritualibus*.[26] Manuel Gonzalez-Tellez (+ after 1673) seems to have been the first canonist to accept the view of Suarez, although he mentioned that John Duranti (+ 1589) had held the theory before him.[27] Following him, Pirhing,[28] De Lugo,[29] Schmalzgrueber,[30] and Wernz[31] did little more than reproduce the doctrine of Suarez, and they simply referred to him to substantiate their view.

Pirhing discussed the question of a novice who had a contagious disease concerning which he kept silence when he was questioned

---

[24] Suarez, *ibidem*, n. 7.

[25] Suarez, tr. VII, *De religione*, lib. 5, c. 8, n. 8—*Opera Omnia*, XV, 333.

[26] *Commentaria in Quinque Libros Decretalium* (4 voll., Venetiis, 1692), lib. III, tit. 31, c. 1, n. 20.

[27] *Commentaria Perpetua in Singulos Textus Quinque Librorum Decretalium* (5 voll. in 4, Venetiis, 1699), lib. I, tit. 40. c. 6.

[28] *Jus Canonicum*, lib. III, tit. 31, n. 121.

[29] *Opera Omnia* (7 voll., editio summo studio ac diligentia mendis expurgata), Tom. I, *De Justitia et Jure* (Venetiis, 1718), Disp. XXII, sec. VII, n. 115 (hereafter cited *De Justitia et Jure*).

[30] *Ius Ecclesiasticum*, lib. III, tit. 31, n. 165.

[31] *Ius Decretalium*, III, n. 642.

before his reception. Such a defect did not invalidate the novitate or the profession, he held, if the disease was of such a nature that it would cease after proper remedies had been used for one complete year. But if it was not cured in that time, the individual who had obscured it could be ejected from the monastery even after he had made his profession.[32] Over and above these observations, however, the novitiate was not considered as invalidly entered upon under the influence of fraud, unless the deceit had resulted in substantial error, and then only if the deception was not dispelled before the actual profession.

---

[32] *Jus Canonicum,* lib. III, tit. 31, n. 121.

PART II

Canonical Commentary

CHAPTER IV

The Origin and Scope of the Impediment of Force, Fear, and Fraud

Canon 542, 1°. Invalide ad novitiatum admittuntur: Qui religionem ingrediuntur vi, metu gravi aut dolo inducti, vel quos Superior eodem modo inductus recipit.

The present Code of Canon Law, for the first time in general ecclesiastical legislation, extends the invalidating effects of physical violence, grave fear, and fraud to the act of entering the canonical novitiate, as well as to the profession of religious vows. In the pre-Code law these effects were applied solely to the act of religious profession itself, and, indeed, only to that of solemn vows. But the Church, as the zealous guardian and protector of the souls in its care, has always shown itself most solicitous that those who take this most serious and most sacred step do so as complete masters of their choice. The novitiate itself was established for the purpose of assuring greater liberty and fuller knowledge in those seeking entrance into the religious state of life. And, by casting up the bulwarks of censure[1] and careful interrogation[2] even about the act of entering this preliminary state, the Church has signified that its intention has ever been the same, namely, that this act be as freely placed as the act of religious profession itself.

The sacred character of the choice of the religious mode of life demands full and complete liberty in the one who selects it. For, in choosing to consecrate himself entirely to the divine service, man, as St. Thomas observed, offers himself as a true holocaust to God, giving to Him his entire self, his life, his senses, the property he possesses.[3] In so doing he performs an act of perfect

[1] Conc. Trident., sess. XXV, *de regularibus*, c. 18.

[2] Conc. Trident., sess. XXV, *de regularibus*, c. 17.

[3] *Sancti Thomae Aquinatis Doctoris Angelici Opera Omnia iussu impensaque Leonis XIII, P. M. edita* (Romae: 1882-); *Summa Theologica* (Romae: 1888-1906), II-II, q. 186, a. 1.

charity.[4] But such an act, in order to be perfect, demands not only freedom of choice, but also spontaneity of desire. For, as Pope Nicholas I observed, there is nothing of good in the act of embracing the religious state unless it is freely, deliberately, spontaneously willed.[5] Without clear knowledge and perfect freedom of decision, there can be no true sacrifice.

The historical evolution of this impediment establishes the fact that the chief aim of the Church in legislating against coerced entry into religion has always been twofold: to protect the full freedom of the individual in assuming the grave obligations placed upon one by this state,[6] and to preclude the unhappy effects which are usually consequent upon coerced acceptance of these obligations.[7] Implicit in these two reasons is the desire of the legislator to protect the involved individual from any unjust influence on his inherent right to determine his own activity.[8] But, over and above the protection of the private rights of individuals, the present impediment of force, fear, and fraud is likewise designed to protect the common good, lest perhaps through the use of these unjust agencies, those who are useless, or positively harmful, to the religious institute into which they are forced or tricked into entering, give rise to worldliness within, and scandal from without.[9]

Different from the case of religious profession, the nullifying effects of coercion and fraud upon the canonical novitiate are

[4] *Summa Theologica,* II-II, q. 189, a. 3, ad 3.

[5] C. 4, C. 20, q. 3—Jaffé, n. 2835.

[6] Cf. c. 9, C. 20, q. 1.

[7] Cf. c. 4, C. 20, q. 3; also Schaefer, *De Religiosis ad Normam Codicis Iuris Canonici* (4. ed., Città del Vaticano: Typis Polyglottis Vaticanis, 1947), p. 427; Berutti, *Institutiones Iuris Canonici* (6 voll., Voll. II, III et VI, Taurini-Romae: Marietti, 1936-1943), III, 139; Jardí, *El Derecho de las Religiosas* (2. ed., Vich: Editorial Seráfica, 1927), p. 203; Blat, *Commentarium Textus Codicis Iuris Canonici* (5 voll. in 7, Romae: apud "Angelicum," 1921-1938. lib. I, 1921; lib. II, ed. altera, 1921; lib. II, partes II et III, 3. ed., 1938; lib. III, Pars I, 2. ed. aucta et emendata, 1924; lib. III, partes II-VI, 2. ed., 1934; lib. IV, 1927; lib. V, 1924), lib. II, 594; Suarez, tr. VII, *Re religione,* lib. 6, c. 3, n. 5—*Opera Omnia,* XV, 400 (hereafter these works will be cited respectively *De Religiosis, Institutiones,* and *Commentarium*).

[8] Schaefer, *loc. cit.;* cf. also n. 788, p. 429.

[9] Blat, *Commentarium,* lib. II, 594.

derived solely from the positive ecclesiastical law.[10] The reason for this observation lies in the very nature of these two acts. For the religious profession constitutes a true bilateral contract which gives rise to reciprocal obligations and duties of a grave nature; on the part of the religious institute it gives origin to the obligation of recognizing the professed as one of its members towards whom it is obliged and over whom it has certain rights; on the part of the professed, it gives rise to the obligation of living according to the rule and constitutions of the institute, with the consequent rights and duties arising therefrom.[11] Thus the profession, containing an implicit contract, once validly entered upon, is productive of irrevocable obligations of a serious nature. Natural equity and justice demand that one who has been physically or morally constrained, or fraudulently duped, to effect such a contract must be restored to his pristine state of liberty, and freed from such unwanted obligations, by the very fact that his right to self-determination has been seriously impaired through the violent or deceitful action of another.[12] Hence, whenever consent which is given to a religious profession represents the product of one of

---

[10] Wernz-Vidal, *Ius Canonicum ad Codicis Normam Exactum* (7 voll. in 8, Voll. III, VII, 1. ed., Vol. VI, 2. ed., Voll. II et V, 3. ed., Romae: apud Aedes Universitatis Gregorianae, 1933-1949), III, 198; Schaefer, *De Religiosis,* p. 427; Biederlack-Führich, *De Religiosis* (Oeniponte, 1919), p. 114; Larraona, "Commentarium Codicis," *Commentarium pro Religiosis* (ab anno 1935: *Commentarium pro Religiosis et Missionariis,* Romae, 1920-), XVII (1936), 11. (Hereafter Wernz-Vidal's work will be cited *Ius Canonicum,* and *Commentarium pro Religiosis* and *Commentarium pro Religiosis et Missionariis* will be cited *CpR* and *CpRM,* respectively.)

[11] Bidagor, "De dolo et eius effectibus in admissione ad novitiatum et professione religiosa," *Periodica de Religiosis et Missionariis,* 8 voll., Brugis, 1905-1919 (Vol. I: 1905, 2. ed., 1911; II et III: 1907, 2. ed., 1911; IV: 1909, 2. ed., 1913; V: 1911, 2. ed., 1913; VI: 1912; VII: 1912-1914; VIII: 1919); ab anno 1920: *Periodica de Re Canonica et Morali utilia praesertim Religiosis et Missionariis,* 7 voll., Brugis, 1920-1927 (Vol. IX: 1920; X et XI: 1922-1923; XII: 1923-1924; XIII: 1924-1925; XIV: 1925-1926; XV: 1926-1927); ab anno 1927: *Periodica de Re Morali, Canonica, Liturgica,* Brugis (1927-1936) Romae (1937-); Vol. XVI, 1927- , XX (1931), 64* (hereafter cited *Periodica*).

[12] Wernz-Vidal, *Ius Canonicum,* III, n. 248, p. 198; Biederlack-Führich, *De Religiosis,* p. 114; Schaefer, *loc. cit.*

these agencies, the profession is invalid by reason of the natural law.

The same weighty reason, however, does not obtain in the case of forced entry into the canonical novitiate. For the obligations in this act are only tentatively assumed, as a preliminary preparation, as it were, for the definite and final formation of the actual contract of profession itself. The aspirant who enters the novitiate retains the complete freedom either of remaining or of departing if he so pleases. And the institute receiving him likewise retains a complete liberty either to accept or to reject him at the completion of or during the period of his noviceship. Hence, these two acts are not of the same juridic nature, although for the juridical perfection of either a full consent is required in the same identical manner, in one, however, by reason of the natural law, in the other, by reason of the positive will of the legislator.[18]

Although the text of canon 542, 1°, employs the terminology, *"qui religionem ingrediuntur . . ."*, entry into religion in this case consists solely of entry into the novitiate, as is obvious from the context in which this text is found. Consequently, if a candidate has

---

[18] A distinction must be drawn, however, between the nullifying effects of grave moral violence and the effects produced by the agency of fraud. For, whenever deceit is used in procuring consent to this act, it may result in a substantial deception concerning the nature of the object towards which consent is to be directed. In such an eventuality the novitiate as well as the profession would be rendered invalid by reason of the natural law.

However, since the law, when treating of the effects proper to fraud alone, as distinct from those arising from the error it induces, usually considers the deception resulting from this agency as pertaining merely to the accidental qualities of the object or act to be willed, it is not incorrect to speak of the invalidity of the novitiate when it is occasioned through fraud as likewise stemming from the positive will of the legislator, and not from the natural law. Badii (1884-1938) seems to be the only author who maintained that the novitiate would be invalid by reason only of the positive law, even in the case of a substantial deception. This view, however, is not shared by other canonists, who, in treating of fraud in the novitiate, as well as in other juridical acts, point to the basic distinction drawn above. Cf. Badii, "Il dolo nel Codice di Diritto Canonico," *Il Diritto Ecclesiastico* (Romae, 1890-), XL (1929), 313; Wernz-Vidal, *Ius Canonicum,* III, 199; Schaefer, *De Religiosis,* p. 429; Cappello, *Summa Iuris Canonici* (3 voll., Voll. I et II, 4. ed., Vol. III, 3. ed., Romae: apud Aedes Universitatis Gregorianae, 1945-1948), III, 158.

been morally constrained to enter the postulancy, his consent is not automatically voided by the law, and his subsequent entry into the novitiate is not rendered invalid thereby, provided he ceases to be coerced and freely of his own choice decides to enter the religious life some time before his actual investiture with the habit of the novitiate. Since the postulancy is not absolutely necessary for the validity of the novitiate, the novitiate is unaffected by its lack of proper form or coerced performance.[14] Evidently, however, superiors must be solicitous that when candidates enter upon their postulancy they do so with complete freedom and full deliberation. Creusen even recommends that it would be prudent to keep written proof of this fact.[15]

To be an impediment to the novitiate, violence, grave fear, and fraud must efficaciously procure the actual entry of the candidate in such a way that it must be considered as the sole and principal reason for his entry. If these agencies are only extrinsically related to this act, as, for example, if they merely serve to hasten the entry of one who would have entered even if they had not been present, though perhaps not so quickly, this fact alone would not make the consent given under their influence invalid.[16] It must be noted, however, that sometimes that which in the abstract seems only extrinsically related to the act of consent to enter may in a concrete case be intrinsically essential to the placing of this act. Thus, violence must be considered as intrinsically affecting the consent itself if, for example, one desired to enter religion, but not the particular institute into which he was forced; or if he desired to enter a monastery, but had no desire to enter the particular one he was constrained to enter; or if he wished to enter one class of a religious institute but was forced into another. Whether or not the violence in these cases plays an essential or non-essential rôle is a matter of fact in each individual case.[17]

---

[14] Schaefer, *De Religiosis,* n. 769, p. 415; Larraona, "Commentarium Codicis," *CpRM,* XVII (1936), 12; Creusen, *Religious Men and Women in the Code* (translated by Edward Garasché, 4. Eng. ed. by Adam Ellis, Milwaukee: Bruce Publishing Co., 1942), n. 177, p. 132.

[15] Creusen, *loc. cit.*

[16] Schaefer, *De Religiosis,* p. 427; Creusen, *op. cit.,* n. 179, p. 134; Larraona, *ibidem,* p. 13.

[17] Larraona, *ibidem,* note 173.

Although the law on coerced entry into the canonical novitiate in canon 542, 1°, and that on coerced religious profession in canon 572, § 1, 4°, are closely parallel to each other, they differ in one respect. It makes no difference legally whether constraint is brought to bear on the aspirant seeking entry or the superior receiving him in a coerced entry into the novitiate; in both cases the act is invalid. But in the law on coerced profession, no mention is made of the invalidating effects of grave violence or fraud in this act with relation to the superior who receives the profession. In view of this fact some authors hold that a profession would remain fully valid if the superior receiving it was forced to do so under duress or led to consent to it under fraud.[18] Others maintain, on the contrary, that in spite of the fact that no mention is made of the effects of duress on this act when it is applied to the superior only, the profession, as the novitiate, is invalid.[19] This latter opinion seems solidly probable because of the implicit contract involved in the profession, the text and context of this canon, and the opinion of accepted authors before the present Code.[20]

Since the primary and principal reason why invalidity is decreed to fall upon a novitiate entered upon through one of these agencies is to safeguard the full deliberation and perfect liberty of both the candidate and the superior performing it, it is entirely irrelevant whether the force, fear, or fraud which gives rise to it is induced by either party in the transaction, or by a third party. Formerly, especially with regard to the element of fraud, legal redress was

---

[18] Vermeersch-Creusen, *Epitome Iuris Canonici* (3 vols., Voll. II et III, 6. ed., Vol. I, 7. ed., Mechliniae-Romae: H. Dessain, 1940-1949), I, 535-536; Coronata, *Institutiones Iuris Canonici* (5 voll., Voll. I, II, III et IV, 2. ed., Taurini: Marietti, 1936-1945), I, n. 591, p. 754; Biederlack-Führich, *De Religiosis*, n. 90; Schaefer, *De Religiosis*, n. 953, p. 548; Creusen, *Religious Men and Women in the Code*, n. 226, 4°, p. 173; Larraona, "Commentarium Codicis," *CpRM*, XVII (1936), 12 (hereafter Coronata's work is cited as *Institutiones*).

[19] Wernz-Vidal, *Ius Canonicum*, III, n. 303, pp. 269-270; Beste, *Introductio in Codicem* (3. ed., Collegeville: St. John's Abbey Press, 1946), p. 388.

[20] Oesterle, "De relatione inter metum gravem et invaliditatem novitiatus et professionis," *CpR*, XV (1934), 407-411; Hostiensis, *Commentaria*, ad c. 12, X, *de regularibus et transeuntibus ad religionem*, III, 31, n. 13; Reiffenstuel, *Ius Canonicum*, lib. 3, tit. 31, n. 161.

granted to those who had been induced to give consent to a contract through its use, only when the other party in the transgression was responsible for its use. Under the present law, however, it is the agencies themselves that are primarily proscribed and outlawed inasmuch as they represent the cause from which the defective consent arises, and hence it matters not whether they are employed either by the superior or by the candidate against the other, or by an extraneous person against one or both of them, unknown to, or even contrary to, the will of the one benefited by their use.[21]

Finally, it is most important to point out that the invalidating effects attached to coerced entry into the novitiate in no way extend to the giving of prudent advice or counsel to one who shows signs of a divine vocation to this mode of life. Both St. Thomas and Suarez declared that it was not only licit to admonish another to embrace the religious life, but that it was a praiseworthy act, meritorious of a great reward.[22] Whenever parents, confessors, or spiritual directors prudently advise young persons in their charge to enter religion when they show an inclination to and apt qualities for the religious life, they are in reality fulfilling a most sacred duty placed upon them by reason of their position. And both prudence and respect dictate that children should seek out the wise counsel of their elders and give full consideration to the advice of the latter whenever they are contemplating taking this very important step in their lives. Prudent and cautious inducement is not moral constraint; the latter results only when the inducement is so inordinate as to interfere with the volitional liberty of an aspirant to a serious degree, or to preclude true internal consent.[23]

On the other hand, one who averts another from entering religion by violence, grave fear, or fraud sins against justice and is bound to make restitution to the religious institute or to the aspirant

---

[21] Vermeersch-Creusen, *Epitome Iuris Canonici,* I, 500; Berutti, *Institutiones,* III, 139; Coronata, *Institutiones,* I, n. 570, 710; Cappello, *Summa Iuris Canonici,* II, 46; Wernz-Vidal, *Ius Canonicum,* III, 200; Cervia, *De Professione Religiosa* (Faventiae: apud Societatem Thypographicam Faventinam, 1938), p. 81, note 1.

[22] S. Thomas, *Summa Theologica,* II-II, q. 189, a. 9; Suarez, tr. VII, *De religione,* lib. 5, c. 8, n. 10—*Opera Omnia,* XV, 323.

[23] Schaefer, *De Religiosis,* n. 789, p. 430.

if through this unjust action he causes a notable material injury to either.[24] If, however, only counsel, importunate persuasions, or promises are used, charity would be violated.[25] For entry into religion must be considered as a great good, the gift to God of a soul, and if one effectively and unjustly averts another from this good act without sufficient reason, one in reality inflicts upon such a person a very real harm.[26]

---

[24] Prümmer, *Manuale Iuris Canonici* (4. ed., Friburgi Brisgoviae: Herder and Co., 1927), p. 269.

[25] C. Marc, *Institutiones Morales Alphonsionae* (18. ed., 2 voll., Lugduni, 1927), II, n. 2140, p. 647.

[26] Cocchi, *Commentarium in Codicem Iuris Canonici* (8 voll. in 5, Voll. II, III, IV et VIII, 4. ed., Vol. VII, 3. ed., Augustae Taurinorum: Marietti, 1937-1947), IV, 106 (hereafter cited *Commentarium*). Cf. Schaefer, *De Religiosis,* n. 789, p. 431.

CHAPTER V

THE NATURE, DIVISIONS, AND EFFECT OF FORCE AND FEAR

Preliminary to the actual study of the effects of force and fear on the validity of the act of admission or reception into the canonical novitiate, it will be advantageous to recall these two legal notions, their divisions, and their effect on juridical acts in general, both for the purpose of clarity and for a more detailed analysis. Since the specific nature of the juridical act involved in admission into the novitiate does not differ essentially from any other juridical act of a physical or moral person when accepting obligations or assuming a juridical status, the general principles determining the juridical value of other acts performed under the influence of duress will also be applicable to this particular act.[1]

ARTICLE I. THE NATURE, DIVISIONS, AND EFFECT OF FORCE

A. *The Nature of Force*

The term force, in its broadest signification, designates either strength or might as it exists in itself or else as it is actively exerted against another. In this latter aspect, it is synonymous with violence, and is therefore defined by St. Thomas as an action which has its beginning from without and in which the one upon whom it is exerted does not in any way concur. Or, better, it is an extrinsic determination which is contrary to the natural inclination of someone or something.[2]

As a legal element, or in so far as it is considered as an infringement upon the self-determination of a human being, force (*vis, violentia*) is defined in the Roman legal sources as *maioris rei*

[1] Peinador, "De ingressu in statum religiosum, iure naturali invalido," *CpR,* XV (1934), 142-151, 281-290; *CpRM,* XVI (1935), 388-395, 444-452; cf. also Goyeneché, *Iuris Canonici Summa Principia de Religiosis* (Romae: Tip. Pol. "Cuore di Maria," 1938), n. 48, p. 82 (hereafter cited *De Religiosis*).

[2] *Summa Theologica,* I, q. 82, a. 1.

impetus qui repelli non potest, an attack by some overpowering agency greater than can be resisted.[3] This legal notion, borrowed from the ancient Roman sources by the medieval glossators,[4] has been constantly and consistently repeated in canonical jurisprudence ever since.[5]

Since it is impossible to force the human volitive faculty as such to elicit an act proper to itself alone through the application of any extrinsic violence,[6] the only type of violence envisioned under this legal notion of force is corporal propulsion directed to the procuring of a purely external action. For only those acts of the will which are put into execution by some other power external to the will itself, as the external senses and nerve centers of the body, are capable of frustration by means of an impetus from an external principle.[7]

The glossators observed that the terminology *"vis physica"* is synonymous with *"vis"* of the Roman sources, since it is always procured by means of physical contact with its victim.[8] And, since it presupposes that the intensity of the impetus is so superior as to defy resistance, they likewise noted that it might be referred to as *"vis absoluta,"* in the sense that it excludes all volitional concurrence on the part of the victim in the act which it effects.[9] Joannes Andreae, in the schema he used to compare the concepts of *vis* and *metus,* noted that force is distinct by reason of its source, its intensity, and its effect: it proceeds from a corporal propulsion, is of

---

[3] D. (4.2) 2.

[4] *Glossa ordinaria, casus* ad c. 4, X, *de his quae vi metusve causa fiunt,* I, 40; Hostiensis, *Summa Aurea,* tit., *de his quae vi metusve causa fiunt,* n. 1; Joannes Andreae, *Novella,* ad c. 5, X, *de his quae vi metusve causa fiunt,* I, 40; Panormitanus, *Commentaria,* in tit., *de his quae vi metusve causa fiunt,* n. 1.

[5] Sanchez, *Disputatio de Sancto Matrimonii Sacramento,* Lib. IV, Dis. I, nn. 1, 2; De Lugo, *De Justitia et Jure,* Disp. XXII, sec. VII, n. 115; Pirhing, *Jus Canonicum,* lib. I, tit. 40, n. 1; Schmalzgrueber, *Ius Ecclesiasticum,* lib. I, tit. 40, n. 1; Reiffenstuel, *Ius Canonicum,* lib. I, tit. 40, n. 1.

[6] S. Thomas, *Summa Theologica,* I-II, q. 6, a. 4.

[7] S. Thomas, *Summa Theologica,* I-II, q. 6, a. 6, ad 1.

[8] *Glossa ordinaria* ad c. 5, X, *de his quae vi metusve causa fiunt,* I, 40.

[9] *Glossa ordinaria, loc. cit.*

such intensity that it cannot be repelled, and results in a purely external act.[10]

This analysis shows that three factors go to make up the juridical notion of force. First, it supposes that the violent action has its origin totally from an extrinsic principle through the medium of physical contact.[11] It is of no significance whether the extrinsic principle of this propulsion is a free agent or a natural cause,[12] so long as it is directly and physically applied to the victim himself.[13]

Secondly, the dominance of the external agent must be exerted to such a degree that the victim is incapable of resisting it. For it is of the essence of violence that the power of the active agent employed exceed that of the passive agent in such a way that his entire capacity becomes subject to it.[14] It is obvious that the objective degree of such force will vary according to the capacity of the subject concerned; a child cannot resist with as much strength as can a man.[15]

Thirdly, the legal concept of force supposes that the resultant external act is executed without any volitional concurrence on the part of the victim suffering the force and that, moreover, it is totally repugnant to his natural inclination.[16] It presupposes, therefore, that the will does not remain merely negatively indifferent, but that a positive act of dissent is registered.[17] For if the will remains merely passive in the action, internally at least, it must be considered as virtually in agreement by showing itself willing to suffer the violent performance of the act.[18]

Since force, by its very nature, necessarily derives from outside its victim, the juridic notion does not in any way include irresistible impulses which may arise internally from abnormal propensities such as obsessions or phobias. Although these too may either

---

[10] *Novella,* in c. 5, X, *de his quae vi metusve causa fiunt,* I, 40, nn. 15, 16.

[11] *Summa Theologica,* I-II, q. 6, a. 6, ad 1.

[12] Blat, *Commentarium,* lib. II, 42.

[13] Coronata, *Institutiones,* I, 179.

[14] S. Thomas, *Summa Theologica,* I, q. 82, a. 2, ad 2.

[15] Coronata, *Institutiones,* I, 178-179.

[16] *Summa Theologica,* I, q. 82, a. 1; I-II, q. 6, a. 6, ad 1.

[17] *Summa Theologica,* I-II, q. 6, a. 4, ad 2; Beste, *Introductio in Codicem,* pp. 158-159.

[18] *Summa Theologica,* I-II, q. 6, a. 3; I-II, q. 6, a. 5, ad 2.

minimize the voluntariness of an act or totally destroy it, they must rather be considered under the heading of psychic disturbances than under the legal notion of extrinsic force.[19] Likewise, it seems, such phenomena as hypnosis and terror cannot be included here, though some authors appear ready to include them.[20] For terror is in reality a momentary mental incapacity and not a defect of the will. It is a state in which the intellectual excitement has mounted to such a degree that every form of reasoning is impossible, thus rendering the intellect absolutely incapable of discharging its normal functions. In such a state the will can neither dissent nor consent; it is temporarily incapacitated.[21] The same holds true for hypnosis which is a pathological state, not of the physical, but of the psychological faculties.[22] Furthermore, it is highly doubtful, according to accepted authorities, whether one acting under hypnotic suggestion could be forced to place an act utterly against his will.[23]

In the light of these preliminary notions, the term force, when used with reference to the placing of a juridical act, means one thing only: an overpowering physical impetus used to compel another to perform an action which is totally opposed to his will. It is with this signification that it is referred to as a species of violence which nullifies entry into the canonical novitiate.

B. *The Divisions of Force*

The concept of force as outlined above is that of absolute force, that which is completely invincible with perfect opposition of the will. Strictly taken, this is the only type of violence which falls within the limits of the legal concept of force.[24] But besides absolute physical force there is another type referred to as relative or moral

---

[19] Salsmans, "Circa vitia consensus," *Jus Pontificium* (Romae, 1921-1940), X (1930), 104.

[20] Wernz-Vidal, *Ius Canonicum*, V, 625; Berutti, *Institutiones*, II, 52, note 2.

[21] Giacchi, *La violenza nel negozio giuridico canonico* (Milano: Dott. A. Giuffrè, 1937), pp. 15-16.

[22] Giacchi, *op. cit.*, p. 19.

[23] Allers, "Some medico-psychological remarks on canons 1068, 1081, and 1087," *The Jurist* (Washington, D. C., 1941-), IV (1944), 378-380.

[24] Cf. Ojetti, *Synopsis Rerum Moralium et Juris Pontificii* (4 voll., Romae, 1909-1914), s. v. *vis*, n. 4107; Coronata, *Institutiones*, I, 179.

force, that which is not of such superior strength as to defy resistance. In the external forum, relative force denotes some slight external compulsion which is not insurmountable and which therefore does not take away complete liberty of action. In the internal forum, it may also denote some externally insurmountable compulsion to which the will does not interiorly dissent.[25]

It is obvious that relative or moral force cannot be considered as a species of the legal concept of force as outlined above except analogically, in so far as it likewise operates through the medium of physical contact. It does not physically necessitate, but rather creates a situation in which the will in each given moment of its presence is faced with the necessity either of resisting or of yielding to its pressure. Hence, in so far as it engenders a trepidation of will in its victim, it coincides with the active aspect of the concept of fear. It is not however identical with it, for the active agent of fear may or may not operate through the medium of physical contact. In ultimate effect, however, since the act resulting from moral force is *involuntarium secundum quid,* it does not substantially differ from the effect of fear. For the purpose of clarity, and to conform with the common usage, whenever force is referred to in this present work, it will signify only absolute physical violence, unless the contrary is noted.

C. *The Effect of Force*

Juridical acts done through absolute physical compulsion, or force of such intensity that it cannot be resisted, are invalid by their very nature. The person who acts under such violence is not master of his own act, but rather he acts as the mere tool of the exterior agent.[26] The act itself is merely a mechanical physical reaction to

---

[25] Regatillo, *Institutiones Iuris Canonici* (2 voll., Vol. I, 2. ed., Vol. II, 1. ed., Santander: Sal Terrae, 1942-1946), I, 135 (hereafter cited *Institutiones*); Maroto, *Institutiones Iuris Canonici* (2. voll., Vol. I, 3. ed., Romae: apud "Commentarium pro Religiosis," 1921), I, 459 (hereafter cited *Institutiones*); Noldin, *Summa Theologiae Moralis* (5. ed., 3 voll., Ratisbonae, Romae et Neo Eboraci, 1904), I, 51; Merkelbach, *Summa Theologiae Moralis* (3. ed., 3 voll., Parisiis, 1938), I, n. 68, p. 73.

[26] Beste, *Introductio in Codicem,* p. 159; Michiels, *Principia Generalia de Personis in Ecclesia* (Lublin, Polonia: Universitas Catholica, 1932), p. 502 (hereafter cited *Principia Generalia*).

an external impulse in which the will takes no part. Hence, it cannot be imputed to the individual as the principle from whom it proceeds, and is, therefore, totally bereft of moral or juridical value.[27] It cannot even be considered as a juridical act except in external appearances only,[28] and hence canon 103, § 1, of the present Code considers such an act as if it were non-existent.[29]

It is to be noted, however, that these observations are true only if the violence is in reality absolute. The amount of active resistance which must be employed against violence before it is considered as insurmountable differs in the internal and the external forums. In the internal forum, or if one considers the morality of an act, force is termed absolute only when the victim has in reality resisted the violence not only with internal dissent, but also, in so far as he is morally bound and able, by employing such external means as might efficaciously frustrate the attack, and nevertheless has failed in his attempt to do so.[30] In the external forum, however, or in reference to the juridical efficacy of the act, it is not necessary that the force be in fact externally resisted (internal resistance being always presupposed), but it suffices according to the explicit words of canon 103, § 1, and the definition itself, that "it cannot be resisted." In other words, so long as the victim foresees that resistance is useless to impede the effect of the violence, he need not externally have manifested his repugnance.[31]

If, in spite of the fact that the external force is insurmountable, the will of the victim nevertheless concurs, the legal consequences of such an act differ from the moral consequences. In the internal forum, the external act is voluntary, and hence, if sinful, morally imputable. In the external forum, however, the act is considered as invalid, for the lawgiver is concerned with externals, and the consent in this instance, though present, is not manifest externally.[32]

---

[27] Gasparri, *Tractatus Canonicus de Matrimonio* (2 voll., editio nova, Romae: Typis Polyglottis Vaticanis, 1932), II, n. 832, p. 48.

[28] Coronata, *Institutiones,* I, 179.

[29] Canon 103, § 1. Actus, quos persona sive physica sive moralis ponit ex vi extrinseca, cui resisti non possit, pro infectis habentur.

[30] Michiels, *Principia Generalia,* p. 503.

[31] Michiels, *loc. cit.;* Maroto, *Institutiones,* I, 460.

[32] Michiels, *op. cit.,* pp. 503-504; Maroto, *loc. cit.;* Blat, *Commentarium,* lib. II, 42.

Finally, if it is a case in which the external force is not of such a degree that it cannot be resisted, the will of the passive agent is presumed to concur in the resultant act and hence it is considered as valid. In practice, however, these acts may be treated as acts done through grave and unjust fear, since the element of fear is usually present in them. They may therefore be liable to rescission by a competent authority.[33]

ARTICLE II. THE NATURE, DIVISIONS, AND EFFECT OF FEAR

A. *The Nature of Fear*

In its general philosophical sense, the term fear signifies an irascible movement of the sensitive appetite stimulated by the perception of some sensible evil represented in the imagination as imminent. As such, it is predominantly prevalent in the sensitive faculties of the human composite and is more properly referred to as *passio timoris.*[34] Purely sensitive fear directly affects the activity of the sensitive organism, especially the memory and the imagination, and indirectly, through these, the intellect and the use of reason. If it is vehement, and especially if it emerges suddenly, it may either more or less diminish or even totally destroy the mental capacity of its victim.[35] In this latter case, it is referred to as terror.[36]

Juridically, however, or in so far as it is considered as a morally determining force upon the human will, fear, or *metus,* is defined in the Roman sources as *instantis vel futuri periculi causa mentis trepidatio,* a perturbation or anxiety of the mind arising from the apprehension of some imminent or future danger.[37] The juridical notion considers fear only as an irascible affection of the superior faculties of the soul, or more precisely of the will, as distinguished from the purely sensible concept of fear. Abstracted from the physical and organic commotion which perhaps may accompany it,

---

[33] Michiels, *op. cit.,* p. 503; Maroto, *loc. cit.*

[34] S. Thomas, *Summa Theologica,* I-II, q. 25, a. 4.

[35] Michiels, *Principia Generalia,* p. 505.

[36] Giacchi, *La violenza nel negozio giuridico canonico,* p. 17.

[37] D. (4.2) 1.

such fear is considered as prevailing merely in the rational faculties in so far as it is a trepidation effected in the mind, or more precisely in the will, through the intellectual apprehension of some threatening harm from which the will recoils. As such, it does not in itself impede the objective and deliberative judgment of reason, nor does it totally destroy freedom of choice.[38]

Whenever the agent of the impending evil engendering this psychological disturbance is another human being who wishes, by means of it, to produce a result counter to the spontaneous self-determination of the victim upon whom it is wrought, this mental trepidation properly takes on the character of moral or impelling violence, in the sense that it morally compels the will of its victim to place an act which ordinarily he would be unwilling to place.[39] It may likewise be referred to as a form of conditioned violence, *coactio conditionalis,* under these same circumstances, since the adverse agent, by threatening the evil which gives rise to the fear, places the victim under a conditioned necessity either of complying with his demand on the one hand, or of bearing the threatened harm from which he recoils on the other.[40] Ordinarily, such fear does not destroy the self-determination of its victim; it merely reduces the spontaneity of his act.

The legal notion defined above, therefore, represents only the passive aspect of the concept of fear when it is considered as a form of moral violence. It is this passive aspect, or the psychological disturbance effected in the mind by the apprehended danger, that is of chief concern to jurists, since it is under this guise that fear proximately affects the will. In the active sense, fear is nothing other than the objective threat giving rise to this mental trepidation. It is in this latter sense that the terms force and fear are considered as correlatives by some authors, as cause to effect, since the objective cause of fear may at times be occasioned by relative physical force. But, as noted above, this is not necessarily so. For fear may be, and generally is, caused without any physical contact between the aggressor and his victim. The adverse agent rather works

---

[38] Michiels, *Principia Generalia,* p. 505.
[39] Wernz-Vidal, *Ius Canonicum,* I, 45; Regatillo, *Institutiones,* I, 135.
[40] Gasparri, *Tractatus Canonicus de Matrimonio,* II, n. 833, p. 49.

through the medium of an objective threat of harm or evil without its physical application.[41]

Although the juridical definition of fear mentions only the disturbance occasioned in the mental faculties through moral coercion, without any explicit allusion to the movement of the sensitive appetite which ordinarily accompanies this affection of the soul, this does not signify that legally fear is considered as something totally abstracted from the concomitant physical reaction which accompanies it, as some authors seem to have taught.[42] Because of the very nature of the human composite, any disturbance of the mental faculties will as a rule be accompanied with some sensible or nervous alteration which will be more or less vividly realized depending upon the physical and nervous condition of the individual and the nature of the threatening danger. *Mental trepidation* therefore must be more properly understood as directly affecting the intellectual faculties and indirectly the sensitive nature of the subject in whom it is found.[43] And hence, the *metus* of the canonists, concretely considered, is an emotional state which pervades the whole human composite. Rudolph Allers has recently defined this concept as "the emotional response to the awareness of a great danger the nature of which is known, even if imperfectly, and which is conceived as imminent and, at the same time, as not absolutely unavoidable."[44] It is in this sense that it is understood in this present work.

Finally, the words of the definition *"instantis vel futuri periculi causa"* indicate the source of juridical fear as well as the fact that there must be a true causal connection between the objective threat of the active agent and the resultant subjective alteration.[45] The characteristics with which the objective danger must be vested, and the circumstances which must surround its infliction in order to

---

[41] Gasparri, *loc. cit.;* Michiels, *Principia Generalia,* p. 504.

[42] Cf. e.g., Bouquillon, *Theologia Moralis Fundamentalis* (Brugis, 1890), n. 333, p. 609.

[43] Claeys Bouuaert, "De metus influxu," *Jus Pontificium,* VI (1926), 105-106; Michiels, *Principia Generalia,* p. 505.

[44] Allers, "Some medico-psychological remarks on canons 1068, 1081 and 1087," *The Jurist,* IV (1944), 372.

[45] Michiels, *Principia Generalia,* p. 506.

establish this causal relationship legally, will be discussed at length in the commentary below.

B. *The Divisions of Fear*

Canonically, fear may be divided by reason of its origin, by reason of the manner in which it is inflicted, and by reason of the degree to which it is effected. By reason of its origin, fear assumes the nature of the cause from which it proceeds. If fear arises from some cause internal to the person, it is referred to as fear from within or *metus ab intrinseco*. Such, for example, would be fears which arise from the consideration of the pains of hell, from qualms of conscience, or from the threat of a malignant disease. If fear has its origin in some external cause, either necessary or free, it is referred to as fear from without or *metus ab extrinseco*. Examples of fear arising from external natural causes are the fears arising from an earthquake, a shipwreck, or a fire, or an epidemic of a virulent disease which is rife in a locality. Extrinsic fear, in so far as it is considered as coming from a free agent, is none other than that which is derived from the threatening action of another human being.[46]

With relation to the manner in which fear is inflicted, that which is caused by a free human agent may be divided into that which is justly and that which is unjustly employed. Fear is considered as justly inflicted whenever it is used for a reason which merits it, by a competent authority having the right to do so, and in accordance with the prescripts of the law.

---

[46] Michiels, *Principia Generalia*, p. 505; Maroto, *Institutiones*, I, 461; Chelodi-Ciprotti, *Ius Canonicum de Matrimonio* (5. ed., Vicenza: Societa Anonima Tipografica Editrice, 1947), p. 143 (hereafter cited *De Matrimonio*); Beste, *Introductio in Codicem*, p. 161.

Some canonists prefer to present the above made distinction in a different manner, defining intrinsic fear not only as that which arises from within the victim, but also as that which comes from a necessary cause, whether internal or external to the subject, or from some natural event, the existence of which does not depend upon a free human agent. Extrinsic fear under this division is simply that arising from a free agent. Cf. Vermeersch, "De metu qui, saltem ex lege positiva, excusat ab obligationibus vitiato consensu susceptis, praecipue de metu ab intrinseco vel extrinseco," *Periodica*, XVII (1928), 141*-143*.

Fear is unjustly inflicted whenever the virtue of justice is violated in some way or other. This may happen when the evil threatened is substantially unjust, as is the case when it is injurious to the rights of the one who incurs it, i.e., it is not merited through any fault on his part, or when it is brought to bear without an adequate reason. It is then referred to as unjust *quoad substantiam*. It may also happen that fear, even though substantially just, becomes unjust by reason of the concrete circumstances surrounding its infliction. Such would be the case, for example, when the person inflicting it is not a competent authority with the right to do so or when, even though he be competent, he uses his authority in an illegitimate manner. The consequent fear is then termed unjust *quoad modum*.[47]

Fear may also be unjustly inflicted by reason of the end for which it is employed. This division is of great importance in a consideration of forced entry into the religious state. Fear is unjust by reason of the end whenever the one inflicting it has the right to do so for some particular purpose, but in reality makes use of this right for the purpose of obtaining some other end than that for which he may legitimately apply the fear, or else for the purpose of procuring for himself some unfair advantage totally disproportioned to his right to threaten the evil. A typical example of such unjust fear is blackmail, whereby the one threatening to divulge some hidden crime employs a legitimate threat for the purpose of obtaining some totally unfair advantage of another.[48]

By reason of the manner of its infliction, fear may also be divided into that which is directly and that which is indirectly inflicted. It is directly inflicted when it is intended for the procurement of some particular act. It is indirectly inflicted when it is not intended for the extorting of the particular act placed by its victim, but, while it is exerted for one purpose, the passive subject towards whom it is directed, rather than submit to the evil occasioned by it, and simply for the purpose of liberating himself from the impending evil, selects to execute another act different from the one demanded.[49]

---

[47] Michiels, *Principia Generalia*, p. 506.

[48] Michiels, *loc. cit.*

[49] Regatillo, *Institutiones*, I, 136; Beste, *Introductio in Codicem*, p. 161; Michiels, *op. cit.*, p. 508.

By reason of the degree to which it is effected, fear is divided into that which is grave and that which is slight. Grave fear may be either absolutely or relatively so. Absolutely grave fear is that which would effectively actuate any man whomsoever gifted with the ordinary strength of resistance. Relatively grave fear is that which, though in itself not considered as grave by other human beings, is grave with regard to a certain individual as the result of a lack in his subjective capacity of resistance or in view of the circumstances surrounding the infliction of the fear. Light fear is the opposite of grave fear. Hence, it is that which proceeds from a threat slight in itself, or at least with respect to the person threatened, or, even though serious in itself, it is neither imminent nor unavoidable for the individual against whom it is brought to bear.[50]

Finally, a further distinction may be drawn between fear which is antecedent and fear which is concomitant, according as an act is performed because of fear or merely with fear. In the former case the fear is the whole cause of the action; in the latter, the action is merely occasioned through its use.[51]

C. *The Effect of Fear*

Outside the case of complete loss of control over the mental faculties through terror,[52] the essential voluntariness of an act of the will is not destroyed through fear. For the very notion of fear, as outlined above, presupposes that the one acting because of it forms a true judgment and makes a free choice.[53] He selects that which to him appears to be the lesser of two evils, though he would

---

[50] Claeys Bouuaert, "De metus influxu," *Jus Pontificum,* VI (1926), 106.

[51] Cappello, *Tractatus Canonico-Moralis de Sacramentis* (3 voll. in 5, Vol. III, 3. ed., Augustae Taurinorum-Romae: Marietti, 1933), III, n. 603, p. 685 (hereafter cited *De Sacramentis*).

[52] Whenever fear is so vehement as to terrorize its victim, thus paralyzing his faculties and totally destroying his deliberation and consequent free election, it cannot any longer be considered as fear in the juridical sense. It is rather a temporary physical incapacity. When fear is considered as a form of moral violence, it essentially supposes both judgment and freedom of choice. Cf. Giacchi, *La violenza nel negozio giuridico canonico,* pp. 15, 16.

[53] Wernz-Vidal, *Ius Canonicum,* V, n. 486, p. 625.

not select to submit to it were it not necessary precisely to avoid the greater evil feared.[54] Hence the essential conditions for a voluntary act are satisfied, since not only that which is willed for its own sake is voluntary, but also that which is wished for the sake of something else.[55] This truth was frequently evidenced in the medieval glosses by the common adage: *coacta voluntas voluntas est.*[56]

Fear, nevertheless, minimizes the voluntariness of the act, as is clearly demonstrated through a consideration of the influence it has upon the intellect and will. For when a person is under duress, the mind, shackled in its proper operation by the vivid phantasm created in the imagination by the impending danger, and rendered less capable of resisting because of the disturbed state of the whole human organism, vacillates between the various impressions which solicit it. Judging that which appears to it as the lesser evil under the circumstances as here and now to be desired in so far as it is a medium of impending the greater evil, it so exhibits it to the will. The will, being a blind faculty, though naturally inclined to desire good and avoid evil, presently chooses one course of action in preference to another merely as a means of escape, and thus indirectly gives way to the vexation itself.[57]

It is evident that the voluntariness of the resulting act is greatly modified; it reflects a mixed character, partly voluntary, partly involuntary. For, considered in itself, outside the actual circumstances of the case, the course of action submitted to by the will is really repugnant to it and would never have been desired for its own sake. But, presented in the circumstances of fear, it becomes voluntary not so much under the species of good to be desired, but as the more preferable of two evils. Though freely chosen, it is not spontaneously desired. Canonists, following the terminology of St. Thomas,[58] refer to such an act as voluntary *simpliciter* but in-

---

[54] Beste, *Introductio in Codicem,* p. 159.

[55] S. Thomas, *Summa Theologica,* I-II, q. 6, a. 6, ad 1.

[56] *Glossa ordinaria* ad c. 2, X, *de his quae vi metusve causa fiunt,* I, 40, s. v. *coacta voluntas.*

[57] Claeys Bouuaert, "De metus influxu," *Jus Pontificium,* VI (1926), 106.

[58] *Summa Theologica,* I-II, q. 6, a. 6.

voluntary *secundum quid,* i.e., involuntary outside the actual case proposed to the will.[59]

Since consent, though modified, is not absent when the will acquiesces through fear, the act in which it intervenes is in itself valid according to the natural law[60] and at the most is capable of rescission. If this is true in the natural law, there is much more reason for the legislator to regard it so in the positive law, lest obligations become too easily cast off and contracts too easily broken under the pretext that the juridical act giving rise to them was vitiated because of fear.[61] Hence, the general principle is enunciated in the present legislation in Canon 103, § 2, that acts performed because of grave and unjust fear are considered valid, unless the law clearly decrees otherwise, though they may be rescinded by a competent authority.[62] The principles of equity and justice demand that one suffering such a violation of his rights should be freed of all obligations arising from it and restored to his previous state.[63]

In order, however, that one may enter a plea of invalidity, or claim the right to the rescission of an act performed through fear, the fear under which the act was performed must qualify as juridically relevant. It must be vested with certain specific qualities, objectively demonstrable, which establish it not only as the true cause of the act, but also classify its infliction as a violation of the right to self-determination of the individual. These qualities, first outlined in the Roman sources, have remained constant and well-defined in canonical jurisprudence ever since they were first accepted by the medieval glossators.

First, the only type of fear with relation to its origin which is considered as relevant is that which is extrinsically caused by an-

[59] Sanchez, *Disputatio de Sancto Matrimonii Sacramento,* lib. IV, Dis. I, nn. 1, 2; De Lugo, *De Justitia et Jure,* Disp. XXII, sec. VII, n. 115; Reiffenstuel, *Ius Canonicum,* lib. I, tit. 40, n. 1; Schmalzgrueber, *Ius Ecclesiasticum,* lib. I, tit. 40, n. 1.

[60] Wernz-Vidal, *Ius Canonicum,* II, 46; Regatillo, *Institutiones,* I, 136.

[61] Michiels, *Principia Generalia,* p. 514; Claeys Bouuaert, *ibidem,* p. 107.

[62] Canon 103, § 2. Actus positi ex metu gravi et iniuste incusso vel ex dolo, valent, nisi aliud iure caveatur; sed possunt ad normam can. 1684-1689 per iudicis sententiam rescindi, sive ad petitionem partis laesae sive ex officio.

[63] Wernz-Vidal, *Ius Canonicum,* II, 46.

other free human agent. Roman Law,[64] the glosses on the *Corpus Iuris Canonici,*[65] and canonical jurisprudence in general, both past[66] and present,[67] have constantly insisted upon this point.

Secondly, with relation to its intensity, fear must be engendered to a grave degree before it is considered as having attained a modifying effect upon the human will. The Roman praetor adopted an abstract norm for this degree which he described as that fear which would move a *homo constantissimus,* or a most resolute man.[68] Later the glossators attenuated the norm of the praetor to that fear which would move a *homo constans,* or a man gifted with ordinary constancy.[69] Following the Council of Trent, the relative norm for ascertaining this degree was commonly accepted by canonical writers in the same sense it is held today.[70]

Finally, to produce its juridical effect, the fear must be unjustly inflicted. The fundamental consideration in determining that an act performed through fear is invalid lies in the fact that fear is a violation of and an infringement upon the self-determination of a human being. It is only when the rights of an individual have been violated that fear merits the invalidating effects attached to it by law. Hence, canonical doctrine,[71] again in agreement with the

[64] D. (4.2) 9; D. (4.2) 7; C. (2.19) 9.

[65] *Glossa ordinaria* ad c. 7, X, *de his quae vi metusve causa fiunt,* I, 40, s. v. *per testes;* Hostiensis, *Commentaria,* ad c. 17, X, *de regularibus et transeunti bus ad religionem,* III, 31; Joannes Andreae, *Novella,* ad c. 17, X, *de regularibus et transeuntibus ad religionem,* III, 31, n. 4.

[66] Sanchez, *Disputatio de Sancto Matrimonii Sacramento,* lib. IV, Dis. XII, n. 2; Pirhing, *Jus Canonicum,* lib. I, tit. 40, n. 10; Schmalzgrueber, *Ius Ecclesiasticum,* lib. I, tit. 40, nn. 2, 8.

[67] Cf., e.g., Michiels, *Principia Generalia,* p. 505.

[68] D. (4.2) 6.

[69] *Glossa ordinaria* ad c. 2, X, *de his quae vi metusve causa fiunt,* I, 40, s. v. *coactus;* Hostiensis, *Commentaria,* in c. 1, X, *de his quae vi metusve causa fiunt,* I, 40, s. v. *evaginato gladio;* Joannes Andreae, *Novella,* ad c. 6, X, *de his quae vi metusve causa fiunt,* I, 40.

[70] Sanchez, *Disputatio de Sancto Matrimonii Sacramento,* lib. IV, Dis. I, nn. 12-23; De Lugo, *De Justitia et Jure,* Disp. XXII, sec. VII, nn. 110-111.

[71] *Glossa ordinaria,* ad c. 2, X, *de his quae vi metusve causa fiunt,* I, 40; De Lugo, *De Justitia et Jure,* Disp. XXII, sec. VII, n. 152; Schmalzgrueber, *Ius Ecclesiasticum,* lib. I, tit. 40, n. 2.

Roman theory,[72] has always demanded an unjust infliction of fear before an act is null *ab initio* or liable to rescission.

Canon 103, § 2, is, as it were, an epitome of all the canonical doctrine of the ages concerning these various requirements which much be fulfilled before the fear qualifies as having attained the effect attached to it by the law. Mention is made in this canon, it is true, only of the elements of gravity and injustice in juridically relevant fear, but since it is impossible for the element of injustice to be present unless through the intervention of another human agent, this general norm in the present legislation likewise demands, at least implicitly, that fear, to produce a juridical effect, must arise from a free extrinsic cause.

In order to defend the individual against unjust interference in his right to self-determination, the positive law, by way of exception to the general principle that acts performed under grave fear are merely rescissible, declares certain juridic acts *ipso iure* null and void. These acts, now listed explicitly in various places in the present Code, enjoy this special protection of the law either because of their indissoluble character, or in view of the sacredness of the obligations they involve, or in consequence of the possible harm to the common welfare which may flow from their coerced performance.[73] Inasmuch as these acts effect a juridic status which gives rise to grave obligations, they demand not only an act of the will which has as its object the manifestation of consent, but likewise the will to accept and effect that which such a manifestation entails. And since an act placed under moral coercion is primarily concerned with the mere manifestation of consent, the law decrees automatic invalidity for such acts when placed under duress.[74]

The Church wishes individuals who assume grave obligations to be complete masters of their choice; hence the law is extremely sensitive to any undue influence on the free self-determination of individuals when placing one of these nine acts as listed in the Code, and renders them null and void whenever they represent the product of the unjust coercion of another. It is with one of these nine acts that the present study is concerned, that of entry into the religious state, or acceptance into the canonical novitiate.

[72] D. (4.2) (3.1); cf. also D. (4.2) 21.

[73] Claeys Bouuaert, "De metus influxu," *Jus Pontificium,* IV (1926), 109.

[74] Giacchi, *La violenza nel negozio giuridico canonico,* p. 83.

CHAPTER VI

The Effects of Force and Fear on Entry Into the Canonical Novitiate

ARTICLE I. THE EFFECTS OF PHYSICAL VIOLENCE

As the study of the nature of absolute physical violence in the preceding chapter revealed it to be such that it excluded all possibility of a human act, little more need be said concerning its invalidating effect upon the act of entry into the canonical novitiate. An action performed through force is merely an *actus hominis,* with no moral or juridical value whatsoever. Mere physical propulsion is incapable of affecting the internal integrity of the spiritual faculties, and hence, even though it may result in an external action which runs contrary to the inclination of the will, it cannot result in procuring true internal consent. And since the very nature of absolute physical force totally precludes internal consent, a novitiate entered upon through such violence is obviously without juridical substance.

Even in the hypothesis that the aspirant actually gives internal consent under such physical constraint, his entry would nevertheless be invalid. For, in the external forum it does not matter whether the victim of force in reality shows external repugnance to it; it suffices for the force to be of such a nature that he could not resist it were he to try.[1] Although most authors make no mention of the effect of relative physical force upon entry into the novitiate,[2] or else seem to presuppose that such force does not cause invalidity in this act,[3] Michiels[4] and Berutti[5] advance the opinion that any

[1] Maroto, *Institutiones,* I, 460; Michiels, *Principia Generalia,* p. 503.

[2] Cf., e.g., Beste, *Introductio in Codicem,* p. 364; Regatillo, *Institutiones,* I, 365; Creusen, *Religious Men and Women in the Code,* n. 179, c, p. 134; Vermeersch-Creusen, *Epitome Iuris Canonici,* I, 499.

[3] Larraona, "Commentarium Codicis," *CpRM,* XVII (1936), 13; Schaefer, *De Religiosis,* p. 427; Cervia, *De Professione Religiosa,* p. 82.

[4] *Principia Generalia,* p. 504.

[5] *Institutiones,* II, 52, note 1.

extrinsic force whatsoever, even that which is relative in nature, suffices to annul this act. This opinion does not lack solid probability in view of the terminology employed in canon 542, 1°. For, whereas canon 103, § 1, specifies that physical force, in order to vitiate a juridical act totally, must be *"extrinseca, cui resisti non possit. . ."*, the canon which deals with a forced entry into the canonical novitiate employs the terminology *"vi . . . inductus,"* without further qualifying the force required for a nullifying effect as an absolute force, even though it does specify with regard to fear on the other hand that it must be a *"metus gravis."* However, the opinion of Larraona and Schaefer seems more probable, namely, that physical violence which is not absolute does not in itself vitiate this act, but inasmuch as it generally does give rise to mental trepidation, it may generally be regarded as sufficient for causing the nullity of the act, not by reason of the fact that it is physical force, but rather because it falls under the element of fear.[6]

Although one cannot even at this late day totally preclude the possible employment of physical force for forcing a person into religion, the probability of its occurrence must be regarded as relatively rare. About the only hypothesis in which it could be realized would be that in which an individual is transported to the monastery or convent through sheer physical compulsion, and there is physically constrained to receive the habit. On the contrary, the use of moral constraint is much more likely to happen. Hence it merits a much fuller and more detailed analysis with relation to this act than the element of absolute physical force.

ARTICLE II. THE EFFECTS OF GRAVE AND UNJUST FEAR

From the preliminary study of the effects of grave fear on juridical acts in general in the preceding chapter, it was found that fear, in order to attain its invalidating effect, must be, according to the exact requirements of the law: (a) from without, (b) of grave intensity, (c) unjustly inflicted, and (d) the true efficacious cause which inspires the act. Since the act of entry into the canonical novitiate does not differ substantially from any other juridical act

---

[6] Larraona, *art. cit.;* Schaefer, *loc. cit.*

by which a person assumes a juridical status, these four conditions will be used as the basis for the evaluation of the effect of fear upon this specific act. Consequently, a detailed analysis will be made in the following four paragraphs of (a) the extrinsic origin, (b) the element of gravity, (c) the element of injustice, and (d) the causal relationship which must be present in order to produce a juridically defective act of entry or acceptance into the canonical novitiate. It is important to point out that these four conditions must be collectively co-existent in each particular case and must be verified in the external forum with at least moral certainty to justify the declaration that a novitiate is invalid.

Since the present legislation on the effect of grave moral violence upon juridical acts and transactions understands this term according to the commonly received explanations,[7] and acknowledges the general principles by which the moral and juridical value of human acts performed under its influence may be determined, one must, in treating of these various elements as needed in juridically relevant fear, fall back on the teachings of accepted authors who wrote before the present Code of Canon Law[8] as well as upon present day juridical and jurisprudential doctrine.

A. *Extrinsic Origin*

In the eyes of the law, only that fear which is inflicted by another human agent is of any legal consequence. Subjective fear, whether it arises from auto-suggestion in a highly excitable person, from mere internal suspicion, or from induction, does not claim any juridical consideration. Neither does that fear which arises from super-human forces, or natural events, or is produced through a situation of fact (such as a disease), come under the type of fear which makes a juridical act void or voidable. These principles, enunciated in the Roman sources, universally insisted upon by the medieval glossators, clarified by the post-Tridentine authors,[9] are evidenced in the present Code by the frequent recurrence of the word *"incussus"* in reference to the invalidating effect of fear on

---

[7] Cf. canon 18.

[8] Cf. canon 6, 4°.

[9] Cf. p. 69.

various juridical acts,[10] as well as by the word *"inductus"* in canon 542, 1°, on forced entry into the canonical novitiate.[11] The law effecting invalidity is meant to safeguard the rights of individuals by voiding acts in which injustice has been suffered. But as only an agent endowed with independent self-determination, such as man, can be the source of an injurious action which violates the rights of another, any fear that is not inspired by a free human agent does not work an invalidating effect.

The immediate consequence of this fact is that fear inspired by any other cause than a free human agent does not invalidate the consent of an aspirant seeking entry into religion or of a superior receiving him. Thus, a novitiate entered upon through the pressure of fear arising from pure imagination, groundless worries, poor health, or the individual's own personal reflection or meditation does not fall under the invalidating effects of this canon. Neither does that fear which is occasioned by some internal disorder in the body, as the presence of a malignant disease, or that which arises externally from some natural peril, such as a virulent epidemic rife in a locality, or from some natural event, as an earthquake, a shipwreck, or other catastrophes, invalidate entry into religion. Even though entry under these conditions may not result from the best motives, and even though it may in fact result in doing the individual harm, it cannot in any way be construed to be the result of extrinsic coercion such as is needed to invalidate this act. These are clear deductions from the general principles governing the effect of fear in juridical acts in the law, as stated above, and are universally held among authors today.[12]

---

[10] Michiels, *Principia Generalia,* p. 506.

[11] Biederlack-Führich, *De Religiosis,* p. 150, note 1.

[12] Cf., e.g., Coronata, *Institutiones,* I, 710; Beste, *Introductio in Codicem,* p. 364; Schaefer, *De Religiosis,* p. 428; Wernz-Vidal, *Ius Canonicum,* III, 198; Vermeersch-Creusen *Epitome Iuris Canonici,* I, 499; Cocchi, *Commentarium,* IV, 110; Pejška, *Jus Canonicum Religiosorum* (3. ed., Friburgi Brisgoviae: Herder, 1927), p. 80; De Meester, *Juris Canonici et Juris Canonico-civilis Compendium* (3 voll. in 4, Vol. II, editio nova, Brugis: Desclée et Sii., 1923), II, 431 (hereafter cited *Compendium*); Oesterle, *Praelectiones Iuris Canonici,* Vol. I (Romae: apud Collegium S. Anselmi, 1931), 288-289.

Fanfani seems to be the only author who is of the opinion that even intrinsic fear may invalidate the novitiate if it can be proved in the external forum. He, indeed, enunciated this principle with regard to the religious profession, but since canons 572 and 542 parallel each other in this regard, it seems that he held the same view with regard to the novitiate.[13] He advances two reasons for this view. First, he argues, the law does not distinguish, therefore neither should we distinguish. And secondly, he says, the Church has signified how much complete freedom is to be desired in the act of entering religion by penalizing anyone who forces this act with the most severe penalty of excommunication. But intrinsic fear diminishes the freedom and spontaneity of one performing this action as much as extrinsic fear. Therefore it seems that intrinsic fear should not be excluded from nullifying the act of entering the religious state.

The first of these arguments quickly disintegrates when one considers the wording of canon 542, 1°, in the light of canon 103, § 2. For if one considers canon 103, § 2, as a general norm operative not only in the juridical acts mentioned in the second book of the Code, but applicable also to all juridical acts of physical or moral persons anywhere mentioned in the Code, as indeed it seems one must,[14] the validity of the argument drawn from the use of the general term *"metus gravis"* in canon 542, 1°, disappears. For once the legislator has laid down the general principle that fear must be incurred from the act of an extrinsic free agent, as the wording of canon 103, § 2, clearly demonstrates, then there is no further need for him to explicitly refer to this fact again wherever he specifically lists a juridical act in the law as invalid if performed through fear, unless there is some particular reason for doing so.

---

[13] Fanfani, *De Iure Religiosorum ad Normam Codicis Iuris Canonici* (2. ed., Taurini-Romae: Marietti, 1925), pp. 271, 272 (hereafter cited *De Iure Religiosorum*).

[14] Cf., e.g., Michiels, *Principia Generalia,* p. 1: ". . . in can. 87-107 quasdam praeponit normas, ad rectam totius libri secundi, *immo et totius Codicis intelligentiam necessarias* . . ." (Italics supplied by the writer); Oesterle, "De relatione inter metum gravem et invaliditatem novitiatus et professionis," *CpR,* XV (1934), 395.

As a matter of fact, the law refers to the extrinsic origin of fear explicitly in only one case, that of matrimony.[15]

The second argument is likewise without foundation. For, if the lawgiver wished to establish entry into the novitiate as an exception to the general demand for an extrinsically caused fear, he should have clearly indicated his intention of doing so, as he could easily have done by adding such a phrase as *"metus, etiam ab intrinseco"* to this canon. In the absence of such a positive declaration, it seems evident that one must conclude that only that fear which is qualified to render any other juridical act void or voidable is qualified to render the novitiate invalid. Hence, only fear inflicted by an extrinsic rational agent, acting wrongfully and for the purpose of compelling another to act, nullifies entry into the canonical novitiate.

It may happen at times, however, that the fear arising in a particular individual seems to be the result of both a necessary and a free cause conjointly. The question then arises whether this fear is to be considered as invalidating because of the intervention of a free human agent. To solve such a case it is necessary to distinguish between the intervention of a human agent as the true cause of the fear or merely as its occasion. If the human agent is the true cause, it is invalidating; if he is merely the occasion, it does not invalidate.

A practical example of such a case would be that of an aspirant who seeks entry into religion because of fear of eternal damnation stirred up in him by the words of a confessor or a preacher vividly portraying the dangers of life in the world. If the confessor or preacher merely makes the individual concerned more conscious of these evils by recalling them to his mind, even though he may somewhat exaggerate them in doing so, his intervention is certainly merely the occasion of the fear. The motives he presents to such an individual are impelling enough in themselves; his intervention adds nothing to their force.[16] Whenever a third party merely draws the attention of some individual to evils, natural or

---

[15] Canon 1087, § 1.

[16] Cf. Jombart, "De ingressu ex metu," *Periodica,* XII (1923), (55)-(56); Wernz-Vidal, *Ius Canonicum,* III, 198; Larraona, "Commentarium Codicis," *CpRM,* XVII (1936), 14, note 176.

supernatural, which are in themselves designed by God to inspire fear, he certainly cannot be considered as the cause of the resulting fear, but only its occasion.[17]

The only possible exception this hypothesis might suffer would be that of a confessor or a preacher who deliberately induced a person of simple character, deeply religious and of tender conscience, to enter the novitiate by convincing him that unless he did so he most certainly would lose his soul. The fear in this case is directly caused by the confessor through a deliberate and gross misrepresentation of fact to compel the individual to enter religion. His intervention in this case ceases to be merely the occasion of the entry, and becomes its true cause. But as Vidal (1867-1938) remarked, the novitiate in this case would be invalid rather on account of the substantial error and the fraud employed than on the count of fear.[18]

B. *The Element of Gravity*

The second condition necessary for the fear to invalidate entry into religion is that it be grave. Since the essence of fear as a juridical element lies in the fact that it is an extrinsically incited, subjective emotional state which exerts pressure against the human will, diminishing in proportion to its intensity the spontaneity of the will's act, it is evident that the determination of the degree of fear which is or was present in coerced entry into the novitiate is of the utmost importance in declaring the nullity of this act. And yet the element of gravity in fear is no less difficult to define in theory than it is to ascertain in practice.

It is impossible to prove that an act of the will as such is or was of an abnormal nature when performed under the influence of fear. An act of the will cannot be described: it can only be observed by introspection, and even there it proves rather elusive.[19] One can,

---

[17] Vermeersch, "De metu qui, saltem ex lege positiva, excusat ab obligationibus vitiato consensu susceptis, praecipue de metu ab intrinseco vel extrinseco," *Periodica,* XVII (1928), 143*.

[18] Wernz-Vidal, *Ius Canonicum,* III, 198.

[19] Allers, "Some medico-psychological remarks on canons 1068, 1081, and 1087," *The Jurist,* IV (1944), 329.

however, arrive at a morally certain evaluation of the intensity of mental trepidation incurred by a given individual, and its consequent influence upon the decision made by him in a given instance, through a careful and detailed analysis of the nature of the impending evil under which he acted, the circumstances surrounding its infliction, the imminence of its eventuation, and the subjective nature of the one upon whom it is wrought.[20] Consequently, jurisprudential and juridical doctrine has built up certain abstract norms to serve as a criterion for formulating a morally certain judgment in this matter. By fitting the facts of each individual case into the framework of this theory, one may effectively demonstrate defective consent by proving that, under existing conditions of the individual, a normal act of the will generally could not arise. It is to this point that the whole theory of canonical doctrine in this matter is directed.

Both present day juridical doctrine[21] and canonical jurisprudence[22] continue to designate the degree of intensity in fear at which internal consent is considered as efficaciously precluded by the technical terminology of the glossators and the Roman sources, namely, that degree at which an otherwise prudent and resolute man would be certainly influenced in his action or deterred from his resolve. Applying this norm to forced entry into religion, one may say in general that the fear must be regarded as grave in this act whenever the mental trepidation engendered by an impending evil is of such a nature and intensity that it efficaciously moves an otherwise relatively prudent and constant person to choose to enter religion against his or her natural inclination to do so.

Thomas Sanchez (1550-1610) enumerated and explained five conditions which must be verified concurrently in order to qualify fear as grave: (a) the evil threatened must be grave in itself;

---

[20] S. R. R., *Neapolitana, Nullitatis Matrimonii,* die 9 iul. 1936, coram Stanislao Janasik, dec. IX, n. 3—*Sacrae Romanae Rotae Decisiones seu Sententiae, quae iuxta Legem Propriam et Constitutionem "Sapienti Consilio" Pii PP. X prodierunt, cura eiusdem S. Tribunalis editae* (Romae, 1912-   ), XXVIII (1936), 71 (hereafter cited *Decisiones*).

[21] Cf., e.g., S. R. R., *Mediolanen., Nullitatis Matrimonii,* die 8 aug. 1929, coram Francisco Morano, dec. XLIX, n. 2—*Decisiones,* XXI (1929), 411.

[22] Cf., e.g., Gasparri, *Tractatus Canonicus de Matrimonio,* II, 55; Michiels, *Principia Generalia,* p. 509.

(b) the estimation of the gravity of the evil must be based upon a solid judgment, and not a fickle one; (c) the aggressor must be powerful enough to execute his threat; (d) the aggressor must be known as one who customarily carries through his threats; (e) the victim must be unable to deliver himself easily from the aggressor either by fleeing or by seeking aid.[23] These five conditions, however, are conveniently reducible to the first two mentioned, since the last three enumerated are merely further subdivisions of the second.[24] Hence, the essential requisites for grave fear are twofold: the objective evil threatened must be of a serious nature, at least with regard to the person suffering it, and, at the same time, the passive agent must be firmly convinced that the danger of its application is truly imminent and that he cannot deliver himself from it.[25]

According to the first of these conditions, the evil must be of a serious nature in its objective reality, either absolutely or relatively so. Under ordinary circumstances, evils trivial in nature cannot be regarded as productive of mental trepidation sufficiently acute to interfere with volitional liberty.[26] The objective evil threatened must at least exist as a reasonable foundation for the subjective mental agitation which arises from it. Mere empty suspicion, subjectively formulated on a very fragile objective basis, can scarcely be considered as sufficient to produce an act juridically deficient in its proper effect.[27] The law tends to protect individuals against unjust aggression, not against the effects of subjective, groundless suspicion.

Certain objective evils are considered by the law as absolutely grave by their very nature, in so far as they are regarded in the common estimation of all men as sufficient to perturb mentally any individual whatsoever. The most commonly enumerated examples of evils of this type are death by violence, bodily torture, long and

---

[23] *Disputatio de Sancto Matrimonii Sacramento,* lib. IV, Dis. I, nn. 12-23.

[24] Reiffenstuel, *Ius Canonicum,* lib. I, tit. 40, n. 19.

[25] Gasparri, *Tractatus Canonicus de Matrimonio,* II, 55; Wernz-Vidal, *Ius Canonicum,* V, 626; Chelodi-Ciprotti, *De Matrimonio,* n. 118, p. 143; Cappello, *De Sacramentis,* III, 686.

[26] Sanchez, *Disputatio de Sancto Matrimonii Sacramento,* lib. IV, Dis. I, nn. 11-13; Reiffenstuel, *Ius Canonicum,* lib. I, tit. 40, nn. 21, 25.

[27] Schmalzgrueber, *Ius Ecclesiasticum,* lib. I, tit. 40, nn. 2, 16, 17, 18.

severe imprisonment, exile, rape, the loss of liberty, the loss of the major portion of one's property or of the means of support, disinheritance, long and harsh ill-treatment, expulsion from home, the loss of one's honor, good name, or social position.[28] This list, however, is neither exhaustive nor exclusive. For it would be well nigh impossible for one to enumerate specifically all the various forms which human depravity may assume in working harm upon another when intent upon depriving him of his volitional liberty.[29] Rather, the evils of this list merely serve as a standard or norm by which the seriousness of other possible evils may be evaluated.

It is immaterial whether one of the above recounted threats, or their equivalents, are placed directly against the one induced to give consent or against another closely related to him by ties of blood, esteem, or love.[30] Thus if some grave hardship or even death would befall one's parents, or the members of one's family, or close friends, or even servants, unless one gave consent to enter religion, one must generally consider such an individual influenced in his act by absolutely grave fear in the same manner as if he himself were to be the victim of the threatened harm. In such a situation the threat is particularly apt to abolish freedom inasmuch as the individual is apparently made responsible for and the cause of another's misfortune. And the closer his relationship is with the person who is thus threatened, the deeper will be his emotion.[31]

Whenever one of the afore-mentioned evils or of their equivalents is threatened, no matter who the subject of it may be, the law presumes that the resulting fear is absolutely grave. This presumption, however, must yield to the truth if the concrete facts of the case prove that, in spite of the presence of one of these impending evils, grave fear, nevertheless, did not arise from it. Though, gen-

---

[28] *Glossa ordinaria,* ad c. 1, X, *de his quae vi metusve causa fiunt,* I, 40, s. v. *non timore mortis;* Sanchez, *Disputatio de Sancto Matrimonii Sacramento,* lib. IV, Dis. V, nn. 4-29; Gasparri, *Tractatus Canonicus de Matrimonio,* II, 55; Michiels, *Principia Generalia,* p. 509.

[29] Sanchez, *ibidem,* nn. 1-11.

[30] Sanchez, *ibidem,* Dis. IV, nn. 1-10; Reiffenstuel, *Ius Canonicum,* lib. I, tit. 40, n. 19; Schmalzgrueber, *Ius Ecclesiasticum,* lib. I, tit. 40, n. 3; Michiels, *Principia Generalia,* p. 509.

[31] Allers, "Some medico-psychological remarks on canons 1068, 1081, and 1087," *The Jurist,* IV (1944), 329.

erally, these evils are objectively grave, it may happen in certain instances that they give rise to only slight trepidation, because of peculiar personal qualities of the subject suffering them.[32] Thus, for example, to most persons the threat of the loss of one's honor, good reputation, or social position constitutes a perfectly overpowering threat, especially when the individual concerned enjoys the good estimation of his fellowmen or a relatively high social standing. If, however, the calumniator or detractor threatens to divulge some fact of little or no importance to the person threatened, or if the exposé would not noticeably impair his relations with others or seriously bar him from his social standing, the fear engendered by such a threat must be regarded as only slight. Circumstances must decide the gravity of a threat of this type in each individual case.[33]

Hence, it is only by means of a penetrating individual analysis that one can determine whether or not the evil threatened did in fact cause grave fear. It is also obvious that the same objective norm cannot be used invariably for judging the sufficiency of the threatened evil as resulting in this effect. Men react to objectively identical situations each according to his own personality and history. What in one merely arouses the will to fight, to another is overwhelming violence. Hence, it may happen that an evil, though commonly considered as trivial by the average person, may become relatively grave when evaluated in the light of the personal qualities or characteristics of a particular individual.[34] The physical and psychological make-up of the person concerned will, in fact, play the principal rôle in the determination of the degree of emotional reaction incited by an impending evil.[35] And since subjective characteristics will vary greatly according to age, sex, general health,

---

[32] Gasparri, *Tractatus Canonicus de Matrimonio,* II, 55-56; Michiels, *Principia Generalia,* p. 509.

[33] Sanchez, *Disputatio de Sancto Matrimonii Sacramento,* lib. IV, Dis. V, nn. 11, 13, 14, 15.

[34] Sanchez, *ibidem,* nn. 2-5; Reiffenstuel, *Ius Canonicum,* lib. I, tit. 40, n. 20; De Lugo, *De Justitia et Jure,* Disp. XXII, sec. VII, nn. 110, 111, 113, 135.

[35] Michiels, *Principia Generalia,* pp. 509, 510.

talents, integrity of morals, and range of education of the passive agent, so too will the objective evil that is postulated for verifying the presence of grave intimidation differ according to the circumstances of each case.[36]

One must, therefore, carefully evaluate the gravity of the objective threat in the light of all the special affections and dispositions, habitual or temporary, of the passive subject which augment or reduce his ability to resist the intense mental intimidation procured by it. Thus a young woman, by her very nature physically and psychologically more delicately fashioned than a young man, is generally less capable of resisting the onslaught of violent emotion. Likewise, one of a timid nature or frail physical constitution will generally be more easily overcome by a fear-inspiring threat than one of a more robust condition. One who is sick is more easily intimidated than one in the state of health. One who has just suffered some grave psychological crisis, as a deep sorrow, a nervous breakdown, or mental shock, will generally acquiesce more easily to vexation than one who has not been harassed by such mental strain. Evils which may only slightly affect a mature person, may completely destroy the mental equilibrium of a youth or an old or feeble person. Supersensitiveness, a melancholic disposition, a tendency to hysteria, mental weakness, all must be taken into account when one establishes the degree of agitation registered in any individual by the threat of an impending evil. In order to render an equitable judgment, one must carefully weigh all the evidence presented and prudently evaluate it in the light of the principles of equity, jurisprudence, and psychology. It is only by carefully counterbalancing the gravity of the threatened evil against the greater or lesser strength of character found in the passive subject

---

[36] S. C. de Prop. Fide, instr., *De Processu Matrimoniali*, 1883—*Collectanea S. Congregationis de Propaganda Fide* (2 voll., Romae: Typographia Polyglotta Vaticana, 1907), n. 1587, nn. 36-40, especially n. 37. This instruction is constantly quoted in decisions of the Sacred Roman Rota as a basis for the subjective norm for evaluating the degree of fear. Cf., e.g., S. R. R., *Versalien., Nullitatis Matrimonii,* die 13 febr. 1937, coram Andrea Jullien, dec. XI, n. 2—*Decisiones,* XXIX (1937), 86; S. R. R., *Nullitas Matrimonii,* die 1 mart. 1938, coram Caesare Pecorari, dec. XIV, n. 4—*Decisiones,* XXX (1938), 129.

that one may arrive at a morally certain estimation of the degree to which the presence of fear influenced his volitional acts.[37]

Over and beyond the objective relative gravity of the threat, the law demands that the one against whom it is directed be morally persuaded of its imminent eventuation, or at least that he be soundly convinced of the reasonable probability of its infliction unless action is taken. For unless such a reasonable conviction exists in the mind of the one fearing, he cannot be said to be truly activated by the presence of a grave danger. The law supposes that the fear-inspiring act is the product of a solid judgment that, unless it is placed, harm must be sustained. It is upon this point that the difference between constancy and inconstancy hinges under the classical norm measuring grave fear as that which would move a constant man. For, as St. Thomas said, a constant man is prevailed upon to act only from a strong probability that an evil impends; an inconstant one is enticed to action even on a fickle surmise or slight provocation.[38]

The strength and soundness of this subjective conviction will rest mainly upon the verification of four concomitant circumstances surrounding the objective threat. First, the threat of a grave evil must have been actually placed. The line of demarcation, however, between a virtual and an actual threat is sometimes very thinly drawn. The harm does not have to be actually inflicted as long as there is a reasonable probability that it will be inflicted in the near future.[39] A vain suspicion or induction that another may inflict a grave evil unless a certain line of action is pursued does not as a rule give rise to action-compelling fear such as is demanded by the law.[40] If this suspicion is well founded, however, it may at

---

[37] Sanchez, *Disputatio de Sancto Matrimonii Sacramento,* lib. IV, Dis. IV, nn. 1, 4; Reiffenstuel, *Ius Canonicum,* lib. I, tit. 40, n. 79; Schmalzgrueber, *Ius Ecclesiasticum,* lib. I, tit. 40, n. 2; Wernz-Vidal, *Ius Canonicum,* II, 46; Regatillo, *Institutiones,* I, 135; Michiels, *Principia Generalia,* p. 510; cf. also S. R. R., *Alexandrina Armenorum, Nullitatis Matrimonii,* die 23 iun. 1936, coram Joanne Teodori, dec. IV, n. 2—*Decisiones,* XXVIII (1936), 42.

[38] *In IV° Sent.,* dist. 29, q. 1, a. 2.

[39] Cf. S. R. R., *Romana, Nullitatis Matrimonii,* die 20 iun. 1936, coram Andrea Jullien, dec. XLI, n. 2—*Decisiones,* XXVIII (1936), 386.

[40] Sanchez, *ibidem,* Dis. I, n. 15.

times produce this effect.[41] Neither does it suffice that the evil, though threatened, will not be executed until some distant future time at which the victim foresees that he will most probably be able to escape its application.[42]

Secondly, the adverse agent must be powerful enough to carry out his threats, at least in the reasonable estimation of the person fearing. This condition does not mean that he can in fact fulfil his threat, but that the one fearing believes reasonably that he can, though perhaps in reality he may not be able to do so because of some reason unknown to the victim of the fear.[43]

Thirdly, the passive subject must prudently believe that the threatening agent has every intention of actuating his threat unless he obtains the consent he demands. The probability of this intention will depend greatly upon the personality and habits of the one threatening. If he is a loquacious individual, or one constantly given to menacing language, but one who seldom if ever carries through his word, a threat, even of a grave evil, falling from his lips can scarcely be counted as sufficient to induce grave fear. A father who is in the habit of constantly threatening disinheritance of his daughter on the slightest provocation, but who never in reality carries through any of his threats, can scarcely be considered as one who instills grave fear by means of his threats. On the other hand, if the aggressor is known as a harsh character who usually carries through what he threatens to do, his threatening action is easily prone to incite grave fear.[44]

Fourthly, the person victimized by fear must be unable to deliver himself easily from the power of the aggressor or from the grave evil threatened against him. As long as this condition exists a strong presumption remains that the person is and continues to be influenced in his action by the presence of grave violence.[45] If, on

[41] Sanchez, *ibidem,* n. 17.

[42] Michiels, *Principia Generalia,* p. 510.

[43] Sanchez, *ibidem,* n. 19; Schmalzgrueber, *Ius Ecclesiasticum,* lib. I, tit. 40, n. 3, 2°; Reiffenstuel, *Ius Canonicum,* lib. I, tit. 40, n. 19; Michiels, *loc. cit.*

[44] Sanchez, *ibidem,* n. 20; Reiffenstuel, *loc. cit.;* Schmalzgrueber, *loc. cit.*

[45] Schmalzgrueber, *ibidem,* n. 3, 4°; Reiffenstuel, *ibidem,* nn. 104-107; cf. S. R. R., *Nullitatis Matrimonii,* die 16 oct. 1936, coram Andrea Jullien, dec. LXIII, n. 2—*Decisiones,* XXVIII (1936), 596-597.

the contrary, the person could easily have made known his plight to a parent, relative, friend, pastor, or other reliable persons, such as his master of novices or superior, and does not do so, a strong presumption is created to the contrary, i.e., that he was in reality not acting under duress when entering the novitiate. He is not obliged to seek this help, however, if he foresees that it will be of no avail, though such a condition is hard to visualize under the present law.

Another very real factor which may and generally does contribute to the intensity of fear instilled in very sensitive characters is the reverential deference which the passive agent may or must bear towards the person attempting to influence his volitional activity. Whenever this deference gives rise to mental anxiety lest one offend or cause pain to the person who holds this place of authority over him, it takes on the character of that mental trepidation properly qualified as reverential fear.[46] When this fear arises solely from the respect which is due to parents or superiors, or, at the most, from some slight indignation or displeasure which they may register when a child or subject acts contrary to their wishes, with little or no immediate danger of an evil befalling them for not acquiescing to the expressed desires, it is termed purely reverential fear. If such reverential fear is accompanied with relatively serious extrinsic threats or vexations originating from the one in authority, so that its intensity is gravely augmented to an acute degree, thus qualifying it as a true hardship oppressing the will of its victim, then it is referred to as qualified or mixed reverential fear.[47]

Fundamentally, purely reverential fear is something good: it is the natural product of filial piety and reverence which is due to one who is vested with authority; it flows from a deep realization of the basic truth, arising from the very nature of the relationship, that the one who is subject to another has an obligation to pay proper respect and becoming honor to the one who is superior.

---

[46] Davis, *Moral and Pastoral Theology* (4 vols., New York: Sheed and Ward, 1935), I, 29-30; Payen, *De Matrimonio in Missionibus* (3 voll., Vol. II, 2. ed., Zi-Ka-Wei: Typographia T'OU-SE-WE, 1936), II, n. 1683 (hereafter cited *De Matrimonio*); Michiels, *Principia Generalia,* p. 511.

[47] Payen, *De Matrimonio,* II, n. 1683; Michiels, *Principia Generalia,* p. 511.

This relationship can at times, however, exercise a very real influence in diminishing liberty of choice and action in the inferior by inducing him to do or to omit a thing out of fear of offending or grieving the one who is in authority. The natural repugnance experienced and the sense of shame enkindled in anyone when he resists his parents or superiors can easily induce him to comply with their wishes, even though in so doing he acts contrary to the spontaneous inclination of his own will.[48] This dread of offending or giving pain to another, especially if it arises from a deep-seated respect or devotion, can constitute an obstacle to spontaneous choice, even of a state of life.

Generally, however, it must be accounted as only a slight obstacle, though obviously the intensity of trepidation aroused by such reverential deference will vary greatly with the circumstances and temperament of the persons involved.[49] For the confusion experienced in a child or a subject when he circumvents the command of a parent or a superior, though it may constitute an evil affecting the person, will generally not of itself give rise to more than a minor degree of anxiety, especially when it is foreseen that no grave repercussions will fall upon one for so acting and the displeasure registered in the one in authority can easily and quickly be placated. Hence, in the external forum, reverential fear must be regarded as insufficient of itself to cause juridically defective consent on the part of one entering religion.[50] But it is obvious from the very nature of such fear that it must be regarded as an aggravating circumstance which may greatly increase the intensity of fear arising from an extrinsic threat placed by the one in authority. For the will, rendered more pliable by the respect and love which it bears towards the agent of the threat, is more easily solicited to give consent to that which he desires or demands. Hence, reverential fear must be taken into account when evaluating the gravity of even common fear in any case.

---

[48] Wernz-Vidal, *Ius Canonicum,* V, 626-627; Payen, *loc. cit.;* Michiels, *loc. cit.*

[49] Sanchez, *Disputatio de Sancto Matrimonii Sacramento,* lib. IV, Dis. VI, n. 14; Reiffenstuel, *Ius Canonicum,* lib. I, tit. 40, n. 95; Schmalzgrueber, *Ius Ecclesiasticum,* lib. I, tit. 40, n. 4; Wernz-Vidal, *Ius Canonicum, loc. cit.*

[50] Michiels, *loc. cit.;* Payen, *loc. cit.;* Chelodi-Ciprotti, *De Matrimonio,* n. 119 bis.

Although, generally, purely reverential fear of itself merely constitutes an aggravating circumstance which may or may not enhance the degree of fear, qualified reverential fear under particular conditions may seriously interfere with volitional liberty and create a serious obstacle to true consent, in the same manner as grave fear arising from any grave objective threat. Reverential fear assumes the nature of grave fear whenever a parent or a superior, in attempting to influence the will of a child or a subject to perform or omit a certain act, employs such immoderate and severe means to this end that a true moral hardship is created for the child or the subject unless he acquiesces to their wishes.[51]

With relation to entry into religion, an individual may be said to be gravely coerced to this act through reverential fear, generally, whenever parents or guardians constantly and incessantly vex one with harsh, censorious, and insulting language, insistently reproaching or upbraiding one for not doing as they desire; or whenever they employ importunate, urgent, and oft-repeated entreaties, charging one to desist from one's stubbornness and to comply with their wishes; or whenever they give unmistakable indications of their lasting and enduring indignation, anger, or contempt in the event that one does not enter the religious life.[52] Even though they may not descend to threatening such evils as corporal abuse or inhuman treatment, blows or beatings, deprivation of the necessities of life such as food and clothing, or even disinheritance, which in themselves are sufficient to cause grave fear under ordinary circumstances, such cruel and harsh conduct, coming from one towards whom special respect or love is due, can create a perfectly unbearable moral and mental torture for the young person victimized by it.[53]

---

[51] Sanchez, *ibidem,* Dis. VII, nn. 5-8; Pirhing, *Jus Canonicum,* lib. IV, tit. 1, n. 119; Reiffenstuel, *Ius Canonicum,* lib. I, tit. 40, n. 94; Schmalzgrueber, *Ius Ecclesiasticum,* lib. I, tit. 40, nn. 5, 6; Gasparri, *Tractatus Canonicus de Matrimonio,* II, 57; Wernz-Vidal, *Ius Canonicum,* V, 626-627.

[52] Cf. all the above authors in the place cited. For a clear exposition of the actions and vexations which contribute to the intensity of reverential fear cf. S. R. R., *Messanen., Nullitatis Matrimonii,* die 16 mart. 1937, coram Arcturo Wynen, dec. XIX, n. 2—*Decisiones,* XXIX (1937), 215.

[53] Larraona, "Commentarium Codicis," *CpRM,* XVII (1936), 14, note 175 bis.

This is especially true if such conduct is protracted over a long period of time and when it is foreseen that there is little or no hope of its subsiding in the near future. For, constantly molested, tormented, and vexed by such attacks, one is gradually worn down and eventually may be broken in one's moral resistance. It can make life for its victim so embittered that, in order to relieve himself from its oppression and to bring some peace and quiet back into his life, he is driven to consent to that which is totally against the spontaneous choice of his will. It is quite obvious that if one were to enter religion under such conditions, one would not do so with the full liberty demanded by the law, and consequently one's consent to this act would be void of any juridical effect.[54]

One must carefully analyze both the character of the passive subject and that of the active agent in evaluating the intensity of reverential fear and its consequent effect on volitional liberty. If the one molested by such unjust vexation is a child of a naturally timid and affectionate disposition, he will be much more prone to give way under parental oppression than one of a more stolid character. This is especially true when such a one has led a sheltered life in the close ambit of the family circle and has become so deeply attached to his parents and family that he almost totally depends upon their wishes and advice in moderating even the minutest details of his daily life.[55] Conversely, if the parent or guardian of such a child is severe, imperious, and unbending in character, and one who will not scruple to exert duress to obtain his desires, a strong probability is established that the child or the subject acted through grave reverential fear when entering religion, if there is evidence of the presence of verbal and moral abuse and of the threat of it continuing unless he yields to this demand.[56] It will become a matter of fact in each individual case whether the fear is in reality slight or grave.

---

[54] Schaefer, *De Religiosis*, p. 429; Goyeneché, *De Religiosis*, n. 48, p. 82.

[55] Cf. S. R. R., *Antiochen. Melchitarum, Nullitatis Matrimonii*, die 7 aug. 1937, coram Arcturo Wynen, dec. LXI, nn. 4, 12—*Decisiones*, XXIX (1937), 603, 609; S. R. R., *Nullitatis Matrimonii*, die 7 apr. 1937, coram Henrico Caiazzo, dec. XXIV, nn. 2, 3—*Decisiones*, XXIX (1937), 264.

[56] Cf. S. R. R., *Matriten., Nullitatis Matrimonii*, die 11 iul. 1936, coram Acturo Wynen, dec. L—*Decisiones*, XXVIII (1936), 470; Michiels, *loc. cit.*

C. *The Element of Injustice*

In view of the fact that the term *"iniuste"* is not appended to the terms *"metus gravis"* in canon 542, 1°, on forced entry into the canonical novitiate, a dispute has arisen among authors concerning the element of injustice in the fear postulated as invalidating the novitiate. One school of thought, supported by Vidal and Oesterle and others,[57] maintains that even in the case of forced entry into the canonical novitiate the law, at least theoretically, demands an unjustly inflicted fear, as it does in any other case in the Code. In support of this opinion, these authors advance the following arguments. (a) The fact that the former discipline recognized that licit coercion could be employed to force another into the religious state under certain circumstances,[58] demonstrates that absolutely and theoretically one cannot exclude the possibility of just coercion in this act even today.[59] (b) If one examines the general principle enunciated in canon 103, § 2, and refers for the sake of analogy to parallel places in the Code such as those relating to sacred ordination and matrimony, it seems that one must necessarily conclude that the present discipline, as well as the former, does not consider justly inflicted fear as worthy of any juridical consideration. (c) The primary reason why the law invalidates certain juridical acts by the very fact that they have been placed under grave coercion is not so much the lack of consent involved as it is the need to repair

---

[57] Wernz-Vidal, *Ius Canonicum,* III, 199; Oesterle, *Praelectiones Iuris Canonici,* I, 228; De Meester, *Compendium,* II, 431; Berutti, *Institutiones,* III, 139; Bastien, *Directoire Canonique à l'Usage des Congrégations à Voeux Simples* (3. ed., Bruges: Beyaert, 1923), p. 94 (hereafter cited *Directoire Canonique*); Pejška, *Jus Canonicum Religiosorum,* p. 80; Regatillo, *Institutiones,* I, 365; Cocchi, *Commentarium,* IV, 110; Claeys Bouuaert, "De metus influxu," *Jus Pontificium,* VI (1926), 110; Giacchi, *La violenza nel negozio giuridico canonico,* p. 69; Cervia, *De Professione Religiosa,* p. 85; Brys, *Juris Canonici Compendium* (10. ed., 2 voll., Brugis: Desclée, De Brouwer et Sii., 1947-1949), I, 534.

[58] Conc. Trident., sess. XXV, *de regularibus,* c. 18. The Council inflicted excommunication upon anyone forcing another into religion, *except in the cases permitted in the law.* Cf. *supra,* p. 46.

[59] Wernz-Vidal, *Ius Canonicum,* III, 199, note 19.

the injury sustained by these individuals through such undue influence on the determination of their will.[60]

Another group of authors, of equal weight and authority,[61] defend the opinion that any fear whatsoever, if it is grave and of extrinsic origin, falls within the invalidating effect of this canon, without any regard to the element of injustice. They present the following arguments in favor of this opinion. No distinction is made in canon 542, 1°, between the invalidating effects of justly and unjustly inflicted fear, either in regard to the aspirant or in regard to the superior accepting him. Hence, so it seems, one must conclude that the legislator did not wish to distinguish these effects. Furthermore, if one compares the present canon with parallel canons in the Code where grave fear invalidates juridical acts, it becomes clear that the legislator purposely did not limit what he considered as invalidating fear in this instance to fear that is unjustly inflicted. For the Code makes reference to the injustice of the fear employed in only three out of the nine cases in which it declares an act invalid if placed under the influence of grave fear.[62] And if one examines these three cases, it is found that such a distinction was clearly necessary in those instances because the present legislation, as well as the past, admits of the hypothesis that fear can at times be justly employed in these acts.[63] But, from the very

---

[60] Wernz-Vidal, *Ius Canonicum,* III, 199; Oesterle, "De relatione inter metum gravem et invaliditatem novitiatus et professionis," *CpR,* XV (1934), 398.

[61] Larraona, "Commentarium Codicis," *CpRM,* XVII (1936), 15-16; Schaefer, *De Religiosis,* pp. 428-429; Coronata, *Institutiones,* I, 710; Vermeersch-Creusen, *Epitome Iuris Canonici,* I, 499; Fanfani, *De Iure Religiosorum,* p. 272; Beste, *Introductio in Codicem,* p. 364; Biederlack-Führich, *De Religiosis,* p. 150.

[62] Cann. 185; 1087, § 1; 1307, § 3. The other cases are cann. 169, § 1, 1°; 214, § 1; 542, 1°; 572, § 1, 4°; 1095, § 1, 3°; 2338.

[63] Larraona, "Commentarium Codicis," *CpRM,* XVII (1936), 16, note 179; Schaefer, *De Religiosis,* n. 787, p. 428. These authors develop the following argument in support of the statement above. In canon 185 the renunciation of a benefice is declared invalid under the influence of grave fear *unjustly inflicted.* This observation that the fear must be unjust before it will have an invalidating effect here was necessary because the incumbent of a benefice can at times be justly forced to resign, e.g., under canon

fact that the legislator did make a distinction between the invalidating effects of just and unjust fear in these specific acts, it seems logical to conclude that when he deliberately did not make such a distinction in regard to other acts he meant to signify that the element of injustice in the fear was irrelevant to their invalidity as long as the fear involved was grave and of extrinsic origin.[64]

Although they admit that the opposite view does not lack probability, they argue against the proofs supporting it in the following manner. (a) One can no longer appeal to the earlier law to interpret this canon, since this earlier law has changed. Canon 2352 inflicts excommunication on anyone forcing another into the religious state in any manner whatsoever with total disregard to whether the fear was brought to bear in a just or in an unjust manner, thus abolishing this distinction as it existed under the earlier law.[65] (b) An analogy cannot be drawn between the fear postulated for invalidating the novitiate and the fear postulated for invalidating matrimony; matrimony, even today, as in the former discipline, admits of just coercion. The admission to the novitiate does not. The analogy with the invalidity of sacred orders is correctly drawn, since in this case, as in that of the novitiate, any grave fear whatsoever, even though it may be considered as just in the abstract, is sufficient to liberate one from the obligations incurred through the forced reception of orders. (c) One cannot appeal to canon 103, § 2, as a general norm establishing injustice as a necessary element in invalidating fear throughout the entire Code, for this canon is concerned only with the rescission of an act in itself valid and does not apply to those special cases in which

---

2177, 2°. Matrimony, according to canon 1087, is invalid if it is entered into in consequence of grave extrinsic fear *unjustly applied,* because this contract is not considered as vitiated if entered into as the result of a just coercion. A vow is declared invalid in the law in canon 1307, § 3, if it is the result of grave and *unjustly inflicted* fear; here again the legislator does not preclude the possibility of a just infliction of fear.

[64] Larraona, "art. cit.," *loc. cit.*

[65] Cf. canon 2352. Excommunicatione nemini reservata ipso facto plectuntur omnes . . . qui *quoquo modo* cogant . . . virum aut mulierem ed religionem ingrediendam . . . (italics are the writer's).

the Code itself declares an act without juridic substance, for these acts are mentioned in canon 103, § 2, only by way of exception.[66]

Although the opinion advanced by Larraona does not lack probability, the opinion propounded by Vidal and Oesterle seems, at least theoretically, by far the more probable, namely, that fear, in order to invalidate the novitiate, must be unjustly inflicted. This conclusion is derived from the following premises: a) the *nisi* clause of canon 103, § 2, does not completely abstract acts declared invalid in the law from any consideration in this canon; b) it is the universal teaching of canonists that the element of injustice is essential to the concept of juridically relevant fear; c) the conclusion drawn from the parallel passages in the Code by these authors does not seem warranted.

In the first place, the whole argument of Larraona and Schaefer seems to be founded on the assumption that the *nisi* clause of canon 103, § 2, not only distinguishes those acts which are declared invalid by the law itself from other juridical acts by reason of the effect fear has upon them, but also by reason of the type of fear postulated for effecting invalidity in them and that which is postulated for making other acts liable to rescissory action. Once one accepts this assumption, the reasoning of these authors is certainly correctly formulated. But a careful reading of the text of canon 103, § 2, does not seem to furnish a foundation for such an assumption. For, if one examines the *nisi* clause as it is inserted in the context of this canon, it seems clear that it does not stand in opposition to the type of fear here mentioned as juridically relevant, but rather only to the fact that juridical acts in general are only liable to rescission if performed under fear.[67]

---

[66] Larraona, *loc. cit.:* "Quod dicitur de analogia cum can. 103 admitti non valet, quia ibi metus non producit nisi rescissionem, hic e contra invalididatem [sic!], et ceterum in can. 103 *expresse* sermo fit de metu injusto. In casibus *specialibus* quandoque e contra de ipso mentio non fit."

[67] Canon 103, § 1. Actus, quos persona sive physica sive moralis ponit ex vi extrinseca, cui resisti non possit, pro infectis habentur.

§ 2. Actus positi ex metu gravi et iniuste incusso vel ex dolo, valent, *nisi aliud iure caveatur;* sed possunt ad normam can. 1684-1689 per iudicis sententiam rescindi, sive ad petitionem partis laesae sive ex officio." (Italics are the writer's.)

The purpose of the legislator in canon 103 is to establish certain general principles which will govern the effect of force and fear on the juridical acts of physical or moral persons as anywhere mentioned in the Code.[68] In the first paragraph of this canon he describes the effects of force on a juridical act, and qualifies what is meant by juridical force as that which cannot be resisted. In the second paragraph he evaluates the effect of fear on a juridical act, and qualifies what is meant by juridically relevant fear as that which is grave and unjust. He then proceeds to state that in spite of the presence of such fear, a juridical act is valid. But if the law expressly declares it invalid (when such fear is present), then it is totally without substance from the very beginning. This seems to be the only intelligent interpretation that can be given to the text of this canon.[69] And hence Vidal and Oesterle are quite correct in appealing to canon 103 both for the purpose of analogy and as a general criterion of the demand of the legislator for a fear unjustly inflicted in order to establish it as a cause for nullity and as a foundation for rescissory action as well. For the qualities of juridically relevant fear postulated for establishing an act as liable to rescission do not differ essentially from those which are postulated for effecting its automatic invalidity.

This point of view is further substantiated by the fact that canonical theory of every period, both among the medieval glossators and among the authors immediately preceding the promulgation of the present Code,[70] has always and invariably insisted upon the element of injustice as the basic cause for the nullity or rescission of a juridical act.[71] The statement of Innocent IV, *"si nullum est damnum, nulla fiet condemnatio,"*[72] in relation to juridical acts

[68] Michiels, *Principia Generalia*, p. 504.

[69] If one admits Larraona's interpretation of this *nisi* clause as totally abstracting acts invalidated in the law itself from any consideration here, the canon should be translated as follows: if an act is placed under grave and unjustly inflicted fear it is valid, but if the law expressly declares it invalid, then any type of fear whatsoever invalidates it, except where the law makes special provisions otherwise. This interpretation, it seems, does violence to both the text and the context of the canon.

[70] Cf. *supra*, pp. 69-70.

[71] Giacchi, *La violenza nel negozio giuridico canonico*, p. 59.

[72] *Commentaria in Quinque Libros Decretalium et in Decretales Suas* (Augustae Taurinorum, 1581), lib. V, fol. 73, ad *actio quod metus causa*, n. 1.

is representative of all canonical doctrine on this point in all the centuries before the Code. In fact, of all the various requisites for *metus,* the consideration of its injustice is certainly emphasized more than any other.[73] In the light of this fact it seems highly improbable that the legislator wished to effect such a complete change in the present law as to completely preclude the element of injustice from juridical fear in establishing the invalidity of any juridical act. Hence it seems that this injustice must also be postulated for the fear which invalidates the novitiate.

Finally, if one checks the law on the various acts declared invalid in it, one finds that in every place in which the legislator does not mention that the fear involved must be *"iniuste incussus"* the case is one in which either all coercion is illicit under the present law or else the possibility of having a case of just fear with regard to that act is remote, and hence any reference to this quality of juridically relevant fear would have been useless. Any intimidation with reference to an ecclesiastical election is *per se* illicit.[74] The same holds true for fear employed in relation to the forced reception of sacred orders,[75] entry into the novitiate,[76] and the religious profession,[77] since, by reason of the excommunication inflicted upon anyone who exerts coercion on the performance of these acts in any manner whatsoever, all fear becomes essentially unjust when it is exerted in relation to them. Although one cannot entirely preclude the hypothesis of the applicability of a just fear with reference to acts of ecclesiastical authorities such as assistance at marriage[78] and the remission of penalties,[79] the probability of having a just fear in these acts must be, it seems, regarded as quite remote.[80]

[73] Giacchi, *op. cit.,* p. 68.
[74] Canon 169, § 1, 1°.
[75] Canon 214, § 1.
[76] Canon 542, 1°.
[77] Canon 572, § 1, 4°.
[78] Canon 1095, § 1.
[79] Canon 2238.
[80] It is noteworthy that although Vermeersch-Creusen apply the rule, "where the law does not distinguish, neither ought we," to canon 542, 1°, and declare therefore that all fear invalidates this act, when they take up fear with relation to assistance at matrimony, and the remission of penalties,

Hence it seems that, although the law continues to postulate an unjust infliction of fear for nullifying the entry into religion, it has in effect, in virtue of canon 2352, made all fear unjust when it is applied to this act. This solution does not involve a contradiction. For it is quite possible for the lawgiver to postulate theoretically an unjust fear for the nullifying of an act, and at the same time to declare that all fear with relation to that particular act is unjust. Through the proper correlation of canons 103, § 2, 2352, and 542, 1°, this, it seems, is what he has done with relation to admission to the canonical novitiate.

D. *Causal Relationship*

In order to attain the invalidating effect attributed to it by the law, fear must not only possess the qualities outlined in the foregoing paragraphs, but it must also be so correlated to the actual entry into the novitiate as to be considered as the true motive cause from which this act proceeds. It does not suffice merely to ascertain its concomitant presence; it must be conclusively proved to be the impelling reason that inspired a postulant to seek entry, or a superior to receive him. In other words, a causal relationship must be established between the presence of the fear on the one hand and the actual entry on the other.

This relationship is easily discernible in the case wherein a fear-inspiring threat is deliberately and directly employed for the express purpose of coercing a postulant to enter religion or a superior to receive him. Here the alternative which must exist between bearing a threatened evil on the one hand and complying with the aggressor's demand on the other is obviously present. This would be the case, for example, if someone were to threaten to reveal a hidden scandal from another's past life unless he agreed to enter a monastery, or if a parent were to threaten expulsion from home unless a daughter entered a convent. The coercion in these cases is not only grave and unjust, it is deliberately and directly employed for coercing consent to a given act.

---

they distinguish between the effects of just and unjust fear, whereas the law in these instances makes in its text no distinction between that which is just and that which is unjust. Cf. *Epitome Iuris Canonici,* II, 276; III, 257.

A point which has caused much agitation among canonists, however, is whether the law demands that fear must be directly employed with the intention of extorting a given act, or whether an act is also invalid when it is placed for the purpose of liberating oneself from a grave and unjust infliction of fear, even though that fear was intended for some other purpose by the aggressor than to extort the act as placed by the victim. In the former instance the act is said to be directly coerced; in the latter it is indirectly coerced.

In the period preceding the present Code, Thomas Sanchez, and the majority of canonists, adhered to the theory that an act is to be considered as invalid before the law only when it is the result of fear directly and deliberately inflicted for the purpose of extorting it.[81] Joannes de Lugo and Schmalzgrueber,[82] on the contrary, presented cogent arguments in favor of the opinion that, even if an act is the indirect result of fear, it may be considered as coerced, and therefore invalid.

Following the promulgation of the present Code, this controversy continued among the authors, especially with regard to the contract of matrimony. The law in canon 1087, § 1, declares a marriage invalid if entered into under grave and unjust fear *"a quo ut quis se liberet, eligere cogatur matrimonium,"* whereas the former jurisprudence had always demanded a fear *"directe incussus."* Some authors continued to insist that fear must be deliberately induced for a given purpose before a causal connection is set up between it and the resulting marriage contract.[83]

---

[81] Sanchez, *Disputatio de Sancto Matrimonii Sacramento,* lib. IV, Dis. XII, n. 3; Barbosa, *Collectanea Doctorum tam Veterum quam Recentiorum in Jus Pontificium Universum* (6 voll. in 3, Lugduni, 1637), Tom. II, lib. IV, tit. I, c. 15, n. 3; Fagnanus, *Commentaria in Quinque Libros Decretalium,* lib. I, tit. 40, c. 1, n. 5; Pirhing, *Jus Canonicum,* lib. I, tit. 40, n. 41; Reiffenstuel, *Ius Canonicum,* lib. I, tit. 40, nn. 28, 29; Wernz, *Ius Decretalium,* IV, n. 265.

[82] De Lugo, *De Justitia et Jure,* Disp. XXII, sec. VII, nn. 174-185; Schmalzgrueber, *Ius Ecclesiasticum,* lib. I, tit. 40, n. 28.

[83] Cf., e.g., Wernz-Vidal, *Ius Canonicum,* V, n. 501, p. 633; Claeys Bouuaert, "De metus influxu," *Jus Pontificium,* VI (1926), 110; Vlaming, *Praelectiones Iuris Matrimonii* (2 voll., Vol. II, 3. ed., Bussum in Hollandia:

Others, however, maintained that as long as the marriage contract represented the necessary means of escape, and indeed generally the only one, it is invalid even though the active agent inflicting the fear did not intend it for this particular purpose.[84]

This latter opinion was declared to be the true one by Cardinal Gasparri in the 1932 edition of his treatise on matrimony. He revealed that the phrase of canon 1087 had been deliberately selected by the consultors in formulating this canon for the purpose of also embracing the theory that the indirect infliction of fear sufficed to nullify this act, provided that the marriage contract represented the necessary means of liberating oneself from the unjust vexation.[85] In the years following this statement by him, there has been a marked change in the decisions of the Roman Rota in favor of his view. Whereas formerly mention was usually made that fear had to be directly inflicted, since 1932 a number of decisions have been rendered in which indirect fear is likewise admitted as relevant to the nullity of this act, provided that the marriage contract represents the necessary escape from the impending evil.[86]

Paulus Brand, 1921), II, n. 539, pp. 158-159; Regatillo, *Ius Sacramentarium* (2 voll., Santander: Sal Terrae, 1945-1946), II, 328-330; Noval, *Commentarium Codicis Iuris Canonici,* Liber IV, *De Processibus* (2 voll., Vol. I, Augustae Taurinorum-Romae: Marietti, 1920), I, 233 (hereafter cited *De Processibus*).

[84] Cf., e.g., Roberti, *De Processibus* (2 voll., Vol. I, 2. ed., Romae: apud Custodiam Librariam Pontificii Instituti Utriusque Iuris, 1941), I, 694; Chelodi-Ciprotti, *De Matrimonio,* n. 119, p. 144; Cappello, *De Sacramentis,* III, 689; Vermeersch-Creusen, *Epitome Iuris Canonici,* II, 264; Petrovits, *The New Church Law on Matrimony* (Philadelphia: John J. McVey, 1919), n. 424, p. 312.

[85] *Tractatus Canonicus de Matrimonio,* II, n. 856, p. 61. For a very thorough and complete analysis of this whole controversy both from the historical and critical standpoint cf. M. Wyszynski, "Utrum metus indirecte incussus dirimere possit matrimonium," *Jus Pontificium,* X (1930), 193-200; XI (1931), 42-51; XII (1932), 43-52; XIII (1933), 52-63. This author concluded that the legislator not only did not leave the efficacy of indirect fear a moot question in the law, but definitely and decisively decided in favor of admitting it, at least with regard to matrimony.

[86] Cf., e.g., *Westmonasterien., Nullitatis Matrimonii,* 25 iul. 1932, coram Guillelmo Heard, dec. XXXVII, n. 3—*Decisiones,* XXIV (1932), 350; *Nullitatis Matrimonii,* die 12 dec. 1925, coram Andrea Jullien, dec. L, n. 2—

Must one, then, in the light of these facts, declare a novitiate invalid if it is entered into under indirect coercion? Creusen[87] and Bastien[88] explicitly stated that the novitiate would not be invalid under such duress. Other canonists pass over this point in silence in their commentary on this canon.[89] Larraona, Oesterle, and Schaefer, however, defend the opinion that even in the case wherein entry into the novitiate is the indirect result of fear it would be invalid. They hold this opinion to be the more probable one and, in practice, safe.[90] The opinion of these authors seems well founded both by reason of the intrinsic juridical arguments which support it and by reason of the extrinsic juridical proofs which may be derived from various parallel texts of the present Code. Giacchi, in his study on the effect of fear in juridical acts, presents two cogent arguments in favor of the theory that all juridical acts are as invalid under indirect fear as they are under direct fear. His arguments also apply to the act of entering the canonical novitiate.

An act performed through indirect fear, he argues, is no more voluntary than an act performed through direct fear, if that act represents a necessary refuge from an impending evil. For the essence of moral coercion consists in the fact that an individual is placed in such a circumstance that he must necessarily either

---

Decisiones, XVII (1925), 401; *Nullitatis Matrimonii,* die 11 maii 1926, coram Ubaldo Mannucci, dec. XXII, n. 2—*Decisiones,* XVIII (1926), 175-176; *Transilvanien., Nullitatis Matrimonii,* die 6 aug. 1929, coram Arcturo Wynen, dec. XLVI, n. 2—*Decisiones,* XXI (1929), 386; *Lincien., Nullitatis Matrimonii,* die 5 dec. 1933, coram Arcturo Wynen, dec. LXXII, n. 3—*Decisiones,* XXV (1933), 608-609; *Romana, Nullitatis Matrimonii,* die 22 dec. 1937, coram Andrea Jullien, dec. LXXIV, n. 2—*Decisiones,* XXIX (1937), 783.

[87] *Religieux et Religieuses d'après le Droit Ecclesiastique* (3. ed., Bruxelles-Parisiis: Beauchesne, 1924), n. 145, p. 130.

[88] *Directoire Canonique,* p. 94.

[89] Cf., e.g., Coronata, *Institutiones,* I, 710; Wernz-Vidal, *Ius Canonicum,* III, 199; Beste, *Introductio in Codicem,* p. 364; Brys, *Juris Canonici Compendium,* I, 534; Pejška, *Jus Canonicum Religiosorum,* p. 80; De Meester, *Compendium,* II, 431; Blat, *Commentarium,* lib. II, 594.

[90] Larraona, "Commentarium Codicis," *CpRM,* XVII (1936), 16-17; Oesterle, "De relatione inter metum gravem et invaliditatem novitiatus et professionis," *CpR,* XV (1934), 407-411; Schaefer, *De Religiosis,* p. 429.

choose to place some undesired act or else to suffer some grave evil threatened by an external aggressor. But such an alternative is in fact verified in acts placed both under direct and indirect fear, in the above mentioned sense. For the only real difference between a person acting under the influence of direct fear and one acting under indirect fear lies in the fact that the latter has more avenues of escape open to him than the former.

Whereas the one directly coerced is faced with the dilemma of either placing one specific act or of bearing a threatened evil, the one indirectly coerced is faced with the choice of either placing one of several acts or else suffering an impending evil. But if in reality all the various acts presented to him as avenues of escape are not desired by him any more than the act that is demanded, his choice of any one of them is not more voluntary than if he had been forced to choose an undesired act under direct fear. In both cases the one reason why the act is placed is to escape the threatening evil; the fear of the evil is the one motive cause inspiring the act. Furthermore, it is not simply the freedom of election that is destroyed even under directly inflicted fear, but rather it is the full internal will as needed for effecting a juridical act that is wanting. Although the one indirectly coerced has the option of placing several different acts, he has no internal will of placing any one of them.[91]

Secondly, he argues, a true causal connection is not lacking between the iniquitous threat of an unjust aggressor and an act indirectly inspired through fear of that threat. For by the very fact that a grave and unjust fear-inspiring threat is employed by an aggressor to coerce another, the one victimized by such a threat must either elect to perform the act demanded and suffer the evil threatened, or else devise a means of escaping them both. Now, whether he decides to place the act demanded, or to use one of the avenues of escape open to him, his will is no less determined in its choice by the impending evil in one than in the other. For each of the several means of escape presented to him, by the very fact that they are perceived as a necessary means of evading the threatening evil, is potentially the effect of the unjust threat. And

---

[91] Giacchi, *La violenza nel negozio giuridico canonico*, pp. 76-77.

once he has actually made his choice of one or the other, the unjust fear enkindled by the threat exerts its full pressure on the actual determination of his will in no less degree whether he selects to perform the act demanded, or another not specifically intended, but necessary if he is to liberate himself from the unjust vexation. Hence, in effect, the unjustly inflicted threat of the aggressor is as devastating to the free determination of the will of the victim in indirect fear as in direct fear.[92]

To these arguments of Giacchi, Roberti adds a third to prove that the nature of juridical fear as a type of moral coercion does not demand that the fear be intentionally employed to extort the specific act placed. Different from the element of force, he argues, it is the passive aspect of the concept of fear that is primarily considered in the law, namely, the actual effect which the emotion of fear produces upon the will of the passive agent. No mention is made in the present Code either explicitly or implicitly of the intention of the active agent in inflicting the fear. For the primary aim of the lawgiver in legislating against fear is to protect the free exercise of the rights of the one victimized by it. Whether or not those rights have been in reality violated does not depend upon the intention of the aggressor, but rather upon the effect his unjust action has upon the will of its victim. And since, as was pointed out above, this effect is the same whether fear directly extorts a given act or whether it indirectly demands the necessary executing of an act other than the one demanded, the resulting act is ***simpliciter voluntarium*** but ***involuntarium secundum quid*** regardless of whether the person inflicting the fear did or did not intend to effect such an act. Hence, his purpose and design are no longer to be considered in the law when it decrees the invalidity of juridical acts placed under fear.[93]

Alongside these intrinsic juridical reasons an extrinsic juridical argument may also be built up from the various texts of the Code in favor of this opinion. For the legislator was certainly cognizant of the old difference of opinion on the juridical effects of direct

---

[92] Giacchi, *op. cit.*, p. 79.

[93] Roberti, "De metu indirecto quoad negotia iuridica praesertim matrimonium," *Apollinaris* (Romae, 1928-), XI (1938), 559.

and indirect fear when he formulated the present law. He could easily have employed the classic expressions of the pre-Code canonists by postulating a direct infliction of fear, had he so desired. Yet no such reference is made either explicitly or implicitly in the general norm of canon 103, § 2, or in the canons on the process for the rescission of juridical acts under fear,[94] or in any one of the nine instances in which an act is declared invalid by the law itself if performed under the influence of grave and unjust fear.[95] This, coupled with the fact that in at least two places in the Code he explicitly admits the relevance of indirectly inflicted fear as long as it is the cause of an act, creates a strong probability that he has revamped the former discipline on this point in the law.[96]

For according to canon 169, § 1, 1°, a vote cast in a canonical election is declared invalid in the law if the elector casting it is either directly or indirectly influenced in his selection through grave fear. The law clearly admits the relevance of indirectly inflicted fear in this case.[97] But since canon 169 is nothing else than an application of the general norm of canon 103, § 2, to the juridical act of voting in a canonical election, it seems one must logically conclude that such fear is likewise admitted under the general norm of canon 103.[98]

The former discipline has been changed with regard to the contract of matrimony in canon 1087, § 1, as has been explained, so that indirectly inflicted fear is likewise relevant in declaring the nullity of this act. But if fear indirectly induced can have a nullifying effect on this act, which enjoys the favor of the law,[99] there

---

[94] Canons 1684, 1685.

[95] Cf. *supra*, p. 90.

[96] Oesterle, *ibidem*, p. 400; Roberti, *De Processibus*, I, 695. Vidal admitted this opinion with regard to juridical acts generally, even though he denied it with regard to matrimony. Cf. Wernz-Vidal, *Ius Canonicum*, II, 47, note 6.

[97] Maroto (*Institutiones*, I, n. 398) described indirect fear under this canon as "tendens per se ad alium finem v.g. ad damnum quodlibet vel gravamen electoribus infligendum, a quo ut se liberent electores, ferunt suffragium in favorem persecutoris vel alterius ceterae personae."

[98] Oesterle, "art. cit.," *CpR*, XV (1934), 400.

[99] Cf. canon 1014.

is much more reason to believe that it likewise nullifies other juridical acts, which do not enjoy the special favor of the law.[100]

In the light of these observations, it seems juridically sound to maintain that the novitiate likewise is invalid if entered upon even under the indirect influence of fear, even though the active agent inspiring the fear has no intention of forcing this particular act. This interpretation of the law does not mean that the alternative between entering religion or suffering a grave evil does not need to exist to produce this invalidating effect, for otherwise no one could be said to be forced to enter. But as long as such an alternative does exist at least in the mind of a person victimized by grave and unjust fear and he perceives that an entry into the novitiate is either the only refuge from the evil that threatens or one of several, each of which is in his estimation a greater evil, true internal consent is lacking. It does not matter whether or not the person causing the fear intends to place the aspirant or the superior in such a particular circumstance, as long as his conduct in reality sets up such an alternative for the one against whom his unjust coercion is brought to bear.[101]

A hypothetical case might serve to illustrate and establish this point. Let it be supposed, for example, that a timid young lady, having lived a shielded life, is confronted by domineering parents with the proposition either of entering marriage with a man of their choice or else of suffering expulsion from home and loss of all right to her inheritance. Looking to both the threat of her parents and the proposed marriage as grave evils, she perceives that the only alternative available to her under the circumstances is to enter a convent. Her consent to entering the convent is certainly not the product of a free choice; it is the result of an undesired choice foisted upon her by the iniquitous conduct of her parents, who were unjustly infringing upon her rights. Her entry under such circumstances, it seems, would be invalid. The spontaneous internal consent needed for a juridically valid act of embracing the religious state is wanting.

---

[100] Oesterle, *loc. cit.*

[101] Michiels, *Principia Generalia,* p. 519; Berutti, *Institutiones,* III, 139, Cocchi, *Commentarium,* IV, 111.

Although for the most part the foregoing doctrine has been developed with regard to the aspirant seeking entry into the religious state, the same principles apply with equal force to the superior admitting him. Thus it does not matter whether the one who is the author of the unjust fear actually intends to coerce the superior to receive a specific candidate. As long as the aggressor places the superior in such a position that the latter cannot liberate himself from the unjust threat except by admitting the candidate in question, the superior's decision is actually the result of fear, and therefore invalid.

CHAPTER VII

THE NATURE, DIVISIONS, AND EFFECT OF FRAUD

Before entering upon the actual discussion of the juridic effects of fraud when it is employed to induce a candidate to enter the canonical novitiate, or a superior to receive him, one must consider this legal element in itself in order to make a brief study of its nature, divisions, and effects. Since the legal theory on the element of fraud as it is presented in the present Code does not depart substantially from the theory as held by the authors anterior to the promulgation of the Code, one must for the development of this concept draw upon pre-Code sources as well as on contemporary jurisprudence.

ARTICLE I. THE NATURE OF FRAUD

Etymologically, and in the most primitive sense, the term fraud (*dolus* in Latin, δόλος in Greek) designates any ruse or artifice employed to deceive another. Since, in this general sense, the term could be used either with a good or an evil signification, it was generally customary in early times to qualify it further with an adjective to determine its moral character. Consequently, the Roman sources drew a distinction between legitimate fraud, *dolus bonus,* which was a trick employed for a good purpose, such as the deception of a thief or of one's enemy in war, and illegitimate fraud, *dolus malus,* which was a deceitful action employed to derive some unfair advantage of another.[1] Through common usage the latter signification became so identified with this term itself as to become the exclusive sense in which it was used, and the former connotation has almost completely passed into desuetude.[2] Although some modern authors continue to refer to this ancient distinction, they do so for the sole purpose of demonstrating that the present

---

[1] D. (4. 3) (1. 3).

[2] Fransen, *Le dol dans la conclusion des actes juridiques,* p. 12.

notion of fraud contains the element of injustice essentially, as distinct from the ancient general signification of this term.[3]

Some authors draw a distinction between the Latin terms *dolus* and *fraus,* using the latter term to designate the involuntary deception of another, and the former to designate the voluntary deception.[4] This distinction, however, does not seem to be well founded in the present law, since these two terms are employed indiscriminately in the various canons of the Code.[5]

The fundamental notion of fraud, though it is not defined in the Code, corresponds in every respect to the ancient Roman notion of *dolus malus,* which was copied by the medieval decretists and decretalists into their glosses,[6] and which has been used by canonists ever since as likewise representing the canonical concept of this legal element.[7] Hence, juridically, one may define fraud as any craft, deceit, or malicious contrivance intentionally employed to circumvent, dupe, or deceive another [*omnis calliditas, fallacia,*

---

[3] Ojetti, *Commentarium in Codicem Iuris Canonici* (4. voll., Vol. II, Romae: apud Aedes Universitatis Gregorianae, 1928), II, 153 (hereafter cited *Commentarium*) ; Toso, *Ad Codicem Iuris Canonici Commentaria Minora* (5 voll., Voll. II et V, Romae: apud "Jus Pontificium," 1922-1927), II, 50 (hereafter cited *Commentaria*) ; Coronata, *Institutiones,* I, 182-183. Although the first schema of the present Code used the terminology *dolus malus,* the final approved edition has dropped all reference to the moral character of the fraud, since whenever this term is used in the sense of a device employed to create an error from which defective consent follows, it must always be considered as illegitimate in the eyes of the law. Cf. Gasparri, *Schema Codicis Iuris Canonici* (4 toms in 2 voll., Romae: Typis Polyglottis Vaticanis, 1913), I, 30, canon 16; p. 210, canon 413.

[4] Toso, *Commentaria,* II, 36-37.

[5] Cf., e.g., Cann. 52; 2361; 2049; 98, § 1; 729. Cf. also Fransen, *Le dol dans la conclusion des actes juridiques,* pp. 373-374. It must be pointed out here, however, that the term *dolus* itself is employed in two distinct meanings in the present Code. Here it designates the deliberate will to deceive another; under the penal law of the Code it signifies the deliberate will of violating a law. Cf. canon 2200, § 1.

[6] *Glossa ordinaria* ad c. 3, X, *de emptione et venditione,* III, 17; Hostiensis, *Summa Aurea,* tit. *de dolo et contumacia,* II, 14; Reiffenstuel, *Ius Canonicum,* lib. II, tit. 14, n. 3; Schmalzgrueber, *Ius Ecclesiasticum,* lib. II, tit. 14, n. 1.

[7] Cf., e.g., Coronata, *Institutiones,* I, 182; Vermeersch-Creusen, *Epitome Iuris Canonici,* I, 206; Regatillo, *Institutiones,* I, 136; Wernz-Vidal, *Ius Canonicum,* III, 51.

machinatio ad circumveniendum, fallendum, decipiendum alterum adhibita].[8] Or, more precisely, especially with reference to a juridic act, one may likewise define it as "the deception of another, deliberately and fraudulently induced, for the purpose of prevailing upon him to perform a certain determined juridic act."[9]

Whereas the first of these definitions represents the active aspect of the juridical notion of fraud, in so far as it looks primarily to the source from which it stems and the means employed for attaining its end, the second definition represents the passive aspect of this notion, in so far as it looks to the effect produced in the person towards whom such action tends.[10] Both aspects are essential to the juridic notion of fraud when it is considered as a source of defective consent. Just as subjective deception which does not result from objective malicious maneuvers does not constitute a fraud, so neither do these illicit maneuvers in themselves unless they succeed in obtaining the subjective deception towards which they tend. Consequently, authors generally present these two aspects of this juridic notion as correlatives, since in reality they stand as cause to effect.[11]

An analysis of the juridic notion of fraud reveals that it is made up of four constituent elements: it consists of the use of *apt means, fraudulently* and *deliberately set into motion, to create or to sustain an error* in the mind of another, *whereby he is enticed to perform or not to perform a certain juridic act.* A brief discussion of these various elements will aid in gaining a more clear delineation of the exact concept of the notion of juridical fraud, as well as in ascertaining more precisely the juridical effects flowing from it.

First, the means employed must be such as to be prone by their very nature to lead into error the one upon whom they are wrought; they must, in a word, possess objective aptitude to procure the end towards which they are directed.[12] It is only when the means employed are capable of creating a plausible impression upon the

---

[8] D. (4. 3) (1. 2).

[9] Michiels, *Principia Generalia,* p. 535.

[10] Cf. Fransen, *op. cit.,* p. 376.

[11] Cf. Michiels, *loc. cit.;* Oesterle, *Praelectiones Iuris Canonici,* I, 65; Wernz-Vidal, *Ius Canonicum,* VI, 278, note 3.

[12] D. (4. 3) 7, fr. 10; Michiels, *loc. cit.;* Fransen, *op. cit.,* pp. 376-377.

individual they hope to deceive that they can properly be qualified as a sufficient basis for fraudulent error, which is the primary effect of fraud and the medium through which it works. Unless they are of such a nature as to create a reasonable foundation for credibility, one can scarcely classify them as prone to deceive, and hence it would be impossible to establish a causal relation between them and the act which they may induce.

One cannot establish an absolute or precise norm by which one may ascertain whether or not the means employed must be judged as sufficient to classify them as a source of juridical fraud. One must rely to a great extent upon the various concrete circumstances which make up each individual case in evaluating their aptitude to create a fraud. For that which to one, in view of his natural or cultivated sagacity, is easily discernible as a ruse, to another, less gifted by nature or less erudite by culture, may prove to be a true source from which fraudulent error may arise. Consequently, one must in establishing the aptness of the means employed, take into account all the personal characteristics of the one upon whom the trickery is practiced, such as age, sex, educational background, natural ability, and, in general, all those mental or moral qualities which may either greatly increase or lessen his ability to perceive insincerity in the speech or conduct of another.[13]

The actual means used, however, may be either positive or negative in character. Under certain conditions, one may effectively deceive even by purely negative action, as when one dissimulates or keeps silent concerning certain facts so as to entertain or sustain an error which is already known to exist in the mind of another.[14] Generally, however, mere silence cannot be counted as a true source of fraud unless there exists a moral obligation to speak out concerning those things about which another is known to be in error when assuming obligations or placing a juridical act.[15] This obliga-

[13] Michiels, *op. cit.*, pp. 535-536; Fransen, *op. cit.*, p. 377; Noval, *De Processibus*, I, n. 338, p. 221; Badii, "Il dolo nel Codice di Diritto Canonico," *Il Diritto Ecclesiastico*, XL (1929), 310.

[14] Fransen, *loc. cit.;* Michiels, *loc. cit.;* Ojetti, *Commentarium*, II, 154; Roberti, *De Processibus*, I, 691.

[15] Bidagor, "De dolo et eius effectibus in admissione ad novitiatum et professione religiosa," *Periodica*, XX (1931), 63*.

tion may arise from the law itself, as when it charges one with the duty of imparting the required information to another, or it may arise from the very nature of the position one holds over another, as for example when a confessor is directing souls to religion.

Following the outline of the Roman definition given above, authors generally enumerate three forms which the artifice of the deceiver might assume when he wishes to create a fraudulent error in the mind of his victim, namely, craft, deceit, and the use of a malicious plot. One is said to deceive through craft (*calliditas*) when he deliberately nurtures an error in the mind of another through his silence concerning the truth. One is said to make use of deceit (*fallacia*) whenever, while feigning good counsel, he deliberately misrepresents those facts which, as he knows or suspects, will influence the consent of another. One is said to employ a malicious plot (*machinatio*) whenever through his insincere action he creates a false impression upon another.[16] Generally, whenever fraud is employed for the purpose of influencing a juridical act, it assumes the guise of good counsel whereby the individual is induced to perform the act or not to perform it.[17]

Secondly, the means employed must not only be apt in nature, they must be fraudulently used. For fraud is juridically reprehensible only when it tends to violate that fundamental good faith which is the essential basis for all social relations among men. Hence, the mere use of such acts or speech which, though insincere, do not tend to create an unjust error in the minds of others cannot be counted as fraudulent in nature. For example, when a merchant merely exaggerates the good qualities of his wares to attract more buyers, he is not ordinarily judged guilty of fraud; his action does not in itself violate basic good faith, since all know and admit of the legitimacy of such action. On the contrary, whenever one presents false documents, such as false certificates of birth or forged passports, or if one designedly employs ambiguous phraseology to trick another in a commercial contract, or if one were to keep

---

[16] Pirhing, *Ius Canonicum,* lib. II, tit. 14, n. 1; Reiffenstuel, *Ius Canonicum,* lib. II, tit. 14, n. 8; Schmalzgrueber, *Ius Ecclesiasticum,* lib. II, tit. 14, n. 2; Wernz-Vidal, *Ius Canonicum,* VI, 278; Michiels, *op. cit.,* p. 535; Bidagor, *ibidem,* p. 62*.

[17] Wernz-Vidal, *loc. cit.*

silent in a case wherein the law demands that one reveal certain hidden facts, it is quite evident that such means, by their very nature, tend to violate the good faith of all.[18]

Thirdly, the purveyor of the fraud must intentionally set these fraudulent means to work for the precise purpose of deceiving another so as to derive some unfair advantage of him.[19] Fraud violates the rights of an individual only in so far as it proceeds from the illicit action of another. It is precisely this ill will which changes a material act of deception into a formal act of fraud. The specific malice proper to fraud is none other than the very will to deceive, whereby the subject of such deception suffers some harm. The bad will of the agent who employs fraudulent means does not necessarily have to extend to the harmful effects which may flow from such an act extorted through fraud. It is essential and sufficient that he merely intend to lead another into error and thereby dispose him to place an act of consent.[20]

Since malice is an essential requisite for the true notion of juridical fraud, it follows that whenever one deceives another without any malicious intent his action cannot be described as juridical fraud. This would be the case, for example, if one were to create a set of objective circumstances inadvertently which do in fact give rise to an error on the part of another, or if one were to lead another into error when counseling him for the reason that one is in error oneself.[21] In such an eventuality the juridical effects of such acts must be judged, not by the principles governing the effects of fraud, but rather by the principles regulating the effects of simple error.[22]

Finally, the objective and intentional use of fraudulent maneuvers, even though illicit in itself, does not constitute an act of juridical fraud, such as will either preclude or minimize juridical consent, unless it succeeds in inducing into error the one against

---

[18] Cf. Michiels, *Principia Generalia,* p. 536; Fransen, *Le dol dans la conclusion des actes juridiques,* p. 376.

[19] D. (4. 3), 18, fr. 3; Michiels, *loc. cit.;* Fransen, *op. cit.,* p. 377; Schmalzgrueber, *Ius Ecclesiasticum,* lib. II, tit. 14, n. 2.

[20] Ojetti, *Commentarium,* II, 154; Badii, "Il dolo nel Codice di Diritto Canonico," *Il Diritto Ecclesiastico,* XL (1929), 310.

[21] Pirhing, *Jus Canonicum,* lib. II, tit. 14, n. 81.

[22] Wernz-Vidal, *Ius Canonicum,* II, 51, note 10.

whom it is directed. For the law is primarily concerned with the element of fraud in so far as it constitutes an unjust interference with man's inherent right to self-determination. Since it is precisely in the error which it induces that fraud is able to attain this effect, the illicit maneuvers of another are not juridically reprehensible as an act of juridical fraud when such an error is not in fact created.[23]

In itself, fraudulent error does not differ from any other error which may arise from some natural cause. It is distinct, however, by reason of its efficient cause: it is essentially the product of the illicit action of another and is, therefore, by nature, unjust. Fraudulent error, therefore, is none other than illicitly induced error.[24] Since it is through the medium of the error which it induces that the element of fraud works its vitiating effect upon consent, the terms fraud and fraudulent error may be used interchangeably in practice as representing the same concept, since in reality they stand as cause to effect.[25]

ARTICLE II. THE DIVISIONS OF FRAUD

Canonically, fraud may be divided by reason of the error it induces or by reason of the rôle which that error plays in influencing consent to a juridic act. By reason of the error it induces, it is divided into substantial fraud and accidental fraud. Fraud is substantial whenever it succeeds in so misrepresenting an object or the nature of an act as to conceal its essential nature or substantial qualities, thus creating a false notion concerning its very essence. Fraud is termed accidental, if it succeeds in obscuring only some of the accidental qualities of the object or act while the knowledge of the substantial or essential elements remains unaffected by it.

Divided with relation to the influence it exerts upon the will in placing a juridical act, fraud is termed either antecedent (*causa dans*) or concomitant (*incidens*). Fraud is said to be antecedent

---

[23] Fransen, *Le dol dans la conclusion des actes juridiques*, p. 378.

[24] Pirhing, *Jus Canonicum*, lib. II, tit. 14, n. 2; Schmalzgrueber, *Ius Ecclesiasticum*, lib. II, tit. 14, n. 12; Reiffenstuel, *Ius Canonicum*, lib. II, tit. 14, n. 5; Wernz-Vidal, *Ius Canonicum*, VI, 278, note 3.

[25] Wernz-Vidal, *loc. cit.*

whenever the object obscured or misrepresented by it constitutes the impulsive cause for which a juridical act is placed; if the truth had been known concerning it, consent would certainly have been withheld. It is to be noted that one may have a case of antecedent fraud in which the object obscured is not substantial either by nature or by stipulation. Fraud is called concomitant, or incidental, whenever it exerts no appreciable influence on the determination of consent, so that the one acting under its influence is so disposed that, even had the fraud not been present, he would nevertheless have desired the object or placed the act, even though perhaps not quite so promptly or quite so easily.[26]

ARTICLE III. THE EFFECT OF FRAUD

The fundamental juridic reason for which the element of fraud is proscribed in the law is not so much that it induces defective consent as it is that it constitutes an infringement upon the juridic liberty of the individual against whom it is employed. The principal reason why juridic acts performed under its influence are declared in the law to be either void *ab initio* or else voidable through rescissory action is not that essential consent is lacking in these acts, since generally such is not the case, but rather it is that they have been unjustly extorted through the fraudulent deception illicitly created by another. Hence, their invalidity or rescissibility stems not from defective consent as such, but rather from the injustice inherent in the element of fraud when it succeeds in influencing consent.[27]

Fraud violates the juridic liberty of an individual only in so far as it succeeds in exerting a real influence upon his consent in placing a juridic act.[28] And, since it is proximately through the medium

---

[26] Cf. De Lugo, *De Justitia et Jure,* Disp. XXII, sec. 6, n. 67; Pirhing, *Jus Canonicum,* lib. II, tit. 14, n. 2; Reiffenstuel, *Ius Canonicum,* lib. II, tit. 14, n. 8; Schmalzgrueber, *Ius Ecclesiasticum,* lib. II, tit. 14, n. 15; Michiels, *Principia Generalia,* p. 536; Maroto, *Institutiones,* I, 464.

[27] Cf. Lefebvre, "Dol en droit canonique actuel," *Dictionnaire de Droit Canonique* (publié sous la direction de R. Naz, 10 voll ou 60 fascicules, Parisiis: Letouzey et Ané, 1924-), IV (fasc. XXIV), col. 1348 (hereafter cited *DDC*).

[28] Fransen, *Le dol dans la conclusion des actes juridiques,* p. 378.

of the erroneous judgment which it creates in the mind of its victim that it works its vitiating effect upon the will's consent, the immediate, proper, and indispensable effect of fraud is none other than the deception itself which it creates and which serves either as the basis or the inspiring cause for an act of consent. Authors generally point out that it is precisely in the error itself which fraud creates in the mind of its victim that the injurious nature of this tort resides.[29] For by the very fact that one injects such an error in the mind of another, seeking thereby to dispose him to place a juridic act or to deprive him of adequate knowledge so as to entice his consent, one does a real injury to his juridic liberty. Hence, in reality, the injurious nature of fraud flows from and is inherent in the fraudulent error which it produces.

The second effect flowing from the element of fraud, though it is not essential to it, is the damage caused by the juridic act which it unjustly provokes. Although it is not absolutely necessary that such an effect be in reality present in order to establish fraud as the source of invalidity or a basis for rescissory action, it is, nevertheless, an almost invariable consequence of such acts.[30]

The manner in which the element of fraud succeeds in influencing volitional activity, either minimizing or destroying the spontaneity of the will's act, is clear from the very nature of the intimate relationship which exists between the functioning of the intellectual and volitive faculties of man. For the will, though naturally inclined to good and averse to evil, is a blind faculty: it is wholly dependent upon the judgment of the intellect to assist it and to guide it in its action. Its acts are qualified as voluntary only in so far as they are the product of a free choice which is guided by the true intellectual knowledge of the object towards which it tends.[31]

---

[29] Fransen, *loc. cit.;* Beste, *Introductio in Codicem,* pp. 157, 159; Toso, *Commentaria,* II, 50, 51; Maroto, *Institutiones,* I, 372. Michiels (*Principia Generalia,* p. 537) seems to draw a distinction between the injustice of fraud and the error which it produces, though he represents both elements as essentially proper to it. Fransen points out, however, that since it is precisely in the deception itself that the malice of fraud resides, it seems that fraudulent error, by its very nature, is essentially unjust, and hence it is superfluous to make a distinction between the effects of fraudulent error and the injustice which is inherent in it.

[30] Noval, *De Processibus,* I, 226; Fransen, *loc. cit.;* Michiels, *loc. cit.*

[31] S. Thomas, *Summa Theologica,* I-II, q. 6, a. 8.

Whereas the element of fear aims at directly destroying the voluntary content of an act by unduly hampering the will in its choice, the element of fraud aims at attaining this effect in an indirect manner, by vitiating or corrupting the intellectual foundation upon which this choice subsists.[32] It tends to interfere directly with the intellectual judgment and indirectly, through it, with volitional consent.[33] While an act extorted through fear represents the product of an irascible movement of the will (it is chosen in preference to an evil which the will would avoid), an act obtained through fraud is the result of a concupiscible movement of the volitive faculty (it is embraced under the guise of good). Fear, therefore, coerces consent; fraud solicits it.

In ultimate effect, however, the element of fraud and that of fear are identical; the consent which flows from these elements (if one excludes substantial fraud), though a *simpliciter voluntarium,* is an *involuntarium secundum quid.* The act would not have been willed had their influence not been present.[34] These elements differ, therefore, only in the manner in which they influence consent. In the element of fear two objects are proposed to the will, one of which it in no way wills, the other of which it does not desire but wills because of fear. Fraud, on the other hand, proposes only one object, but either proposes a different object from that to be willed, or else presents it otherwise than it is in reality. In both cases there is a violation of justice: in fear, because the will is directly coerced, in fraud, because the intellectual knowledge which must direct its acts is tampered with.[35]

Since it is proximately through the medium of the erroneous judgment which it creates that fraud influences volitional activity, its juridical effects derive partly from the nature of the error it produces, and partly from the rôle which that error plays in the actual formation of consent. By reason of the error it engenders, the principles governing the element of fraud do not differ from those regulating the effects of simple error.[36] Consequently, whenever

[32] Regatillo, *Institutiones,* I, 136.

[33] Beste, *Introductio in Codicem,* p. 159.

[34] Pirhing, *Jus Canonicum,* lib. II, tit. 14, n. 3; Ojetti, *Commentarium,* II, 155.

[35] Regatillo, *Institutiones,* I, 136.

[36] Michiels, *loc. cit.*

fraud succeeds in so misrepresenting an object or an act as to cause a substantial error concerning it, the act placed under its influence is invalid not only by reason of the natural law,[37] but also by reason of the positive law.[38] For under such circumstances the will is rendered incapable of placing a true act of consent towards the object to which it is externally directed. The will accepts an object only as that object is represented to it by the intellect. But when the intellect is led to judge the object to be substantially different from that which it is in objective reality, the will internally consents to something totally different from that to which its external consent is apparently directed.[39]

The same principle holds true in an act which is placed through fraudulent error, which does not in itself affect the substance of a transaction or juridic act, but which, by the express stipulation of the party concerned, is made a condition *sine qua non* to consent.[40] For in such a case error is substantial to the act, not by its nature, but by the express will of the one who places it.[41]

In the present legislation, as authors point out,[42] when the law considers the element of fraud and proscribes the effects which are specifically proper to it, though it does not exclude the case of substantial fraud totally, it nevertheless presupposes that a substantial error is not involved. For in such an eventuality the act would be without juridic substance, regardless of whether such an error is or is not the result of fraudulent maneuvers. And the law has already provided a proper remedy for such a case under the

---

[37] Cf. De Lugo, *De Justitia et Jure*, Disp. XXII, sec. 6, n. 67; Reiffenstuel, *Ius Canonicum*, lib. II, tit. 14, n. 16; Schmalzgrueber, *Ius Ecclesiasticum*, lib. II, tit. 14, n. 5; Wernz-Vidal, *Ius Canonicum*, II, 51; Chelodi-Ciprotti, *Ius Canonicum de Personis* (3. ed., Vicenza-Trento: Libreria Moderna Editrice, 1942), p. 169 (hereafter cited *De Personis*).

[38] Cann. 103, § 2; 104.

[39] Cf. Pirhing, *Jus Canonicum*, lib. II, tit. 14, n. 2; Wernz-Vidal, *Ius Canonicum*, II, 49; Cappello, *De Sacramentis*, III, 658.

[40] Ojetti, *Commentarium*, II, 177.

[41] Bouscaren-Ellis, *Canon Law, a Text and Commentary* (Milwaukee: Bruce Publishing Co., 1949), p. 90.

[42] Michiels, *Principia Generalia*, pp. 538-539; Chelodi-Ciprotti, *De Personis*, p. 169; Coronata, *Institutiones*, I, 183.

general norm of canon 104.[43] Rather, in proscribing fraudulent influence in acts, the law is mainly concerned with the case in which fraud produces merely accidental error, but which exerts a more or less determining influence upon volitional consent.

Consent given under fraud, therefore, though qualified, is nevertheless presupposed by the law to be a true act of consent. It is in itself valid not only according to the natural law, but, in the absence of any declaration to the contrary, according to the positive law as well.[44] For, as long as substantial knowledge concerning the nature of an act or a contract is not lacking to one, one's knowledge is essentially sufficient to produce a deliberate intention to accept or to perform it. Consequently, consent which flows from fraud is understood as being a *simpliciter voluntarium* in itself, though it is rendered an *involuntarium secundum quid* whenever the error involved serves to entice the will to consent to that which would have been repugnant to it had the full truth been known at the time of consent.[45] The present Code enunciates the general principle in canon 103, § 2, therefore, that juridical acts performed under the influence of fraud are considered as validly executed unless the law explicitly declares otherwise,[46] although they are liable to rescissory action either upon the petition of the injured party or even *ex officio* if the common good demands it.[47]

However, in order that one may invoke this legal benefit granted by the law to acts fraudulently extorted, certain legal requirements

---

[43] Badii, "Il dolo nel Codice di Diritto Canonico," *Il Diritto Ecclesiastico,* XL (1929), 311; Beste, *Introductio in Codicem,* p. 159.

[44] Michiels, *op. cit.,* p. 538; Roberti, *De Processibus,* I, 690.

[45] De Lugo, *De Justitia et Jure,* Disp. XXII, sec. 6, n. 73; Pirhing, *Jus Canonicum,* lib. II, tit. 14, n. 12; Ojetti, *Commentarium,* II, 154; Beste, *Introductio in Codicem,* p. 159.

[46] Canon 103, § 2. Actus positi . . . ex dolo, valent, nisi aliud iure caveatur; sed possunt ad normam can. 1684-1689 per iudicis sententiam rescindi, sive ad petitionem partis laesae sive ex officio.

[47] The present legislation expressly declares acts to be without substance from the very beginning in four instances, even under the influence of accidental fraud, namely, in canon 169, § 1, 1° (the casting of a vote in a canonical election), canon 185 (the renunciation of an ecclesiastical office), canon 542, 1° (admission into the canonical novitiate), and canon 572, § 1, 4° (the making of a religious profession).

must be verified. These are essentially threefold: the ruse from which the act results must be a true fraud; the erroneous judgment which results from this fraud must exert a determining influence upon one's consent to the act; and the presence of both the fraud and the error which it produces must be demonstrated with at least moral certitude.[48] In the following paragraphs a few observations will be made concerning each of these points.

First, the deceit employed to coerce the act must constitute a true formal act of fraud, that is to say, all the constituent elements of fraud as outlined above in the analysis of this concept must be verified. It does not suffice that the author of the act has been led into error through a simple fault or through negligence. The juridic act must represent the effect of fraudulent maneuvers, intentionally put to work to deceive. Once these maneuvers do succeed in procuring an act of consent, however, it is wholly irrelevant, as far as rescissory action is concerned, whether or not some material injury results from its use.[49] The injury which serves as the foundation for rescission, as pointed out above, does not lie in the material harm done through fraud, but rather in the fact that defective consent results from it. Hence, the latter alone is essential to the availability of the rescissory action.

Secondly, in order that a rescissory action may be invoked, the act must be shown to be the result of fraud. All admit of the relevancy of antecedent fraud to this effect. A controversy has arisen among contemporary canonists, however, upon the precise juridical effects of fraud which exerts only an incidental influence upon the placing of an act. Weighty authorities are to be found on both sides in the issue. One school of thought, adhering to the traditional doctrine commonly accepted anterior to the present Code,[50] is of the opinion that the law has not been changed on this point and that therefore one must continue to postulate that fraud constitute the impulsive cause for an act before its legal effects can be revoked through a rescissory action. The authors who support

[48] Fransen, *Le dol dans la conclusion des actes juridiques,* p. 379.

[49] Fransen, *loc. cit.*

[50] De Lugo, *De Justitia et Jure,* Disp. XXII, sec. 6, nn. 67-87; Pirhing, *Jus Canonicum,* lib. II, tit. 14, n. 4; Schmalzgrueber, *Ius Ecclesiasticum,* lib. II, tit. 14, n. 10; Reiffenstuel, *Ius Canonicum,* lib. II, tit. 14, n. 9.

this opinion are by far the more numerous.[51] Another school of thought, on the contrary, is of the opinion that the wording of the present legislation is such as to argue a change in the law to the effect that even incidental fraud is relevant to the petitioning and conceding of a rescissory action.[52]

The proponents of this latter opinion advance chiefly three reasons for their opinion. First, they argue, the present law has dropped all reference to the former distinction which was wont to be made between the juridical effects of antecedent and incidental fraud. For neither under the general norm of canon 103, § 2, regulating the effects of fraud on juridical acts in general, nor in the canons outlining the process for the rescission of such acts, is there any mention of the need that the fraud involved be determining in character. Under canon 103, § 2, the act which is liable to rescission is simply described as placed *"ex dolo,"* while canon 1684, with reference to the process of rescission itself, simply describes the act as *"dolo circumventus."* But even those acts in which fraud has intervened only incidentally, it is argued, are

---

[51] Roberti, *De Processibus,* I, n. 258, p. 692; "De actione rescissoria ob dolum," *Apollinaris,* III (1930), 143-145; Gillet, "De actione rescissoria ob dolum (can. 103)," *Jus Pontificium,* IX (1939), 323-324; Cappello, *Summa Iuris Canonici,* III, 158; Maroto, *Institutiones,* I, 465; Ojetti, *Commentarium,* II, 154; Bidagor, "De dolo et eius effectibus in admissione ad novitiatum et professione religiosa," *Periodica,* XX (1931), 70*; Vermeersch-Creusen, *Epitome Iuris Canonici,* I, 206; Beste, *Introductio in Codicem,* p. 161; Salsmans, "Circa vitia consensus," *Jus Pontificium,* X (1930), 107; Prümmer, *Manuale Iuris Canonici,* qq. 55, 485; Berutti, *Institutiones,* II, 54; Fransen, *Le dol dans la conclusion des actes juridiques,* pp. 380-385; Lefebvre, "Dol en droit canonique actuel," *DDC,* IV, col. 1349; Lemosse, "Dolus (Evolution historique de la theorie du)," *DDC,* IV, col. 1371; Badii, "Il dolo nel Codice di Diritto Canonico," *Il Diritto Ecclesiastico,* XL (1929), 311; Augustine, *A Commentary on the New Code of Canon Law* (8 vols., Vols. II and III, 1. ed., Vol. VIII, 2. ed., St. Louis: B. Herder, 1919-1924), II, 33; Van Hove, *Commentarium Lovaniense in Codicem Iuris Canonici,* Vol. I, Tom. IV, *De Rescriptis* (Mechliniae-Romae: H. Dessain, 1936), p. 199, note 2 (hereafter cited *De Rescriptis*).

[52] Noval, *De Processibus,* I, 224; Michiels, *Principia Generalia,* p. 540; Wernz-Vidal, *Ius Canonicum,* II, 51, note 11; VI, 279-280; Chelodi-Ciprotti, *De Personis,* p. 169; Coronata, *Institutiones,* I, 183; Toso, *Commentaria,* II, 52.

qualified to fall within this terminology. And thus, by not setting up a clear distinction between the juridical effects of antecedent and incidental fraud, the law has actually extended its proscription against fraud to include the acts placed under incidental fraud as well as the acts determined by fraud. In support of this argument they invoke the principle that, where the law does not distinguish, neither ought we distinguish.[53]

Furthermore, they contend, the principal and primary reason why the law employs juridical sanctions against fraud is to repair the injury which it causes by its malicious interference with the juridic rights of another. The purveyor of the fraud, by the very fact that he is guilty of it, should not be allowed to go unpunished; the common good demands that his delictual action must be outlawed through a destruction of its effect. But, even when the fraud is only of an incidental nature, the injury arising from it cannot be properly repaired, nor can the delict be punished, nor the common good protected, unless the act in which it was present is made liable to rescission.[54]

Finally, it is said, the very nature of the positive juridical order seems to demand that the rescissory action on the count of fraud must rest upon an objective demonstrable foundation, i.e., on the existence of objective fraud itself, and not upon the subjective foundation of the degree to which fraud actually affects internal consent in placing an act. It is almost impossible, they argue, to demonstrate conclusively the actual rôle which fraud plays internally in soliciting consent. Consequently, the present law makes it immaterial whether the fraud is or was actually the impulsive cause of an act or merely incidental in its performance, as long as it can be demonstrated as having been present.[55]

The authors who maintain the traditional opinion, namely, that incidental fraud does not suffice for a rescissory action, oppose the

---

[53] Michiels, *Principia Generalia,* p. 540; Wernz-Vidal, *Ius Canonicum,* VI, 279-280; Coronata, *Institutiones,* I, 183.

[54] Michiels, *Principia Generalia,* pp. 540-541; Wernz-Vidal, *Ius Canonicum,* VI, 280; Noval, *De Processibus,* I, 226; Coronata, *loc. cit.*

[55] Michiels, *op. cit.,* p. 541; Coronata, *Institutiones,* I, 183; Regatillo, *Institutiones,* I, 137. (This latter author merely sums up the two opinions without clearly indicating his own.)

deductions of these authors by attacking the arguments upon which they are based. They point out that the argument which has been built up from the lack of an explicit distinction in the Code between the effects of antecedent and concomitant fraud does not seem to be entirely well founded. For, although the Code does not explicitly make a distinction between these effects, it nevertheless clearly indicates, both in the manner in which it treats of the element of fraud and by the wording of the texts in which it outlines its effects, that it considers this element as relevant only in so far as it does in reality effectively vitiate or influence volitional consent. Thus, under the general norm of canon 103, the purpose of which is to establish the juridic effects of those elements which either preclude or diminish juridic consent, the element of fear and that of fraud are placed on the same juridical footing. But no one is to be found, even among the adversaries of this view, who is willing to admit that fear is sufficient for annulling or making an act liable to rescission, unless it is established as the impulsive cause for which the act was performed. Hence, it seems that one is bound by logical necessity to hold that, unless fraud exerts a noticeable influence upon an act, it cannot be counted as of any relevance as to the rescission of that act. And since incidental fraud by its very nature is understood to have exerted no appreciable influence upon consent in the placing of an act which it merely accompanies, it cannot be construed in any way as constituting an obstacle to volitional liberty. Hence, it seems, it must be excluded from any consideration in canon 103, § 2.[56]

Furthermore, the wording of canon 103 itself seems to support this deduction. For, if one understands the words *"actus positi ex metu gravi"* as requiring that fear must constitute the inducing cause of an act, i.e., that there must be a true causal connection between the fear and the placing of the act, it seems that one must likewise hold that the words *"actus positi . . . ex dolo"* in this same text are to be understood in this same manner.[57] And the wording

[56] Badii, "Il dolo nel Codice di Diritto Canonico," *Il Diritto Ecclesiastico*, XL (1929), 311; Fransen, *Le dol dans la conclusion des actes juridiques*, p. 382.

[57] Gillet, "De actione rescissoria ob dolum (can. 103)," *Jus Pontificium*, IX (1939), 323-324; Roberti, "De actione rescissoria ob dolum," *Apollinaris*, III (1930), 143-144.

of the canons regulating rescissory action on the count of fraud seem to corroborate this view. For canon 1684, § 1, grants this action to one who has been led to place an act *"dolo circumventus,"* while canon 1685, § 2, states that one may institute action against one possessing objects which are *"dolo extortas."* But such a manner of speaking is hardly compatible with the notion of incidental fraud. One can scarcely describe an object as extorted through fraud when it would have been given had the fraud been present or absent. Hence, the wording of these canons seems to exclude the relevancy of anything less than antecedent fraud.[58]

There is also said to be weakness in the second argument presented in favor of the relevancy of incidental fraud, namely, that even in the case of incidental fraud the injury involved cannot be properly repaired unless the act in which it has intervened is set aside. Such a line of reasoning ignores the very nature of the injurious character of fraud. For the injury inherent in fraud in reality lies in the fact that it constitutes an effective interference with the juridic liberty of its victim. But from the very nature of incidental fraud, as pointed out above, it is understood as exerting no telling influence upon the placing of an act of consent, and hence the element of injury, in so far as it does not affect consent, cannot be considered as present in it.[59]

Finally, criticism is directed against the third reason supporting the admission of incidental fraud (namely, that rescissory action must rest upon an objective, not a subjective, foundation) on the grounds that this principle, though valid, is wrongly applied by those who advance it in this connection. For, in the general economy of the juridic order, fraud always contains an internal element, *dolus consistit in animo,* the demonstration of which can be established only by having recourse to conjectures. And though it is true that the proof of the extent to which fraud influenced consent is difficult, it is equally difficult to establish the existence of true fraud itself.[60]

In the absence of any conclusive proof in support of the opinion of those authors who argue a change in the law in favor of the

[58] Gillet, *ibidem,* p. 324; Roberti, *ibidem,* p. 144.

[59] Fransen, *op. cit.,* p. 382; Van Hove, *De Rescriptis,* p. 199, note 2.

[60] Fransen, *op. cit.,* pp. 384-385; Beste, *Introductio in Codicem,* p. 161.

relevance of incidental fraud, it seems that the traditional doctrine on this point must be considered as the controlling factor even today. As observed above, previously to the Code, only when fraud had exerted a determining influence upon an act of consent did it call for proscription from the law. Since there is no clear indication in the present legislation that this traditional view has been discarded, it seems that one must hold, in virtue of canon 6, 4°, that antecedent fraud alone likewise qualifies under the present Code.[61]

Finally, to justify the rescission of an act, not only must true fraud be present with a determining influence upon an act, but the presence must be proved. The proof of the presence of fraud presents a particularly difficult problem, since one is dealing with an element which is based upon the internal intention on the one part, and in internal effect on the other part.[62] Since fraud, by its very nature, presupposes that the one who purveys it acts through ill will, one cannot presume its presence, and accordingly it must be demonstrated. The reason for this observation is evident, since no one is to be presumed evil unless he is proved to be so.[63]

If one excludes the case in which the purveyor of the fraud confesses his guilt, it is impossible to demonstrate the presence of fraud through direct proof. Since it is a moral element, it is incapable of measurement through physical criteria. One can, however, through a careful analysis of the antecedent, concomitant, and consequent circumstances surrounding an individual case arrive at a morally certain judgment that the act placed under those circumstances was in fact the result of fraud. One must, for the most part, fall back upon conjectures and presumptions drawn from the facts of the case, the convergence of which will enable one to come to a con-

---

[61] Gillet appeals to canon 23, ". . . leges posteriores ad priores trahendae sunt et his, quantum fieri possit, conciliandae," in developing the argument presented above. The norm governing the relationship between the anterior and the present law, however, is to be found not in canon 23, but in canon 6. Cf. Gillet, "De actione rescissoria ob dolum (can. 103)," *Ius Pontificium,* IX (1929), 323.

[62] Schmalzgrueber, *Ius Ecclesiasticum,* lib. II, tit. 14, n. 31.

[63] Schmalzgrueber, *ibidem,* n. 30; Wernz-Vidal, *Ius Canonicum,* VI, 280; Michiels, *Principia Generalia,* p. 541; Fransen, *op. cit.,* p. 385; Ojetti, *Commentarium,* II, 159; Beste, *Introductio in Codicem,* p. 161.

clusion concerning the truth in the matter.[64] Fransen points out that many times, though the evidence is not sufficient to prove conclusively the presence of fraud in an act, it may nevertheless demonstrate that the case is one in which there was a lack of sufficient consent.[65]

There is a divergence of opinion among canonists as to whether or not one must demonstrate not only the existence of true objective fraud, but likewise the fact that the victim of such fraud was in fact led into error because of it. Some authors maintain that the proof of the existence of error is no longer necessary, but that it suffices simply to establish the fact that fraudulent maneuvers were employed, and once that fact is clear, the error which is generally consequent upon such action is presumed to exist by the law. They argue that the sanctions invoked against the fraud are imposed not because of the error involved but solely to repair the injury done through the inherent injustice of fraud.[66] Others, holding to the traditional opinion, argue that one must demonstrate not only the fact that fraudulent maneuvers were used in connection with an act, but also that the author of the act was led into error through their use.[67] They call attention to the fact that in reality the reason advanced by those who support the opposite opinion is of no avail, since it is precisely in the error itself which fraud induces that its injurious nature lies. For, since it is proximately through the medium of this error that fraud succeeds in causing an act of defective consent, one cannot be said to have sustained an injury whenever, in spite of the presence of fraudulent maneuvers, one does not act because of the deception.

While Vermeersch-Creusen favor the opinion that, when it is a case of those acts which are merely made rescissible in the Code,

---

[64] Lefebvre, "Dol en droit canonique actuel," *DDC,* IV, col. 1348; Michiels, *loc. cit.;* Regatillo, *Institutiones,* I, 137.

[65] Fransen, *loc. cit.*

[66] Noval, *De Processibus,* I, n. 340, p. 224; Michiels, *op. cit.,* p. 542; Gillet, "De actione rescissoria ob dolum (can. 103)," *Jus Pontificium,* IX (1929), 324.

[67] Fransen, *Le dol dans la conclusion des actes juridiques,* pp. 385-386; Vermeersch-Creusen, *Epitome Iuris Canonici,* I, 206; Lefebvre, *ibidem,* coll. 1348-1349.

one must prove not only the perpetration of fraud but the resulting error as well, they argue that, whenever it is a case of one of those acts which are declared to be automatically invalid in the law itself once the presence of fraudulent maneuvers is proved, then the law presumes that the error did follow, and one is relieved of the burden of proof of the presence of error in these acts.[68] As Fransen and others point out, however, if one is to demonstrate the true causal connection between the presence of fraudulent maneuvers and the act following from them, the same reason exists for demanding the demonstration of the existence of fraudulent error in these cases as in those which are merely amenable to a rescissory action.[69] Furthermore, Vermeersch-Creusen give no reason for making such a distinction. It seems, therefore, that even in cases involving automatic invalidity one must demonstrate that one was in fact induced into error before such acts can be declared invalid.

Summing up these discussions, therefore, one may say that, in order that a juridic act may be considered as invalid or liable to rescission, one must conclusively demonstrate through moral arguments based upon conjectures and presumptions that the act was in fact the result of an erroneous intellectual judgment which was fundamentally created by the intentional maneuvers of another. If such a judgment does not in fact exist in the act, or does not play a determining rôle in its confection, the given consent must be considered not only as valid, but likewise as not liable to rescission through a judicial process.

---

[68] *Epitome Iuris Canonici,* I, 206: "Propria autem vis huius canonis de dolo [Canon 103, § 2] haec nobis esse videtur: allegatio doli qua talis non sufficit ad infirmandum actum, sed error substantialis vel causam dans praeterea demonstrandus est. In casibus autem ubi dolus ex iure actum infirmat, error praesumitur dolum secutus, et satis est ut dolum alleges an vincendam causam, nisi alter probet nullam re vera deceptionem adfuisse."

[69] Fransen, *op. cit.,* pp. 391-392; Michiels, *Principia Generalia,* p. 542; Lefebvre, *ibidem,* col. 1349.

CHAPTER VIII

The Effects of Fraud on Entry Into the Canonical Novitiate

The foregoing general study has served to demonstrate that not only the juridical concept of the element of fraud, but the category of juridic norms within which this element becomes operative so as to cause invalidity or to give rise to rescissory action are both well defined in canonical jurisprudence. These same principles, which govern the effect of fraud upon all other juridic acts placed under the present Code, must be considered as likewise valid with regard to the specific act which is the object of the present study, namely, entry or acceptance in a canonical novitiate. Although this act possesses a special juridic character in consequence of the end towards which it is directed, it does not differ in its essential requisites from any other act which may be placed to obtain a desired legal effect or to establish some definite juridic status. It stands as an exception to other acts in the present Code, not by reason of the nature of the fraud postulated for making the act juridically defective, but only by reason of the fact that the sanction of invalidity invests it automatically whenever it is executed under the influence of fraud.

Hence, a detailed analysis of the element of fraud as an invalidating impediment to the novitiate involves not only a careful study of the element of fraud itself, in so far as it may be realized in this act, but also of the various factors concerning which fraudulent error might possibly be induced with regard to it, and of the rôle which these factors may play in determining the consent of either the superior or the candidate in its confection. The present discussion will, therefore, be directed principally to three points: (a) the nature of fraud as it is envisioned under this impediment, (b) the principles governing the effect of fraud upon consent of an aspirant, and (c) the principles which govern its effect when it is employed against a superior accepting him. These three points will be discussed in detail in the following three chapters.

It is a fundamental principle of interpretation in ecclesiastical jurisprudence that the terms which are employed in the law to manifest the legislator's will and intent to the community must be understood according to the commonly accepted signification usually attached to them in legal matters.[1] The terminology employed in the law may be used in either a strictly juridical sense or in a sense accepted by ordinary usage.[2] But whenever use is made of a term to which a specific juridic signification has been attached in legal matters, as is the case if it is well established in both pre-Code law and canonical jurisprudence, this technical meaning must likewise be considered as the one which is attached to that term in the canons of the present Code, unless the contrary is plainly evident. In virtue of this principle, it is evident that the notion of fraud as a diriment impediment to entry into religion must be held to be identical with the juridic concept of this element as it is commonly understood with reference to other juridic acts, as authors universally concede.[3]

In keeping therefore with the general notion of fraud, this element, in so far as it is constituted as an invalidating impediment to the canonical novitiate, may be defined as *the deception of a candidate or a superior, deliberately and maliciously induced or sustained through the use of apt fraudulent devices, so as to entice the former on the one hand to seek entry into religion, or to dupe the latter on the other to receive him.* Hence, this impediment has

---

[1] Cf. canon 18.

[2] Michiels, *Normae Generales Juris Canonici* (2 voll., 2. ed., Parisiis—Tornaci—Romae: Desclée et Socii, 1949), I, 520 (hereafter cited *Normae Generales*).

[3] Some, in treating of this impediment, merely refer back to their commentary on the general notion of fraud and the principles governing its effects as they outlined them under canon 103, § 2, e.g., Blat, *Commentarium,* lib. II, 594; Coronata, *Institutiones,* I, 710. Others observe that the notion of fraud which falls under this impediment corresponds to the Roman legal notion of this element, which is also the canonical notion, e.g., Schaefer, *De Religiosis,* p. 429; Vermeersch-Creusen, *Epitome Iuris Canonici,* I, 500; Oesterle, *Praelectiones Iuris Canonici,* I, 289. Still others, without further comment, proceed to treat of this impediment as if this notion of fraud were a foregone conclusion, e.g., Cappello, *Summa Iuris Canonici,* II, 46; Berutti, *Institutiones,* III, 139; Wernz-Vidal, *Ius Canonicum,* III, 178.

a twofold aspect, in so far as it may be realized either on the part of the candidate or on the part of the superior. In either case, before the validity of the novitiate may be impugned on the count of fraud, however, all the various essential requisites which go to make up a formal act of juridically relevant fraud must be verified as having been present in any maneuver employed to induce the consent of either the candidate or the superior to this act. As outlined in the preceding general study of the element of fraud, these essential requisites which qualify a maneuver as a formal act of fraud are four in number and must be verified with at least moral certainty to be co-existent, i.e.: (a) the means employed must be prone to deceive, (b) they must constitute a grave violation of good faith, (c) they must be deliberately set into motion to deceive, and (d) deception must in fact ensue from their use. Since these four requisites form the basis upon which one must judge whether or not any maneuvers employed in inducing consent to entry into religion qualify as fraud, it will be necessary to review briefly these various conditions with special application to this specific act.

ARTICLE I. THE ELEMENT OF CLEVERNESS

The first essential requisite which must be verified in order to qualify a maneuver as fraudulent in relation to the novitiate lies in the evaluation of its aptness as a vehicle for deceit. That is to say, either by its very nature or by reason of concomitant circumstances, the medium through which fraudulent deception is alleged to have been employed must represent reasonable objective grounds from which fraudulent error might arise. Both Roman Law[4] and canonical jurisprudence[5] have always and invariably insisted that unless error takes its rise from a ruse which, objectively taken, may be regarded as a reasonable foundation for its inception, one cannot allege a fraud. The reason for this demand is evident, for if one is to establish a causal relationship between the objective

---

[4] D. (4. 3) 7: ". . . nam nisi ex magna et evidenti calliditate non debet de dolo actio dari."

[5] Cf. Fransen, *Le dol dans la conclusion des actes juridiques,* pp. 66, 95, 118-119, 188, 191.

ruse on the one hand and the subjective erroneous judgment formulated on the other, which the very nature of fraudulent deception supposes, one must at least have reasonable objective grounds upon which to base a judgment in the matter. It has ever been a legal principle that the deception, in order to be qualified as fraudulently induced, must be totally the product of extrinsic maneuvers, and not of any levity or fickleness on the part of the one deceived.[6]

In view of the great variety of types of persons and the innumerable means which may possibly be employed in perpetrating a fraud to extort consent to entry or acceptance in the novitiate, it is impossible to establish a precise and absolute norm whereby one may judge the aptness of a maneuver to deceive; rather, its evaluation must be left in the realm of the practical moral judgment of the one who is to render a decision in this matter as to whether or not it qualifies as a plausible ground for credibility under the circumstances in which it is used.[7]

The degree of cleverness which must be present in any ruse to qualify it as an apt artifice of deceit is usually referred to in forensic terminology as that which would influence a *vir prudens.*[8] In reality, nothing more is signified by this technical terminology than the fact that the objective device through which one is led into error must be vested with that degree of cleverness which would ordinarily succeed in deceiving the individual against whom it is employed when acting with the prudence and care which befits his state and condition in conducting affairs of importance.[9] Hence, in practice, on the one hand one must analyze the objective device in the light of the character of the individual using it, and especially the circumstances surrounding its use, in so far as these may render it more or less plausible to the superior or candidate against whom it is employed, i.e., whether the mendacious statement which led to error was made in the course of light banter, or in a serious

[6] D. (4. 3) 1; Fransen, *op. cit.*, p. 377.

[7] Badii, "Il dolo nel Codice di Diritto Canonico," *Il Diritto Ecclesiastico*, XL (1929), 310.

[8] Cf., e.g., Panormitanus, *Commentaria,* ad c. 6, X, *de his quae vi metusve causa fiunt,* I, 40.

[9] Cf. Bidagor, "De dolo et eius effectibus in admissione ad novitiatum et professione religiosa," *Periodica,* XX (1931), 62*.

conversation or solemn attestation. On the other hand, one must likewise take into account all those personal characteristics which may either greatly contribute to or lessen the ability of the victim to see through the insincerity of the objective ruse, such as his or her age, whether the one deceived is young and inexperienced or mature and well versed in affairs; their natural character, whether he or she is naive or adroit; their mental culture, whether they are learned or unread; and any and all other factors which will have a telling effect upon their ability to uncover the fraudulent nature of a device used to induce their consent.[10]

The aptness of the means employed to deceive will, therefore, differ from case to case, depending upon the objective nature of the ruse and the subjective qualities of the individual against whom it is employed. Obviously, a maneuver used to entice a simple and unlettered individual into a monastery as a lay brother needs to be vested with less objective plausibility than will ordinarily be needed for duping a high school or college graduate into the novitiate for the clerical state. An artifice used to induce a young and inexperienced girl into the convent, under ordinary circumstances, needs less objective credibility than one employed, for example, to trick a mature woman who has spent years in the business world into entering it. It is pertinent, however, to observe here that a person who may be well versed in secular affairs may in reality be quite simple and easily misled in matters pertaining to the religious state, since through piety one may be led to be less cautious in this matter than in conducting secular affairs. In ultimate analysis, it is the opinion of the present writer that the criterion which one must adopt in practice in judging the sufficiency of a ruse to constitute a fraud is whether or not the particular candidate or superior against whom it is directed was in fact induced into error through its use, excluding any negligence on his part to preclude deception or any levity inviting it.[11]

---

[10] Badii, *loc. cit.;* Fransen, *op. cit.*, pp. 376-377.

[11] At the same time one must not go so far in adopting the subjective norm as to say that even a very slight objective foundation may at times induce fraudulent error. Although De Lugo advanced this opinion, it seems to be entirely out of favor in present day jurisprudence, and rightly so, since

ARTICLE II. THE EVALUATION OF THE VIOLATION OF GOOD FAITH

Although the juridic notion of a violation of good faith in legal transactions is founded upon the notion of moral bad faith, it is, nevertheless, distinct from it. For the legislator does not consider all transgressions of the moral or ethical order as violations of good faith which are meritorious of his action, but only those which are considered as violations of the juridic rights of individuals and hence as injurious to society. In order, therefore, that a ruse employed to induce another to perform an act may be considered as assuming the nature of fraud, it must be classified as anti-social or anti-juridical in character.[12]

The precise circumstances and conditions under which a ruse must be considered as having exceeded the recognized limits so as to become anti-juridic seem to be one of those factors in fraud which of necessity must be left to the prudent estimation of the one who is rendering a judgment in this matter. Authors use very general phraseology in explaining what is meant by a juridical violation of good faith.[13] It seems that the concept of good faith juridically is based upon canonical equity as well as upon strict justice. That is to say, it not only implies the obligation of refraining from any malpractice which is explicitly reprobated by the law, but it also supposes the sincere desire of not interfering with the juridic liberty or the rights of another. Hence, any maneuver which clearly runs contrary to this sincere intention, which is presumed to exist in all those acting before the law, must be branded as *per se* an infringement upon good faith. At the same time, however, it must be remembered that the law does not consider every

---

if one were to hold this view it seems that the whole juridic order of things would be disrupted; one could not be sure of the soundness of any juridic act. Cf. De Lugo, *De Justitia et Jure,* Disp. XXII, sec. VII, n. 142.

[12] Fransen, *op. cit.,* p. 377; Badii, *ibidem,* p. 307.

[13] Bidagor and Michiels describe a violation of good faith as any circumvention which violates that faith which must serve as the foundation upon which all juridic relations are carried on. (Cf. Michiels, *Principia Generalia,* p. 536; Bidagor, *ibidem,* p. 61*.) Badii refers to it as that which exceeds the limits of tolerated cleverness and connivance. (Cf. Badii, *ibidem,* p. 310.) Fransen says it is the deliberate use of such means in inducing consent to an act as infringe upon the explicit or tacit rules which regulate juridic relationships. (Cf. Fransen, *loc. cit.*)

slight violation of good faith as calling for a sanction against it, but only those which interfere in a serious degree with the juridic liberty of an individual performing an act.[14] Hence, in actual practice, whenever such a violation does occur, it will be easily discernible to anyone who has any adroitness in legal matters.

It is the opinion of the present writer, in the light of these observations, that good faith on the part of a candidate seeking entry into the novitiate of an institute and on the part of an interested third party who attempts to solicit the superior's consent to receive him, obliges them to manifest not only those things which are explicitly represented in the common or particular law as obstacles to valid or licit reception, but also those matters which, from the very nature of this act, are implicitly understood as being of grave importance in determining a superior's consent in accepting candidates. On the part of the institute and on the part of an interested third party who attempts to influence a candidate to enter the religious state, good faith would oblige them not only to manifest sincerely those facts about the religious life which are of grave importance either in general or to the candidate concerned, but also to refrain from any intrigue which may in any way tend to make the individual's choice of the religious state less free or less spontaneous. For, as pointed out above, consent given to entry or acceptance in the religious state must not only be freely given, it must be spontaneous.

At the same time, it is imperative to point out that it is not only lawful but laudable to influence candidates to desire the religious state through personal counsel and direction, by describing its advantages over the lay state and by introducing proper motives for embracing it, as long as in the doing of this the truth is not violated in any way. What is proscribed in the law is not influence which is licitly employed, but that which unjustly extorts consent. Hence, as long as the influence is reasonable, it does not violate good faith.[15] Only if there is a flagrant violation of mutual

---

[14] Badii, *ibidem,* n. 2: ". . . la dottrina giuridica non tiene conto di quelle leggere violazioni della buona fede, commesse per indurre una persona a compiere un negozio giuridico . . ."; cf. Fransen, *op. cit.,* p. 387.

[15] Beste, *Introductio in Codicem,* pp. 364-365.

confidence may one allege fraud. And the same observation holds true with regard to the superior who admits candidates. As long as personal influence is kept within reasonable bounds, one need not be greatly concerned that a violation of good faith has occurred in the presenting of a candidate to one for approval.

ARTICLE III. THE ELEMENT OF MALICE

Granted that apt devices of deceit, which at least externally tend to violate good faith, have been employed in influencing candidates to choose the religious state, or superiors to receive them, unless these means are deliberately and maliciously set to work for the precise purpose of creating a deception there is lacking the formal element upon which rests the whole notion of juridically relevant fraud.[16] Canon law proscribes fraud only in so far as it is recognizable as a morally imputable act. That is to say, it presupposes that the individual who employs fraudulent means does so with a free self-determination accompanied with a sufficient advertence.[17] The external devices through which it is perpetrated are merely presumed to represent the externalization of this internal intent. Though they may serve as a reasonable criterion to demonstrate the certain, evident, and undeniable fact of ill will, without the ill will which they indicate they do not in themselves constitute a fraud.[18]

For the purpose of the present study it is not necessary to dwell upon the nature of the volitional act involved in the perpetration of fraud. Only two points of importance need here be recalled. The first of these is that the intention which is proper to an act of fraud implies the deliberate will to lead another into error through the use of improper means so as to dispose him to conform to the deceiver's will in his juridical action. This is as far as the intention of the deceiver need extend, for it is a veritable injustice in itself to will and to take the proper means to deprive

[16] Fransen, *Le dol dans la conclusion des actes juridiques,* pp. 189, 377.

[17] Badii, "Il dolo nel Codice di Diritto Canonico," *Il Diritto Ecclesiastico,* XL (1929), 306; Coronata, *Institutiones,* I, 183: ". . . dolus semper alicui imputatur."

[18] Badii, *loc. cit.*

another of his full liberty in yielding consent to a juridic act. It is a very real tort in itself to lead a candidate or a superior into error intentionally so as to elicit the consent of the former to embrace religion or to solicit the consent of the latter to receive an undesirable candidate.

Secondly, it is important to note that the intention of the deceiver need not extend to the evil effects, material or spiritual, which may in fact flow from the act which he intends to extort through the erroneous judgment fraudulently induced.[19] Indeed, it seems he may be either totally unconscious of these effects or even think that the particular act which he induces the individual to place represents a good to be desired for him, and yet perpetuate a juridically reprehensible act of fraud. This is a very salient point, especially with regard to the use of fraud to induce consent to entry into the religious state. It was because of a misunderstanding of this truth that the medieval glossators were led so far astray in developing their unique theory of *dolus in spiritualibus,* whereby they held that fraud used to induce individuals to assume the religious state was not juridically reprehensible because of the good end thereby attained.[20] Since the religious state as such represents a state of higher perfection, anyone, especially one of simple though pious character, may easily be misled into believing that the objective good attained by inducing one to embrace this state justifies the means employed in attaining this end.

Hence, it may well happen that the individual who employs trickery in order to induce a candidate to enter religion, or a superior to receive him, may think he is doing one or the other a real service in so acting. This is not too remote a possibility. A hypothetical example might be found in the case of deeply religious, though somewhat ill informed, parents who, cherishing the one desire to see one of their children embrace the religious

---

[19] Fransen, *op. cit.,* p. 377: "Il n'est pas nécessaire que l'on ait en vue de faire subir à autrui un dommage matérial. Le simple fait de vouloir extorquer son consentement suffit à constituer un dol . . ."; Badii, *ibidem,* p. 310: "Non occorre però che vi sia l'intenzione di recar danno alla persona che si viene ad ingannare"; Michiels, *Principia Generalia,* p. 536.

[20] Cf. *supra,* pp. 31-32.

state, should falsely convince one of the latter that he was morally obliged to embrace the religious state because he had been dedicated to God as a child. It is obvious that these individuals do not wish any evil effects which may flow from their action, but only the good that they see in its result. And yet the malice needed to qualify their maneuver as fraudulent, and invalidating if it takes effect, is fully realized. This may also happen on the part of the member of an institute who, perceiving the qualities of intellect and character which would render a certain individual a desirable candidate for his institute, attempts to influence the latter to enter it through the use of unreasonable representations. It is evident that the end desired by the individual is good, but, nevertheless, the means used represent a truly fraudulent intent. Hence, it is wholly irrelevant whether or not the individual perpetrating a fraud intended a good or an evil effect by his action, as long as he deliberately willed to engender deception, and thereby to extort consent.

Finally, on the part of the intellect, the deliberate intention of deceiving supposes that the deceiver possesses at least a reasonably certain knowledge that the truth or fact which is the object of deception is of grave importance to the individual from whom it is to be withheld or to whom it is to be misrepresented, as well as that the means which are utilized to obscure or misrepresent this fact are fraudulent. Vermeersch and others have observed, however, that even a well-founded suspicion that the truth deliberately obscured or misrepresented may certainly exert a determining influence upon the consent of the superior would suffice to establish any deception concerning it as a formal act of fraud, such as would qualify to invalidate the entry of a candidate if it does, as a matter of fact, take effect in inducing consent.[21] The notion of a formal act of fraud seems to imply that the one who perpetrates it must not only have habitual knowledge of the importance of the

[21] Vermeersch-Creusen, *Epitome Iuris Canonici,* I, 500: ". . . qui consulto vitia dissimulat *quae redhibitoria esse suspicatur,* dolum commiserit quo irrita fiat eius receptio . . ."; Creusen, *Religious Men and Women in the Code,* p. 136: "If the postulant has concealed a disease or a family disgrace which he knew *or suspected* would certainly have caused his exclusion, his admission is invalid . . ."; Bouscaren-Ellis, *Canon Law, a Text and Commentary,* p. 260.

fact obscured but also actual advertence to its importance when he misrepresents it. However, once it can be established or presumed that he has habitual knowledge of the importance of the fact, it seems one must hold him responsible in the external forum unless there are clear indications to the contrary.

ARTICLE IV. THE ELEMENT OF DECEPTION

The mere objective presence of fraudulent maneuvers such as have been outlined in the preceding paragraphs, even though they may be deliberately set to work, does not suffice to invoke the sanction of automatic invalidity upon entry in the novitiate. As such, these maneuvers merely represent a potential invalidating agency in this act; they do not become juridically relevant to its actual invalidity on the count of fraud unless they do in reality succeed in efficaciously interfering with the consent of a candidate or a superior in placing it.[22] But, since the proximate medium through which fraud works upon the will in soliciting consent is the erroneous judgment which is created or sustained in the mind of the victim, unless this objective trickery does in reality result in the deception of the candidate or the superior, neither can be said to be induced to perform this act through fraud. For, it is to be remembered that fraud and fraudulent error are identical terms in law when one speaks of this element as a source of defective consent. Hence, the commonly recognized rule—*scienti dolus non fit*[23]—is likewise fully valid with regard to fraud as an invalidating impediment to entry in the canonical novitiate.

As observed above, fraudulent error as such does not differ essentially from any other error residing in the intellect except by reason of the fact that it is illictly induced or nurtured there.

---

[22] Fransen, *Le dol dans la conclusion des actes juridiques,* pp. 377-378: "L'existence du dol objectif, conçu comme nous venons de le définir, ne suffit pas à provoquer la sanction du droit. Il faut encore que ce dol ait réellement influé sur le consentement de l'auteur de l'acte juridique. . . ." Cf. Bigador, "De dolo et eius effectibus in admissione ad novitiatum et professione religiosa," *Periodica,* XX (1931), 63*.

[23] Lefebvre, "Dol en droit canonique actuel," *DDC,* IV, col. 1348.

As long as it may be considered as the product of malpractice at the time consent is given to a juridical act it is immaterial whether the malpractice represents the sole source from which it took its rise or the medium through which it is sustained.[24] Ordinarily, therefore, fraudulent error does not consist in the mere lack of knowledge or in ignorance concerning an object or truth, but rather in the false notion concerning it, in that it is judged to be other than it is in objective reality.

The question presents itself, however, as to whether or not for all practical purposes ignorance which is culpably sustained through fraudulent devices may be considered equal to error in this matter. Although they are philosophically distinct, the legal effects of these two elements are considered as identical before the law.[25] It seems as though ignorance which is deliberately sustained in the mind of a candidate or a superior through the malicious use of fraudulent devices may, for all practical purposes, be considered as of the same juridical effect as fraudulent error. For error, in reality, is the result of ignorance in that it is through the lack of knowledge concerning the truth that one is led to judge an object to be other than it is in reality. Error, therefore, may be properly designated as *ignorance in action.*[26] While ignorance is a lack of knowledge of a thing, error is a false notion concerning it formulated because of a lack of adequate knowledge of it. But when one treats of the performance of an act which requires a practical judgment concerning the object in order that the full consent of the will may be directed towards it, it seems to make no appreciable difference whether one is led to place the act through a lack of knowledge or through false knowledge. Hence, it seems that the law would

---

[24] Fransen, *op. cit.,* p. 376; Michiels, *Principia Generalia,* p. 535.

[25] Wernz-Vidal, *Ius Canonicum,* II, 50: "Quae sanciuntur de dolo cum iis, quae de errore dicta sunt, coordinari debent . . ."; *ibidem,* p. 48: "Error et ignorantia re quidem inter se differunt . . . in iure tamen idem efficiunt." Cappello, *Summa Iuris Canonico,* I, 179: "Error, seu falsum iudicium, ignorantia seu defectus cognitionis . . . in iure aequiparantur." Cf. Chelodi-Ciprotti, *De Personis,* p. 168.

[26] "Consultationes," *Jus Pontificium,* III (1923), 150.

allot the same juridic effects to both ignorance and error whenever either represents the product of fraud.[27]

It may likewise be argued that one who culpably leaves a superior in ignorance concerning some fact which is known to be of decisive importance in determining the latter's consent to admit a certain candidate is in reality creating a potential error which becomes an actual one at the moment the superior gives consent. This observation may be concluded from the very nature of the act of consent which the superior places when performing his function of admitting candidates. For his consent under these circumstances in reality represents a practical judgment that the particular candidate concerned possesses all those qualities which render him worthy of admission. Thus, at least confusedly,[28] he does formulate an erroneous judgment concerning those things which have been fraudulently withheld from him so as to sustain his ignorance concerning them.[29]

ARTICLE V. CAUSAL RELATIONSHIP

Finally, in order to impugn the validity of the novitiate on the count of fraud, it is necessary to ascertain whether a true causal connection exists between the deceitful artifice which may have been present in the act of entering or admitting a candidate to the novitiate and the actual consent given to this act, so that the latter must be considered to have been placed in fact *ex dolo* or under the influence of fraud, i.e., under the influence of the error

[27] Ojetti, *Commentarium,* II, 166: "Et hinc est, quod, quum in quantum attinet ad consequentias iuridicas idem sit alicuius rei aut nullam notionem haberi aut falsam, in iure saepe nulla distinctio fit inter errorem et ignorantiam." Ojetti (1862-1932), indeed, advanced this observation with regard to fortuitous error itself. But since fraudulent error and fortuitous error differ only by reason of their source, it seems that the same principles apply to fraudulent error as well.

[28] Salsmans, "Circa vitia consensus," *Jus Pontificium,* X (1930), 108.

[29] Ojetti seemed to favor this view when he wrote: ". . . ignorantia potest dici causa [actus] per accidens, sicut removens impedimentum." Cf. *Commentarium,* II, 166. Cf. also Maroto, *Institutiones,* I, 750: "Ignorantia mater erroris est et vix in praxi datur actus in quo error ignorantiam non comitetur."

which is engendered through fraud.[80] In other words, the deliberate use of deceitful devices must be so correlated to the erroneous judgment which serves either as the basis or the inspiring cause for consent that this judgment must be considered as having been fraudulently induced.

This correlation is easily perceivable whenever fraudulent maneuvers are deliberately set into motion for the direct and immediate purpose of enticing an individual into the religious state or for the one objective of duping a superior into receiving him. Thus, for example, if a candidate were asked in the formal examination before his acceptance whether or not he is affected by pulmonary tuberculosis and were given to understand that he would not be received if such were the case, then if he were to present a forged medical certificate to the effect that he is free of this disease when he knows full well that he is gravely ill with it, the causal connection between the deception deliberately created by him and the extortion of the superior's consent is plainly evident. For, under such circumstances the deception so created is not only unjust: it is deliberately directed to the procuring of consent to this one act.

The question presents itself, however, as to whether the law demands that fraud must be perpetrated directly and exclusively for the one purpose of soliciting consent to this specific act before the sanction of invalidity falls upon it, or whether the novitiate is likewise invalid whenever consent given at its inception represents the indirect result of fraud, i.e., is induced through an erroneous judgment which is engendered in the mind of a candidate or a superior through malpractice which is *per se* directly employed for the purpose of extorting consent to some other specific act. In other words, does it suffice that there has been merely a casual connection between a fraudulent device and the erroneous judgment which inspires the act of consent, or must there likewise be a formal moral union between the ill will of the one who sets the fraudulent device to work and the specific act of consent extorted through them, even though indirectly?

---

[80] Michiels, *Principia Generalia,* p. 536.

The problem is not purely a theoretical one. Hypothetical cases in which the perpetration of a fraud for some other purpose may indirectly exercise a determining influence upon the consent of a candidate or superior to the inception of the novitiate are not difficult to find. For example, let it be supposed that an individual, in order to obtain admission into a lay college conducted by a certain teaching institute, were to manipulate his former scholastic records, which showed him to be a student of such low calibre that he knew no college would be willing to receive him on the strength of them. Then, after having attended a summer session of this college, he decides to enter the institute itself at the beginning of the fall term and does in fact apply for admission. The superiors upon receiving his petition, knowing that he has been a student in their college, do not ask him for his scholastic record, but instead, unknown to him, they obtain a transcript of his falsified record from the college files (as would be the normal procedure in this matter) and use this record as the basis for their approval of his application as a candidate for their institute, though they certainly would not have received him had they known the truth. In this case the fraud is *per se* intentionally directed against another person for some other end, and yet it is quite apparent that it has exercised a determining influence upon the superiors' consent.

One may think also of a case in which a deception is induced in the same individual but for some other end, and indirectly results in procuring an act of consent to entry or acceptance in the novitiate as well. Let it be supposed, for example, that in consequence of a shortage of sisters to fill this capacity, a certain young woman were to apply to the superior of an institute to work in the capacity of a typist in the offices of the institute. The superior informs the applicant that the gaining of this position will hinge on one condition, namely, that she present letters to the effect that she is a good practicing Catholic and is known to be of good repute. Knowing that her pastor will be most unwilling to give her any such recommendation in view of her protracted immoral conduct in the past, which has given her a bad name, she presents to the superior a forged letter, written on parochial stationery, supposedly by her pastor in a distant town, in which it is declared that she has been a daily communicant of long standing and an extraordinarily pious girl. Upon the reception of this letter the superior gladly gives the girl the position. Later, in order to ingratiate herself with this superior she tells her many other untruths about herself so as to create the impression that she has always been a militant Catholic. But in doing so she has absolutely no intention at the time of entering the institute. Later, however, after having enjoyed the good graces of the superior for several months, she decides to apply for admission into the novitiate, not adverting to the effect her former deception will have upon her acceptability. The superior, however, judging her to be a fit candidate upon the grounds of this deception, consents to accept her in the novitiate of the institute, though she would certainly not have received her had the full truth been known. Is the novitiate of this girl automatically invalid?

Authors, in commenting upon fraud as invalidating the novitiate, seem to indicate in their manner of treating of this impediment that the fraud must be directly perpetrated to obtain this one act before it constitutes a novitiate as invalidly entered upon. Some few expressly state that fraud must be used precisely within the scope of obtaining consent to this act.[31] Others, although they do not make such an explicit statement, after presenting the concept of fraud, merely proceed to exemplify how fraud could be realized in this act by giving a case in which it is used directly for this one purpose.[32] Still others either remain silent concerning the manner

[31] Brys, *Juris Canonici Compendium,* I, 534: "Dolus intelligitur de fallacibus artibus ad decipiendum pro hoc scopo determinato adhibitis."

[32] Beste, *Introductio in Codicem,* p. 364: "Dolus . . . habetur, si candidatus consulto reticuerit vitia . . . aut scienter fingat . . . *ut ingressum obtineat";* Berutti, *Institutiones,* III, 139: ". . . dolo inductus, si illum recipiat quia circa ipsius qualitates physicas vel intellectuales aut morales *de industria* deceptus est"; Larraona, "Commentarium Codicis," *CpRM,* XVII (1936), 17: "Si . . . candidatus . . . aliqua fingat quae vera non sunt vel dissimulet aut reticeat illa quae revera existunt *hac de causa ut ingressus obtineatur qui* alioquin denegaretur, certo dolus existit"; Vermeersch-Creusen, *Epitome Iuris Canonici,* I, 500: "Sic candidatus qui qualitates . . . mentiatur *ut obtineat ingressum* . . . vel qui *consulto* vitia dissimulat . . ."; Oesterle, *Praelectiones Iuris Canonici,* I, 289: ". . . dolus habetur, si candidatus falsa indicia de qualitatibus, de valetudine, de bonis faciat *ea intentione* ut ingressum obtineat . . ." (italics are the writer's).

of causality, or else do not furnish a clear statement to the effect that only direct fraud is relevant in determining the invalidity of the novitiate.[33] It does not seem to the present writer that the same arguments advanced with regard to the relevancy of indirect fear obtain with regard to the element of fraud. For here one is dealing with an element which by its very nature demands not only a causal relationship between it and the extorted act of consent, but likewise a formal one.[34]

At the same time, it must be noted that a clear-cut distinction must be made between the indirect influence of fraud upon this act and the indirect intention of extorting it. For an indirect intention of inducing a candidate or a superior into error so as to influence their consent certainly suffices to qualify fraud as morally and causally united to their consent in the act of entry or acceptance in the novitiate. By an indirect intention here is meant that an individual perpetrates a fraud for some other immediate end which is foreseen and willed by him as a means of obtaining the consent of an individual to enter religion or a superior to receive him.[35] Thus, for example, in the first hypothetical case presented above, if the individual were to manipulate his scholastic record fraudulently for the direct purpose of obtaining entry into the lay college of the institute, while at the same time he foresees, because of the ordinary manner in which his records will be obtained, that this act will induce a superior into error concerning him, his

[33] Cf. Blat, *Commentarium,* lib. II, 594; Cappello, *Summa Iuris Canonici,* II, 46; Creusen, *Religious Men and Women in the Code,* pp. 134-135; Chelodi-Ciprotti, *De Personis,* p. 415; Fanfani, *De Iure Religiosorum,* p. 198; Wernz-Vidal, *Ius Canonicum,* III, 199-200.

[34] Cf., e.g., Ojetti, *Commentarium,* II, 154: "Exinde patet non haberi dolum, de quo hic, nisi machinatio, etc., adhibita fuerit in eum praecise finem, ut alter perficiat negotium, quamvis non sit necesse, ut dolum adhibens foveat intentionem inferendi alii damnum."

[35] It is to be noted that Badii understands the direct and indirect occurrence of fraud in canon 169, § 1, 1°, in much the same manner. Cf. Badii, "Il dolo nel Codice di Diritto Canonico," *Il Diritto Ecclesiastico,* XL (1929), 312: ". . . non è necessario che il dolo sia stato diretto per se stesso allo scopo di estorcere il voto, ma basta che sia stato ordinato a qualsiasi altro fine previsto e voluto dall'agente come mezzo per conseguire la elezione di una certa e determinata persona."

novitiate is certainly invalid. The same principle may be applied to the second case as well. If the young woman has any foreknowledge that the deception which she induces in the superior for the purpose of obtaining a position will or may likewise influence consent with regard to her admission into the institute, her novitiate is certainly invalid. It is to be noted, as stated above,[36] that as long as the individual is conscious that his fraudulent action may influence consent to an act, directly or indirectly, either at the time it is set into motion, or at any time before or during the actual eventuation of the act, the formal will needed to constitute a fraud must be considered as present.

It is imperative to point out here that although the legal notion of fraud is founded upon the presence of internal ill will, the law draws its practical criterion of the presence of malice from the external circumstances surrounding the use of the fraudulent devices. Hence, whenever it can be prudently judged, either by reason of the nature of the deception or of the circumstances surrounding its infliction, that the ill will of an individual not only extended to a certain act directly intended and extorted, but likewise to the influence indirectly exerted by that fraud upon the consent of a superior accepting him, one must hold him responsible for this indirect effect, and his novitiate, it seems, would be invalid.

---

[36] Cf. *supra*, pp. 131-132.

CHAPTER IX

THE EFFECT OF FRAUDULENT ERROR UPON THE CONSENT OF A CANDIDATE

According to the exact wording of canon 542, 1°, the novitiate is rendered automatically null and void whenever a candidate has been *induced* to seek entry into it through the use of illicit representations such as intrigue or fraud. Not every slight deception through which a candidate may be led to seek entry into religion, therefore, may be considered as sufficient to nullify his action. Rather, the wording of the canon makes it very clear that unless the deception created or nurtured in his mind through the agency of illegal trickery exerts a telling influence upon his consent, this consent cannot be considered as juridically defective. Hence, the theory advanced by some authors with regard to the juridical relevance of incidental fraud under the present Code cannot find any application here, as they themselves are willing to concede.[1] Rather, the erroneous judgment illicitly caused through fraud must be either of such a nature, or else have played so important a rôle in determining the consent of the candidate, that he would not have given consent had the truth concealed from him been known when he placed this act.

Hence, in keeping with the general principles governing the effects of fraud upon other juridic acts, once the fraudulent deception has been proved as present in a candidate when seeking entry into the novitiate, the validity of this act will hinge upon two fundamental factors, namely, the nature of the fraudulent deception and the rôle which it played in influencing or inspiring his consent. In the following paragraphs the invalidity of the novitiate will be discussed first under the aspect of the error itself, and secondly under the aspect of the influence exerted by it in determining the consent of a candidate.

[1] Cf. Coronata, *Institutiones,* I, 710: ". . . et his rationibus unice vel principaliter ductus candidatus admittatur fraude deceptus . . ."; Wernz-Vidal, *Ius Canonicum,* III, 199-200.

The first principle one must invoke when estimating the effects of fraudulent deception upon the consent of a candidate is that, if he has been led into substantial error, his consent is invalidly given not only by reason of the provisions of the positive law but by reason of the natural law as well.[2] For under such circumstances the candidate is rendered absolutely incapable of placing a true act of consent, since the object towards which it is externally directed is totally different from that which is represented in his mind. *Nihil enim est volitum, nisi quia et quatenus fuerit praecognitum.*[3] A novitiate entered upon through such an erroneous judgment would be automatically invalid even though it were not the result of deceit, and even though such an error did not constitute the motive cause for entrance into it.[4]

However, the determination of precisely what constitutes a substantial error with regard to the act of entering the novitiate gives rise to a somewhat knotty problem. For one is here dealing with an act whereby there is assumed a juridical status which in view of its very nature has been established for imparting by instruction and trial the essential knowledge which is needed by the faithful for embracing the religious state with full deliberation and preparation. It is quite apparent, therefore, that the law cannot demand the same complete and detailed knowledge of the religious life, either in general or as it is lived in a particular institute, on the part of a candidate entering upon his probation as it does in the novice who is about to assume his vows in the institute. In virtue of this fact it is clear that one cannot use the same norm to judge those errors which must be counted as substantial with relation to the profession and those which must be considered as substantial to the act of entering the novitiate, in preparation for the profession.[5]

In what then does substantial error consist on the part of a

---

[2] Schaefer, *De Religiosis*, p. 429; Wernz-Vidal, *Ius Canonicum*, III, 199.

[3] Michiels, *Principia Generalia*, p. 531.

[4] Cf. p. 114; Peinador, "De ingressu in statum religiosum, iure naturali invalido," *CpR*, XV (1934), 283.

[5] Bidagor, "De dolo et eius effectibus in admissione ad novitiatum et professione religiosa," *Periodica*, XX (1931), 69*; Peinador, *ibidem*, p. 285.

candidate seeking entry into the novitiate? Strictly taken, a juridical act is a human act, legitimately manifest, by which an agent intends to produce a determined juridical effect recognized by the law.[6] Hence the solution to the question as to what constitutes substantial error in this case hinges upon the nature of the intention needed on the part of the candidate for acting validly. Properly analyzed, the act of consent of an aspirant entering the novitiate must be essentially directed to a twofold objective: proximately, he must intend to assume this juridical status in which the religious life, as it is lived in a specific community, is given a true and a serious trial; ultimately, because of the intimate connection between the two acts, his consent must likewise tend to the assumption of the obligations of the religious state as such, and especially as it is practiced in the particular community into which he seeks entry,[7] provided it be willing to accept him at the end of his probation. Consequently, an aspirant may be said to be acting under substantial fraud whenever he is deceived concerning the essential nature of the novitiate itself, or the essential nature of the religious state as such, or even concerning the substantial character of the specific institute into which he seeks entry.[8]

First, substantial fraud may be realized in an aspirant with regard to the nature of the novitiate itself. In general, such would be the case whenever an aspirant had been induced into error or ignorance concerning the fact that the novitiate is a state of serious experimentation of and preparation for the religious life. For if a candidate were to be deprived of knowledge of this fact, then even by reason of the natural law he would be rendered incapable of placing a deliberate act of consent towards assuming the status of the novitiate.[9] It must be noted here, however, that before an erroneous judgment concerning the novitiate can destroy the consent given by a candidate to it, it must have succeeded in obscuring this essential nature of the novitiate to such a degree that the notion which the candidate has concerning it totally differs from

---

[6] Regatillo, *Institutiones*, I, 134.

[7] Peinador, "art. cit.," *loc. cit.;* Bigador, "art. cit.," *loc. cit.*

[8] Peinador, "art. cit.," *loc. cit.*

[9] Peinador, *ibidem*, pp. 285-286.

the reality. For if he retains at least a confused knowledge of the essential nature of the novitiate, then substantial fraud would not be fully realized.[10] The cases in which such total deception occurs must be considered as truly extraordinary. One could adduce as a hypothetical example the case of an aspirant who has been led to believe that the period of the novitiate is merely a year's vacation from study, spent away from his friends and relatives, to see whether he can give them up before embracing the religious state, or who has been induced into believing that the novitiate is in reality only a protracted retreat which does not *per se* tend to the assumption of the religious life as such. Substantial fraud is also conceivable not only with regard to the nature of the novitiate in general but also with regard to its specific character. For example, it seems it would be a substantial fraud if a candidate were tricked into thinking that he was being received as a candidate for the clerical state, whereas in reality he was being received in preparation for profession as a lay brother, or vice versa.

Secondly, substantial fraud may exist through an erroneous judgment illicitly induced or confirmed concerning the essential nature or purpose of the religious state as such, since the consent of a candidate must likewise extend to the act of ultimately embracing this state, if he is found worthy and desires to do so at the completion of the novitiate.[11] Fraud would be substantial if it obscured the essential means, the primary purpose, the fundamental obligations, the permanence, or the necessity of the religious life.[12] Thus it would be a case of substantial fraud if a postulant were deluded into thinking that the religious state is merely a fraternal organization of the faithful, in which, because of the common life, salvation is made easier, but which does not bind those entering it to anything more than the ordinary laity are obliged to observe.[13] It would likewise amount to fraud affecting

[10] Authors compare the knowledge needed to enter the novitiate validly by reason of the natural law to that which is needed to commit a mortal sin with regard to some grave obligation. Cf. Peinador, *ibidem*, p. 145.

[11] Cf. Peinador, *ibidem*, pp. 143-144.

[12] Bidagor, *ibidem*, pp. 68*, 71*; Berutti, *Institutiones*, III, 139.

[13] Peinador, *ibidem*, pp. 285-286.

the substance of the religious state if one surreptitiously convinced another that he could leave this state at will even after he had validly taken vows in it, or if one duped him into thinking that the religious life is an absolute necessity to salvation either for all the faithful in general or for himself.[14] Here again it must be remarked that before the fraud can be considered substantial with regard to the nature of the religious state, the aspirant must be fully convinced that the erroneous judgment concerning these various qualities of the religious state represents its true nature. For if he possessed even a confused knowledge of the objective truth, full substantial deception would not be realized.

Thirdly, fraud would be substantial if it concerned the essential nature of the particular institute into which a candidate seeks entrance, in so far as its specific character affects the general principles of the religious life.[15] In looking to the specific nature of an institute, one must not base one's judgment of what qualities redound to its essential differentiation from other institutes on the legal distinctions found in canon 488, since not all of these distinctions affect the nature of the religious life as it is practiced in these various institutes. Thus, for example, whether a particular community is one of diocesan or one of pontifical approval will not basically affect the character of the religious life as it is lived therein. If such a community was active or contemplative in character before papal approbation, it will generally remain so after. Rather, in judging what pertains to the essential character of an institute one must base one's judgment upon the manner in which the general principles of the religious life are practiced therein.[16]

Hence, for example, the fraud would relate to the substance of the specific nature of an institute if a girl were induced to enter

---

[14] Cf. Bidagor, *ibidem,* p. 68*.

[15] Bidagor, *ibidem,* 71*: "Error substantialis invalidans admissionem est error afficiens generaliora principia vitae religiosae."

[16] The distinctions enumerated in canon 488 are fundamentally technical, legal classifications of the institutes, though they may indirectly affect the nature of the institute as such, e.g., the distinction between clerical and lay institutes.

a community of which she has become fraudulently convinced that it is an institute of simple vows and active life, whereas it is one of solemn vows with strict papal cloister.[17] The same would hold true if a young man were led to embrace a lay institute upon being deceived into believing that it is clerical, or vice versa. It would likewise be a substantial fraud if a postulant were tricked through duplicity into believing that the vows of a particular institute are of such a nature that its members cannot be sent out of their native country, whereas in reality the community is purely missionary and the vow of obedience in the Order obliges the religious to go wherever they are sent.[18] Vidal (1867-1938) held that one might regard a candidate as acting through substantial fraud even in the case in which he has been induced to believe that perfect observance flourished in a particular institute whereas in actuality its discipline was totally relaxed.[19]

Finally, authors are wont to make a distinction between fraudulent error which is objectively substantial in nature and that which is subjectively so. It is termed objectively substantial whenever it concerns an element which either from the nature of the object willed, from a disposition of the law, or from the common estimation of men is held to be a constitutive element of the substance of an act. It is termed subjectively substantial whenever the individual placing an act intends a particular accidental quality to such an extent that he makes it the substance of his consent, i.e., he makes it a "*conditio sine qua non.*"[20] The objects in regard to which a candidate may impose such a condition are innumerable. For example, a case in point would be that of a particular individual who is deceived by his parents into believing that the latter offered him to God as a child and promised that he would enter religion, when, as a matter of fact, they did not make any promise, and this individual clearly states that, unless

---

[17] Wernz-Vidal, *Ius Canonicum,* III, 199.

[18] Cf. Bieter, "The Canon Law on Deceit," *The Ecclesiastical Review* (originally *The American Ecclesiastical Review,* Philadelphia, 1889-1943; Washington, D. C., 1944-), XLVI (1922), 50 (hereafter cited *ER*).

[19] *Ius Canonicum,* III, 199.

[20] Michiels, *Principia Generalia,* p. 529; Ojetti, *Commentarium,* II, 177.

such a promise has been made, he has absolutely no intention of entering the novitiate under these circumstances. Consent would be substantially lacking, since it is without a foundation upon which to subsist.

Prior to the present Code of Canon Law, it was a universal and constant opinion among canonists that entry into religion was invalid on the count of fraud only in the case in which a candidate was so thoroughly deceived concerning the substance of the religious life that he was rendered incapable of placing a true act of consent in relation to it.[21] This doctrine, it is true, was developed primarily with regard to the profession itself, since when the classical canonists spoke of entry into religion they generally understood by this the taking of solemn vows. The question of the invalidity of the novitiate itself because of fraud was either passed over in silence, or else the opinion was advanced that the novitiate might be considered as validly made even though entry into it had been obtained through fraud, provided that the deception so created ceased at some time before the actual taking of vows.[22] The question arises, therefore, as to whether one must consider the fraud which falls under the invalidating sanction of canon 542, 1°, as only substantial fraud exclusively, so that accidental fraud, even though it may have exerted a determining influence upon a candidate's consent in placing this act, would not invalidate it.

Bidagor, in his erudite study of the element of fraud and its effects upon entry into religion,[23] adverting to the traditional doctrine before the Code, was of the opinion that one must consider the present law merely an expression of the former doctrine on this point, since even the preceding discipline demanded that a candidate be perfectly free in choosing the religious state and, nevertheless, all authors affirmed that, unless he was substantially deceived, his entry was not rendered invalid through fraud. He argued that, if this was true with regard to the vows, there is much

---

[21] Cf. *supra*, pp. 42-43.

[22] Cf. *supra*, p. 43.

[23] "De dolo et eius effectibus in admissione ad novitiatum et professione religiosa," *Periodica*, XX (1931), 60*-73*.

more reason for it to hold true with regard to the novitiate, since the candidate's deception can easily be dispelled in the course of the novitiate and hence he does not suffer any grave injury to his juridic liberty.[24] He therefore concluded that accidental error fraudulently induced in a candidate could not with certainty be said to invalidate his entry, even though it be the preponderant reason for his action.[25] At the same time he admitted that if one adhered to the rigor of the law concerning fraud as laid down in canon 103, §2, and canon 104, one might rightly infer that even accidental error, if it was the antecedent cause for entry into the novitiate, might be considered as sufficient to invalidate this act,[26] though he did not favor this opinion.

This latter opinion presented by Bidagor as a possibility is now the one defended by the majority of the canonists, and rightly so, for the provisions of canon 542, 1°, are nothing more than a particular application of the general principles in the present Code governing the effects of fraud upon juridical acts placed under its influence. Hence, just as fraud which is not substantial, but which is established as the efficacious reason for which an act was placed, suffices to qualify the resulting act as juridically defective and subject to rescission, so too must one hold that a fraudulent deception which of itself does not relate to the substance of the religious life or the novitiate, but which, nevertheless, constitutes the determining cause for a candidate's assumption of this status, must be considered as sufficient to establish his action as automatically invalid.[27] This is likewise a well-founded deduction from

---

[24] Bigador, *ibidem,* p. 69*: "Addendum est, argumentis alterius sententiae, errores hos etiam ex dolo provenientes multo facilius purgari in ipso noviciatu; proinde non tam graviter afficere ipsam libertatem ingressus, cuius tuitio tandem ratio ultima mentis legislatoris in canone 542 esse videtur."

[25] *Ibidem,* p. 72*: "Error accidentalis dolo in candidato incussus, determinans eius ingressum non certo admissionem invalidam facere videtur."

[26] *Ibidem,* p. 68*.

[27] Cf. Michiels, *Principia Generalia,* p. 543, note 2: "Hanc quaestionem in tractatu de religiosis ex-professio examinabimus; hic adnotare sufficiat quod opinio auctoris [Bidagor] nobis videtur principiis generalibus can. 103, § 1, potius contraria"; Beste, *Introductio in Codicem,* p. 364: "Dolus hic intelligitur substantialis aut saltem accidentalis dans causam actui"; Fransen, *Le dol dans la conclusion des actes juridiques,* p. 397 (on canon 542, 1°) :

the text of canon 542, 1°, itself. For a candidate, in order to enter a novitiate invalidly, must be *induced* to do so through fraud. But such a manner of speaking is certainly, at the very least, applicable to fraud which constitutes the efficacious reason for which this act is placed, even though it does not pertain to the substance of the religious state itself. Furthermore, Bidagor understood *dolo inductus* as signifying antecedent fraud only when used with relation to the superior accepting the candidates. There seems no reason why it should not be understood in like manner with regard to fraud practiced on the candidate.[28] Hence, it seems logical to conclude that not only substantial fraud invalidates entrance into the novitiate, but accidental fraud as well, provided that it constitutes the impulsive cause for which a candidate consents to this act.

This doctrine, however, gives rise to not a little difficulty in practice. First, it must be borne in mind that a fraudulently induced accidental error may be said to be the cause of an act whenever the one placing it is in reality of that mind at the moment in which he acts that, were the error dispelled or the truth known, he would not act. Under such circumstances the error through which he acts is the immediate cause of his acting, and the act placed by him because of it may be described as totally or principally the product of a fraud.[29] Hence, fraudulent deception may be said

---

"Bien entendu, ce dol doit être principal"; Wernz-Vidal, *Ius Canonicum,* III, 199; Coronata, *Institutiones,* I, 710; Brys, *Juris Canonici Compendium,* I, 534; Oesterle, *Praelectiones Iuris Canonici,* I, 289; Cervia, *De Professione Religiosa,* p. 81; Mayer, *Benediktinisches Ordensrecht in der Beuroner Kongregation* (3 voll., Beuron: Kunstverlag Hohenzollern, 1929-1936), III, 38 (hereafter cited *Benediktinisches Ordensrecht*); Badii, *ibidem,* p. 313; Augustine, *A Commentary on the New Code of Canon Law,* III, 208; Bieter, "The Canon Law on Deceit," *ER,* XLVI (1922), 50; Larraona, "Commentarium Codicis," *CpRM,* XVII (1936), 17: "Quando sermo est de dolo et de ipsius effectibus propriis non tantum abstrahitur ab errore substantiali vel aequiparato, sed hi abesse supponuntur et tantum errorem accidentalem dolum producisse. Ex principio iuris generalis, dolus non invalidat actum sed rescindibilem tantum reddit (c. 103). Inter casus exceptos, in quibus dolus nullum actum reddit noster hic adest, *ingressus in religionem*"; Goyeneché, "Consultationes," *CpRM,* XVI (1935), 233.

[28] Cf. Bidagor, *ibidem,* pp. 70*, 72*.

[29] Michiels, *Principia Generalia,* p. 527.

to provide the reason for the act of entry into the canonical novitiate whenever the one affected by it can, when he knows the truth, sincerely say: "Had I known this, I would not have willed this act."[30] Before, therefore, an object could constitute the impulsive cause for an act of consent, a novice must at least have formulated an erroneous judgment concerning that object, even though indistinctly, and this judgment must be the sole or at least the principal or decisive cause for which he seeks admission into the canonical novitiate.[31]

Secondly, it is of importance to note that not every accidental error must be considered as sufficient objective grounds to establish fraud as the efficacious reason for which this act was placed. To the exclusion of an expressed condition *sine qua non,* the object or the truth about which the candidate is deceived, and regarding which he may claim that it exerted a determining influence upon his consent, must be of such a nature that, with all due consideration for his particular condition or temperament, one may prudently judge it as something which would so influence him when acting with the ordinary discretion befitting his state. For the law does not take into consideration things which are of no consequence either in themselves or, at least, when objectively considered, with regard to the individual concerned.[32] The reason for this observation is obvious, for unless the law demanded that the object obscured represents objectively reasonable grounds for the consent given by an aspirant, there would scarcely be any novitiate which could not be impugned on the grounds of fraudulent deception. At the same time, an individual may give indications of his disposition with regard to a particular factor in the religious life which of itself is not of grave moment, but which because of his temperament takes on added importance as a cause for his entry into a particular institute. Thus, for example, if a candidate had been deceived into believing that a particular institute had only one fast day a week, whereas they have six, the objective grounds to allege a fraud must

[30] Salsmans, "Circa vitia consensus," *Jus Pontificium,* X (1930), 108.

[31] Coronata, *Institutiones,* I, 710: ". . . et his rationibus unice vel principaliter ductus candidatus admittatur fraude deceptus."

[32] Beste, *Introductio in Codicem,* pp. 160-161: *"Minima non curat praetor."* Cf. Mayer, *Benediktinisches Ordensrecht,* III, 38.

be considered, it seems, as in themselves slight, but for a certain individual this fact may be regarded by him as a real hardship in view of his former way of life.[33]

Finally, it must be demonstrated in the external forum that the dispositions of a particular candidate were such that he would certainly not have entered the novitiate had the deception not been present. It may be observed here that a defective intention on the part of a candidate has very slight chance of being proved in the external forum as existing when he entered the novitiate, unless its external manifestation or expression is quite clear and obvious, either from his manner of acting, or from his oral testimony, or from written statements made by him or those near to him. Thus, if he showed absolute repugnance towards the religious state, or even only a negative interest in it; or if he frequently spoke to his friends or family, stating that he would not enter it if a certain fact about an institute was not truly represented; or if he wrote letters to this effect, and then, after he had been deceived concerning those factors which were known to be regarded by him as salient points upon which the determination of his consent hinged, he were to enter the novitiate gladly, the influence of the fraud upon his consent in doing so would be evidently present. In the absence of such external manifestations of his mental attitude it is extremely difficult, if not impossible, to demonstrate the manner which any given fact fraudulently concealed or misrepresented to him had in determining his consent.

Bidagor mentions one inconvenience in this legislation with regard to the novitiate: the outlawing of fraud *causa dans* at the time of entry into the novitiate seems to be disproportionate to the case, especially since the false motives or reasons which may have influenced entry or acceptance in the novitiate will normally be corrected in the course of the novitiate, once the aspirant is in contact with the religious life.[34] Hence he thought it superfluous to outlaw antecedent fraud in this act. But, as Fransen points out,[35] the present legislation is fully justified since the Church, in outlaw-

---

[33] Cf. Fransen, *op. cit.*, p. 398; Bidagor, *ibidem*, p. 67*.

[34] Bidagor, *ibidem*, p. 71*.

[35] Fransen, *Le dol dans la conclusion des actes juridiques*, p. 397.

ing determining fraud even in this act, is merely giving one more indication of its mind that entry into the religious state must be totally spontaneous.

The gamut of possible accidental errors which may suffice to qualify as determining a postulant to enter the novitiate, when fraudulently induced, covers too wide a range to permit an attempt at any specific enumeration. At the most, one can merely indicate various factors about the religious life, or circumstances surrounding a candidate's entry, concerning which any practiced deception may serve to restrict effectively his liberty in making a free and spontaneous choice of the religious state.

Thus the fraudulent accidental error may inspire the consent of a candidate when it involves his personal qualifications for this state, or the extrinsic impelling reason why he should enter. This would be the case, for example, if the parents made their child believe that they had promised to God that he would enter the religious state, when, as a matter of fact, they had not made any such promise,[36] and the postulant entered the novitiate because of this fact, though he certainly would not have done so, had he known that such a promise had not been made. Creusen observes that it would be a case of determining fraud if an individual had been falsely persuaded by another that he had the evident signs of a divine vocation.[37] It must be pointed out with regard to this observation, however, that a mere expression of one's opinion in this matter certainly does not of itself constitute a fraud. In rendering a moral judgment concerning a person's vocation one must not judge his aptitude for the religious state solely in the light of his past, but also with a view to the future training which he will receive and which will greatly enhance his qualifications for it. At the same time, if it is evident from the former life of an individual that he does not have the stability of character, the mental acumen, or the physical health to give a reasonable foundation for an assumption that he may have a vocation, then to persuade him that he has one would certainly constitute a fraud, which, if it is the sole or principal cause inspiring his entry, would certainly invalidate his novitiate. It is to be remembered likewise, however, that if a

[36] Creusen, *Religious Men and Women in the Code*, pp. 134-135.

[37] *Loc. cit.*

person who attempts to influence a candidate to enter the novitiate by telling him that he has a divine vocation is himself in error concerning the essential requisites which point to a vocation, then his deception of the candidate must be charged to ignorance rather than to malicious deceit, and the validity of the candidate's entry into the novitiate must be judged by the principles governing the effects of simple error, not by those covering the effects of fraud.

More often than not the fraudulent deception which induces a candidate to enter the novitiate concerns some factor of the religious life itself, either in general or as it is lived in the particular institute into which he seeks admission. Such would be the case, for example, if relatives were to trick a young man into embracing the religious state so as to obtain his share of an inheritance, by telling him that the vow of poverty practiced therein did not obligate the members to give up their property or its use, but merely required them to make use of it for an honest end and did not prevent them from disposing of it independently of the will of the superior, whereas it is well known to them that such is not the case.[38]

This may occur not only on the part of a third party who has some personal interest at stake in securing the entry of a certain candidate, but it may likewise occur on the part of the religious institute itself. This case is a likely one especially when a superior, in order to solicit the consent of an individual to enter the novitiate, promises to make certain concessions with regard to the rule, the constitutions, or the established policies of the institute, which are either impossible of fulfillment for the reason that they are contrary to the constitutions, or which at least, as can be prudently foreseen, will not be fulfilled.[39] This would be the case, for example, if

---

[38] Cf. Augustine, *A Commentary on the New Code of Canon Law,* III, 208.

[39] Fransen, *loc. cit.:* "En quoi peut-il [le dol] consister? . . . De la part du superiéur: promettre certains avantages factices pour décider un jeune homme, qui sinon s'en éloignerait, à embrasser l'état religieux." Lefebvre, "Dol en droit canonique actuel," *DDC,* IV, col. 1350: ". . . ou bien d'un supérieur (ou d'un tiers) promettant certains avantages factices." Beste, *Introductio in Codicem,* p. 364: "Idem dicendum, si superior usurparet fallaces et dolosas artes, pollicitationes, fraudationes quaslibet ad illaqueandum iuvenem renitentem, qui secus a statu religioso refugisset."

an aspirant stated that he would not enter the novitiate if its members could be sent to the foreign missions, and the superior or another responsible member of the institute were to promise him that he would never be sent out of his native country, whereas they knew full well that the vow of obedience of the Order obliged the religious to go wherever they are sent.[40] Such would be the case if a candidate signified that he would in no way be willing to enter a given institute unless he were to be stationed in a certain city, house, or college of the institute, or under a certain superior, or unless he were employed in a particular occupation such as teaching, parochial work, nursing, or the missionary endeavors of the institute, and the superior, in order to entice him into the novitiate, were to assure him that he most certainly would have his will fulfilled in these matters, though he knew that he could not vouch for such a promise in view of the constitutions or the policy of the institute in selecting the members who would carry on the various occupations in which it is engaged.[41]

The same would hold true if an individual were to manifest that he was so disposed that, if he were not permitted to continue his higher studies after entering an institute, he would not enter it, and if, in order to entice him to enter the congregation, the superior were to assure him falsely that he would be allowed to do so. Or if a candidate were leaving old and sickly parents in the world and emphasized the fact that he did not intend to enter any institute unless he would be allowed to visit them for two months each summer, and if, in order to solicit his consent to entry into his institute, a superior were to promise him with external sincerity that he most certainly would be allowed to do so, whereas the superior knew that according to the constitutions or established policy of the institute he would not be permitted to do so.[42]

Fraud may be considered as of a determining character in cer-

[40] Bieter, "The Canon Law on Deceit," *ER,* XLVI (1922), 50.

[41] Cf. Peinador, "De ingressu in statum religiosum, iure naturali invalido," *CpR,* XV (1934), 288.

[42] These examples, it seems, all fit within the conclusions drawn from the foregoing doctrine on the relevancy of antecedent fraud in invalidating this act. Cf., e.g., Coronata, *Institutiones,* I, 710: ". . . a parte religionis [casus doli] haberetur si ipsi religio describatur ut honores afferens, commoda, ad dignitates ducens etc., et his rationibus unice vel principaliter ductus candidatus admittatur fraude deceptus." Cf. also Augustine, *loc. cit.*

tain cases, even when the general character of the religious life as lived in a certain institute is grossly misrepresented by a member of the institute so as to solicit the consent of an aspirant to enter it. This could be the case, for example, if the candidate were told that the institute does not practice perfect abstinence, whereas the constitutions allow meat to be served to its members but once or twice a year, or if he were induced into believing that the discipline is so relaxed that the superiors would never command him to do anything unless he first gave his consent, or that, although certain austere practices are mentioned in the constitutions, they could never be put in effect because they had remained a dead letter for so long a time. In each of these cases, of course, it is presupposed that the candidate's consent to enter the novitiate is founded upon these factors.

In fine, this discussion may be summed up with a restatement of the principle: if a novice is enticed into the novitiate of a religious institute through a deliberate and gross misrepresentation of the nature of the religious life, or concerning some factor of the religious life as it is lived in the particular institute, even though not substantial, and this factor plays a determining influence upon his will in choosing to enter the novitiate, his novitiate is thereby rendered automatically invalid. It must be borne in mind at the same time, however, that not only must the deception itself continue up to and including the moment in which he is received into the novitiate, but it must continue to be the inspiring cause for which he acts.[48] For it may happen that, although an individual is prompted to seek entry into a certain institute in consequence of fraudulent maneuvers, nevertheless, at the time of the actual entry, he gives his consent absolutely and independently of the deception which originally led him to choose to place this act. However, once it is established that the perpetration of a fraud has exercised a determining influence upon his consent to enter, then in the absence of evidence to the contrary it seems that one must presume that the original deception continues to exert at least a virtual influence upon his actual entry.

[48] Badii, "Il dolo nel Codice di Diritto Canonico," *Il Diritto Ecclesiastico,* XL (1929), 313: "Qui basta avvertire che la perpetrazione del dolo deve essersi verificata al momento dell'ingresso e della recezione nella religione, . . ."

CHAPTER X

The Effect of Fraudulent Error Upon the Consent of a Superior

Canon 542, 1°, not only decrees the novitiate to be automatically without juridical substance from the very beginning when a novice is induced to enter upon it through the agency of fraud, but it likewise affirms its invalidity whenever the superior, because of fraudulent deception, is efficaciously moved to receive an individual into the novitiate whom he would have rejected had the truth obscured from him been known. The same fundamental principles which regulate the juridic effects of fraud upon the consent of a candidate in seeking entry into the novitiate are operative with equal effect and scope with regard to the consent of the superior who receives him.

Hence, as may be gleaned from the above stated principles, whenever a superior is induced to receive a candidate while acting under a substantial deception concerning him, the novitiate of such an individual is rendered null and void not only by reason of the positive law but by reason of the natural law as well. For, under such circumstances, the superior's consent lacks the causative or creative power of effectuating a novitiate not only because the law declares it to be without effect, but primarily because one acting through substantial deception concerning the object to be willed is rendered incapable of placing a true act of consent in relation to it. The deliberate human act, upon which alone the juridic act and effect can be founded, is wanting.

The cases in which a superior may be considered as acting under deception which is objectively substantial in the reception of candidates are reducible, it seems, to the following. First, deception would be substantial if it resulted in an error concerning the person, e.g., if a superior intended to accept a certain individual whose qualities are known to him and approved, while in reality another was substituted in the actual admission. Thus, it would be a case of substantial fraud if Paul were to apply for admission and be accepted, and Peter his twin brother were actually to take the habit.[1]

Secondly, a superior would be acting through substantial deception if he were led into error concerning the substantial qualities of the candidate which redound to an error in the person. The qualities which may be termed as substantial in this connection are those which are demanded either by the natural law or by the positive law, whether general or particular, for the valid reception into a canonical novitiate.[2] This deduction is obvious with regard to those qualities which are demanded by the natural law. Those lacking the use of reason, or who are out of their mind, temporarily or over a protracted period, are evidently excluded from the religious state, since they lack the natural capacity to assume its obligations.[3] Those qualities which are demanded by the positive law, whether general or particular, for the valid admission of candidates relate to the substance of this act because the legislator, by establishing them as legal obstacles to its valid performance, has in effect made them qualities which redound to the substantial worthiness of candidates for the religious state. And, since the object of the superior's consent when admitting candidates into the novitiate is precisely the worthiness of the candidate, any deception concerning the invalidating impediments arising from the positive law renders his consent without substance, since it is outwardly directed to something other than that to which it is internally given. Hence, in the given circumstances, it would be rendered void, not only by reason of the positive law, but by reason of the natural law as well.[4]

---

[1] An error of person does not necessarily invalidate other juridic acts, or even the reception of the sacraments, with the exception of matrimony (canon 1083). But since the object of the superior's consent in receiving candidates is the very person himself, as in the case of the contracting parties in matrimony, an error of person is an error about the essential object of the consent, and as such substantially vitiates it. Cf. Peinador, "De ingressu in statum religiosum, iure naturali invalido," *CpR,* XV (1934), 284.

[2] Peinador, *loc. cit.*

[3] Cf. Wernz-Vidal, *Ius Canonicum,* III, 187.

[4] Peinador, *loc. cit.* This discussion is, in reality, purely academic, since it is wholly irrelevant whether the invalidity of the novitiate under such circumstances derives from the natural or the positive law. The novitiate would be automatically invalid regardless of whether a superior acted through

The same observations are of equal force with regard to those invalidating impediments which appear in the particular constitutions, since each of these amounts to a condition *sine qua non* through which the consent of the admitting superior is legally restricted by the institute which he represents.[5] In the rare case in which a superior might intend to receive a candidate in spite of the presence of one of these invalidating impediments, the invalidity of his action would stem only from the positive law itself, since the essential qualities of a naturally sufficient act of consent would not be wanting.[6]

Finally, it would be a case of substantial fraud if the superior were led into error concerning the class of religious into which a particular individual was being received, e.g., if he was led to think that he was approving the candidate for the lay brotherhood, whereas the documents drawn up for his admission showed him to have been received for the clerical state. In such a case, his consent is directed to a substantially different act than that for which it is externally manifested, since the novitiate made for one class of religious is not valid with relation to another class.[7]

Over and above the case in which the superior's consent is vitiated by reason of an objectively substantial error, it may likewise be rendered without effect by reason of the natural law whenever he has, through a positive declaration, made a certain quality the basis upon which his consent subsists, i.e., he has declared that he is absolutely disinclined to give consent to the admission of any candidate who does not possess a certain quality. Thus, for example, if he were to say, "Although the constitutions of our institute are silent concerning legitimacy, unless a candidate is of legitimate birth, I shall under no condition receive him," such a manner of speaking is tantamount to making this quality a *conditio sine qua non,* which if not verified destroys his consent. The su-

---

ignorance, error, or fraudulent deception in receiving a candidate with one of these invalidating impediments of the common or the particular law. Cf.. canon 16.

[5] Larraona, "Commentarium Codicis," *CpRM,* XVIII (1937), 232.

[6] Peinador, *loc. cit.*

[7] Canon 558.

perior, it seems, may place such a condition not only with regard to the impedient impediments, but likewise with regard to other qualities which would notably affect the candidate's acceptability in the community, depending upon its character and the nature of its work.[8] Thus the superior of a community which is engaged solely in conducting institutions of higher learning may legitimately place such a condition in establishing the scholastic standards with which candidates must have complied before they are admitted.

In addition to these cases of substantial deception, the novitiate is likewise invalid by reason of canon 542, 1°, whenever fraudulent deception is the antecedent cause through which a superior is induced to receive a candidate whom he otherwise would certainly have rejected. For, as was pointed out above, whenever the law proscribes fraud as such, though it does not exclude the possibility of substantial deception, it in reality supposes that such fraud does not occur, since adequate provisions have already been made for such an eventuality through the general norm of canon 104. Rather, it is primarily concerned with those cases in which fraud does not substantially vitiate an act, but rather causes it to be juridically defective through the undue influence which it exerts upon the eventuation of the act. Fraud is proscribed not so much as an agency which precludes consent, but rather as an agency which effectively interferes with the juridic liberty of an individual in placing an act. Hence, in keeping with the general principles governing the effects of fraud upon juridical acts, the novitiate is rendered void of all juridical effect not only when a superior is led to receive a candidate through substantial deception, but also whenever he is duped into receiving him through a fraudulently induced error concerning some quality or truth connected with him which, had it been known, would certainly have served to exclude him. In other words, not only *dolus substantialis* but also *dolus accidentalis causa dans* suffices to bring down the sanction of invalidity upon a canonical novitiate whenever this agency is employed against

---

[8] Cf. Larraona, "Commentarium Codicis, *CpR,* XV (1934), 367, note 27: "Pro diverso Religionem fine speciali ac etiam modis, satis inter se distantibus, quibus eadem denique religiosa perfectio exercetur, dotes ac requisita quae exiguntur in variis Religionibus merito diversa sunt."

the admitting superior, as all authors, including Bidagor, universally admit.[9]

Two essential factors must be proved with at least moral certainty before a novitiate may be declared invalid on the grounds of antecedent fraud. First, it must be demonstrated that the deception under which the superior acted in receiving a candidate was in fact the product of a formal fraud, i.e., the individual who created it in the superior's mind must have done so because he had either certain knowledge or at least a reasonable suspicion that the fact concealed or misrepresented was of grave importance to the superior or the institute in formulating its judgment concerning the qualities of a candidate. For, unless the deception under which the superior acts can be considered as a grave violation of good faith, the principles which govern the effects of fraud do not become operative,[10] but rather the effects of such deception upon his consent must be judged solely by the principles governing the effects of simple error.

Certain facts are by their very nature of such obvious importance with relation to entry into the novitiate of any religious institute that any failure to disclose them or any deliberate misrepresentation with regard to them must be judged as a formal fraud, even though the candidate or interested third party was not charged to reveal them at the time of his or her reception. Among these must be enumerated any grave and protracted illnesses, moral defects of a public nature, or intellectual deficiencies which would certainly render an individual either unworthy or disqualified for the religious state or for admission into the particular institute even by the common estimation of the faithful. But whenever the importance of the condition or quality obscured is not immediately apparent to the one concealing it, his action in doing so must, it seems, be laid to ignorance or error on his part rather than to a formal will to deceive, unless the circumstances indicate the contrary.

---

[9] Cf. all authors cited above, pp. 149-150, in the passages there indicated. Also see Vermeersch-Creusen, *Epitome Iuris Canonici*, I, 500; Bouscaren-Ellis, *Canon Law, a Text and Commentary*, p. 260; Bidagor, *ibidem*, pp. 70*, 72*.

[10] Toso, *Commentaria*, II, 93; cf. Beste, *Introductio in Codicem*, p. 364.

Hence, not every mendacious reply given by a candidate, either in filling out the documents required by the community before his reception, or in replying to the formal oral inquiries put to him before his admission, can be judged as sufficient grounds in themselves to justify a declaration that his novitiate is invalid on the count of fraud. For a lie, in these matters, does not assume the character of juridical fraud unless the importance of the question put to him is clearly evident, or unless he has been previously warned concerning its importance with relation to his acceptance. In other words, an individual cannot be said to circumvent deliberately the will of the superior unless he knows, or at least reasonably suspects, which facts will have an important influence upon the latter's decision to receive or to reject him.[11] When the question put to him seems to be of so trifling a matter that his response to it seems to be of little or no relevance in regard to his reception, one can scarcely charge him with a formal act of fraud when he answers it with a falsehood.[12] Hence, there emerges the grave importance of advising candidates of the precise nature of the point about which they are being questioned, and the influence which it will have upon their acceptance into the community, as well as of the sanction of invalidity which will fall upon their novitiate if they answer it with a falsehood or create a deception concerning it.[13]

On the other hand, however, whenever it can be demonstrated that the candidate knew or at least had reasonable grounds to suspect that a particular fact would have a telling effect upon the decision of the institute to receive him, and nevertheless attempted to create a false impression concerning it, he is to be regarded as guilty of a formal act of juridical fraud, and his acceptance in the novitiate is therefore rendered liable to invalidity if his fraudulent maneuver does in fact take effect.[14] One who is guilty of deliberately employing illicit trickery in a matter which is known to be of some import is responsible for the effects which may flow from its use,

---

[11] Vermeersch-Creusen, *Epitome Iuris Canonici,* I, 500.

[12] Cf. Toso, *loc. cit.*

[13] Vermeersch-Creusen, *loc. cit.;* Schaefer, *De Religiosis,* p. 429; Larraona, "Commentarium Codicis," *CpRM,* XVII (1936), 17.

[14] Larraona, *ibidem,* p. 17, note 182.

whether or not he knew of the invalidating effects attached to such a violation of good faith.[15]

Over and above the verification of the fact that the deception under which a superior labored when receiving a candidate is in reality the product of a formal act of fraud, to hold the novitiate invalid one must demonstrate with moral certainty that this deception exercised a determining influence upon the superior's consent in permitting a novice to enter his institute. For accidental errors concerning the condition or the qualities of a candidate, even though fraudulently induced, do not suffice of themselves to invalidate a novitiate. Unless it can be conclusively demonstrated, or at least reasonably presumed, that the superior who admitted a candidate under its influence would have debarred him from entering had the deception been dispelled before he gave his consent, the validity of the novitiate would remain intact.[16] Once, however, it is clear that the deception was in fact the efficacious reason for the admission of a candidate, nothing more need be proved for justifying the declaration that the novitiate is without juridical substance.

The practical problem presented by this doctrine, however, lies in the precise determination of the circumstances in which a deception concerning some accidental quality in a candidate may or must be considered as having exerted a decisive influence upon a superior's consent in receiving him into the novitiate. The solution to this problem is to be found in a clear delineation of the exact nature and scope of the superior's intent when he consents to the admission of a candidate into his institute. In reality, when a superior gives his consent to the admission of a candidate, that consent presupposes that he has made a practical moral judgment that the individual concerned is a worthy candidate, i.e., that he not only possesses those qualities which are demanded by the divine law, whether natural or positive, and by the ecclesiastical law, whether universal or particular, for a valid and licit entry into religion, but that he

---

[15] Canon 16, § 1.

[16] Bidagor, "De dolo et eius effectibus in admissione ad novitiatum et professione religiosa," *Periodica*, XX (1931), 72*: "Error accidentalis de conditione vel qualitatibus candidati, in Superiore recipiente dolo incussus, dummodo constat vel praesumatur eum non velle recipere in novitiatum nisi immunem a quibuscumque impedimentis, admissionem facit invalidam."

also is endowed with such qualities of character, intellect, and health as will give reasonable assurance that he will be able to carry out his religious duties in the institute with alacrity and with honor, and thus be rendered useful to it in carrying on the particular mission to which it is dedicated. Hence, any quality or lack of quality which would have a notable effect upon his worthiness on any one of these scores must be judged as likewise having a notable effect upon the superior's consent to his admission. Whether or not, however, this effect must be judged as being decisive or determining must be gathered from the gravity of its objective nature or the implications flowing from it, the provisions of the particular constitutions, the recognized policy of the community, and the manifest intention of the acting superior with regard to it.

Generally, as was observed above,[17] the gravity of the truth or quality concealed must be objectively demonstrable. For here as in other acts the law does not take into account things which are of little import, *"nam de minimis non curat praetor."*[18] But at the same time, as Fransen points out,[19] one must not overemphasize the gravity of the objective grounds, so long as the truth obscured through fraud represents something prejudicial to the superior or the institute receiving the candidate. If the quality or the condition which was kept hidden presents reasonable grounds for a presumption that the superior or the institute would have been disinclined to receive him at the time of his reception had the truth not been withheld, then it seems that, unless the circumstances prove the contrary, one must presume that the superior who performed the function of admitting him was of the mentality to exclude him if this condition or quality was not in reality verified.

Although in performing his function of admitting candidates a superior enjoys certain discretionary power in the sense that the ultimate judgment concerning the worthiness of individuals seeking entry into the institute depends upon his opinion whenever the positive law, universal or particular, does not restrict his selection of candidates to those who possess certain particular qualities, one must not consider him as restricting his intention to

[17] Cf. *supra*, p. 151.

[18] Cappello, *Summa Iuris Canonici*, III, 158.

[19] Fransen, *Le dol dans la conclusion des actes juridiques*, p. 387.

a particular quality unless its gravity is clearly evident, or when he has clearly declared his intention with regard to it.

Even in the absence of such a positive declaration, however, as Bidagor rightly observes,[20] one must generally presume that in receiving candidates into the novitiate a superior is of the mind and the will not to receive them if they are impeded from entering by reason either of the universal law or of the provisions of the particular constitutions, unless a dispensation has been obtained from these impedient obstacles. This observation seems fully warranted, especially with regard to the impedient impediments of canon 542, 2°. For, unless there are positive indications to the contrary, one must regard the superior as unwilling to receive any candidate who is impeded by one of these impediments not only because one must suppose that he does not wish to act illicitly,[21] but also because if he deliberately received a candidate contrary to the provisions of this canon he would be rendered liable to the penal sanction of canon 2411,[22] which, though undetermined in its character, is of a preceptive nature in the matter of its application.[23] Furthermore, the constitutions of the various institutes usually contain prohibitions against receiving candidates who are so impeded, and even prescribe determined punishments for superiors who deliberately act contrary to the common law in this matter.[24]

Authors generally make a distinction between the fraudulent withholding of information concerning the existence of any one of the impedient impediments enacted in the universal law, and

---

[20] Bidagor, *ibidem,* pp. 70*, 72*.

[21] Bidagor, *loc. cit.;* Toso (*Commentaria,* II, 96) declared that superiors are bound under grave sin to reject those who are impeded by reason of canon 542, 2°, since this is a grave matter.

[22] Canon 2411. Superiores religiosi qui candidatum non idoneum contra praescriptum can. 542, . . . ad novitiatum receperint, . . . pro gravitate cuplae puniantur, non exclusa officii privatione.

[23] Blat, *Commentarium,* lib. V, 320.

[24] Cf., e.g., *Constitutiones Ordinis Eremitarum S. Augustini* (Romae: Typis Polyglottis Vaticanis, 1926), n. 189: "Superiores qui aliquem destitutum requisitis ad validitatem vel liceitatem admissionis in novitiatum . . . scienter receperint, officio priventur . . . et per triennium maneant inhabiles ad omnia officia cum cura animarum."

inculpable reticence concerning them, stating that if these have been maliciously concealed by a candidate, or through the intervention of a third party, the novitiate would be rendered invalid *provided that such concealment constituted the cause for his reception.* If, however, it did not constitute the cause for his reception, then, although the novitiate would not be rendered automatically invalid through its concealment, nevertheless, if the novice is the guilty party in the deception, the superiors would certainly have reason enough to dismiss him from the novitiate once his fraudulent action is discovered.[25] But whenever it is discovered after the novice has been admitted to his profession that he has deliberately concealed one of these impediments, and it also is established that his deception concerning it was not the cause for his admission, that is to say, he would have been admitted to the novitiate even though the presence of the impediment would have been known, then his profession is not thereby affected, and it seems also that on this ground alone he may be dismissed if he has become simply professed. The presence of one of these impediments, according to Fanfani,[26] would furnish a sufficient reason for petitioning the Holy See for a dispensation from the vows, if the professed himself is willing, or for preventing him from renewing his profession. Some constitutions even make it mandatory for the superiors to dismiss a religious concerning whom there has been deception with regard to one of these impedient impediments, even though he may be bound by simple profession.[27]

It is to be noted that these authors, in stating that deliberate deception concerning one of the impedient impediments renders the novitiate invalid only when it is the cause for the superior's con-

[25] Vermeersch-Creusen, *Epitome Iuris Canonici,* I, 508: "Voluntaria impedimenti dissimulatio graviter quidem culpanda est; et, si dolus causa fuerit receptionis, haec iure positivo, ut supra vidimus, nulla est. Si causam non dederit receptioni, haec quidem valida est, sed culpa, pro gravitate sua, legitimae dimissioni locum dare poterit." Cf. also Beste, *Introductio in Codicem,* p. 368; Fanfani, *De Iure Religiosorum,* n. 180, p. 204; Wernz-Vidal, *Ius Canonicum,* II, 214-215; Larraona, "Commentarium Codicis," *CpRM,* XVIII (1937), 232.

[26] *Loc. cit.*

[27] Cf., e.g., *Constitutiones Ordinis Recollectorum Sancti Augustini* (Romae: Typographia Augustiniana, 1937), n. 224.

sent, make this observation on the supposition that the superior or an institute in a certain case was disposed to receive the particular candidate in spite of the presence of one of these impedient impediments. But, as the same time, it must be remembered, as it was pointed out above, that unless there are positive indications to the contrary one must consider the superior as not disposed to receive candidates so impeded until either the impediment itself has ceased or an indult has been received from the Holy See dispensing from it. Hence, ordinarily whenever one of the impedient impediments is deliberately obscured or misrepresented to a superior, the novitiate is rendered not only illicitly entered upon but also null and void. In ultimate analysis, however, it will depend upon the actual dispositions of the superior or the institute with regard to these impediments, and in practice one would need to sound out these dispositions as they existed when the candidate in question was received if one was called on to determine whether in spite of the prohibition of the law the superior or the institute was prepared to receive him. In such a case a positive avowal of willingness or some equivalent manner of acting on the part of the superior or the institute would disestablish the presumption to the contrary.

If one examines the individual impedient impediments to entry into religion as they are enacted in the universal law, one can readily see that ordinarily no superior would be willing to receive a candidate bound by one of them, even though he may not be conscious of their grave import in the law. For, in detail, no superior must be considered as willing under ordinary circumstances to receive a cleric who is in major orders if he has falsely convinced the superior of having notified his bishop of his intention to enter religion and was doing so with his blessing, when the cleric's ordinary was, as a matter of fact, most opposed to his departure from the diocese since through his departure a large portion of the faithful would be left without care, a care which could be provided for in no other way than by the cleric's return. Likewise it seems indefensible to consider a superior as willing to receive an individual who is bound by grave debts which he is unable to pay and concerning which he remains silent when he is received, unless the institute is disposed to assume any debts to which the candidate in question may have been obligated. One should also not suppose that any institute is willing to receive a candidate who is implicated in public affairs or who holds a position through which the institute may have reason to fear law suits and other annoyances. Similarly one must presume that the superior is opposed to the reception of anyone whose parents or grandparents would be thrown into grave want through a lack of support brought about by the entry of the candidate into religion. The same holds true with regard to parents whose children have need of their care. And in view of the traditional opposition of the Church to a change of rite, one must also regard a superior as unwilling to receive any candidate who is not of the Latin rite. From these observations it becomes apparent that the presumption that the novitiate is generally rendered invalid through the deliberate concealment of any of the impedient impediments as enacted in the universal law has a solid foundation in fact as well as in law.[28]

In virtue of canon 542, 2°, candidates are impeded from entry into the novitiate of a clerical religion in preparation for the reception of orders if they are under any irregularity or simple impediment which would hinder the reception of orders. The question arises as to whether the invalidating effects of fraud would likewise extend to the case in which a candidate voluntarily withheld knowledge of the presence of one of these obstacles. It must first be noted that the prohibition to receive a candidate affected by one of these impediments does not extend to those cases in which they will cease through entry into religion, through profession, through privilege, or through some other operation of the universal law. Thus, for example, since according to canon 984 solemn profession removes the irregularity of illegitimacy, this irregularity would not constitute an impedient impediment to entry into a religious Order, provided that the candidate will have made his solemn profession before the reception of tonsure.[29] The prohibition likewise does not

---

[28] Larraona, "Commentarium Codicis," *CpRM,* XVIII (1937), 232, note 413: "Nullitas potest provenire sive ex impedimento in se quod occultatur, sive *ex dolo* quo admittens circumvenitur. Hic talis esse potest, etsi impedimentum tantum illicitam reddat admissionem, quod haec ex dolo, ad normam Codicis, sit nulla." Cf. Coronata, *Institutiones,* I, 713.

[29] Vermeersch-Creusen, *Epitome Iuris Canonici,* I, 506; Schaefer, *De Religiosis,* p. 445.

extend to those impediments which will certainly cease before the reception of orders, as, for example, the conducting of a business which is forbidden to clerics but which will cease before the reception of orders, provided, of course, that there is no danger of law suits.[30] Outside of these cases the law makes it illicit to receive candidates for the priesthood into the novitiate unless a dispensation has previously been obtained from the irregularity or the simple impediment to orders which gives rise to the impediment to entry into the novitiate.

Coronata,[31] Fanfani,[32] and Goyeneché[33] wish to make a distinction between those irregularities from which the Holy See is generally wont to give a dispensation and those which are not easily dispensed, saying that if one has the intention of petitioning a dispensation from those which are easily dispensed before the reception of orders, the candidate need not be excluded from entering the novitiate in spite of their presence. This opinion does not enjoy the favor of the majority of the canonists. By far the majority of the authors understands canon 542, 2°, as meaning that no one may be admitted into the novitiate if he is bound by an irregularity or an impediment until such time that it has ceased or a dispensation has been obtained from the Holy See, unless it can be foreseen that it will certainly cease before the reception of orders.

It matters not whether the impediment is one easily removed by means of a dispensation or only with difficulty. It is for the Holy See, not for private individuals, to decide if such is the case, and its decision is not to be anticipated or presumed.[34] Vermeersch pointed out the distinction which must be made between these obstacles as hindrances to entry into the novitiate and as hindrances

---

[30] Schaefer, *loc. cit.*

[31] *Institutiones,* I, 715. He cites Fanfani to substantiate his view.

[32] *De Iure Religiosorum,* p. 203.

[33] *De Religiosis,* p. 86. Although this author gives Vermeersch as a reference for this opinion, the 1949 edition (seventh) of the *Epitome Iuris Canonici* (I, 506-507) does not favor this view.

[34] Beste, *Introductio in Codicem,* p. 363; Cappello, *Summa Iuris Canonici,* II, 49; Berutti, *Institutiones,* III, 147-148; Schaefer, *De Religiosis,* p. 445; Cocchi, *Commentarium,* IV, 113; Wernz-Vidal, *Ius Canonicum,* III, 213; Toso, *Commentaria,* V, 99-100; Vermeersch-Creusen, *loc. cit.;* Larraona, "Commentarium Codicis," *CpRM,* XVIII (1937), 150.

to the reception of orders. He interpreted the mind of the legislator here by saying that the law intends first that a dispensation be obtained to permit an aspirant to begin his training, and then, once he has completed it, to permit him to receive orders.[35]

In the light of these observations it seems certain that the invalidating effects of fraud could likewise extend to the case in which one of these impediments or irregularities is deliberately concealed so as to obtain admission into the novitiate, regardless of whether they are easily removed by means of a dispensation or only with difficulty. The presumption is justified, it seems, that the superior is disinclined to receive a candidate who deliberately deceives him concerning the presence of any one of them.

Over and above the impedient impediments arising from the universal law, the constitutions of each particular institute usually contain a number of others which likewise render illicit the entry of a candidate contrary to their provisions. It is to be noted that these impediments bind the superiors of these institutes with force equal to that of those arising from the universal law. The only distinction between them and the ones enacted in the universal law lies in the fact that usually one of the major superiors in the institute is competent to dispense from the former. In some institutes this power is reserved to the supreme moderator alone;[36] in others, the provincial superior is competent.[37]

Since the reception of candidates is a function which has been reserved by the universal law to a major superior,[38] who may be either the provincial or the supreme moderator and who may or may not have the power to dispense from the impediments in the constitutions, one must make a corresponding distinction, it seems, with regard to the effects of fraud practiced on superiors of various

---

[35] "Canon 542, 2°, et dispensatio ab irregularitate," *Periodica,* XX (1931), 136*-137*.

[36] Cf., e.g., *The Rule and General Constitutions of the Friars Minor* (Paterson, New Jersey: St. Anthony Guild Press, 1936), n. 16; Hess, *Manuale de Regula et Constitutionibus Ordinis Fratrum Minorum Conventualium* (Romae: Typis Polyglottis Vaticanis, 1943), n. 256.

[37] *Constitutiones Fratrum S. Ordinis Praedicatorum* (Romae: apud Domum Generalitiam, 1932), n. 75, 2°.

[38] Canon 543.

kinds when these impedient impediments are deliberately concealed by a candidate on being received into one of these institutes. If the superior who admits the candidate is the one who is also designated by the constitutions as competent to dispense from the impedient impediments of the constitutions, and he is generally disposed to do so, one may, it seems, legitimately presume that he is not entirely averse to the reception of the particular candidate concerned, even though the latter has deliberately withheld information concerning this impediment in order to facilitate his entry. If, on the contrary, he is generally not wont to dispense, one must presume that he is not willing to receive the candidate in question. On the other hand, if the admitting superior is not competent to dispense from the impediment, he must generally be considered as not disposed to receive any candidates contrary to its prohibition, since he must not be presumed to will to act illicitly.

Over and above those impediments which are formally established as impedient or invalidating obstacles to entry into the various institutes, the constitutions of each community usually allude to a number of other qualities or conditions, which, although they are not impediments in the strict sense, nevertheless render an aspirant more or less worthy or acceptable to the institute in question. Generally these will treat of the moral qualities or conditions which are to be verified in those who are admitted, in so far as they may furnish more or less reasonable grounds for the assumption that the individual will bear the burdens of the religious life with facility and honor; the intellectual ability of the candidate, in so far as it affects his capability for the religious life in general or his usefulness for the particular end of the institute; and the physical and mental health of the aspirant. As a general rule, the constitutions either direct an admonition or a prohibition against the admission of any candidates who may not measure up to the standards of the particular institute with regard to these various qualities, or else strongly charge the superior who is competent to admit candidates to weigh carefully in the light of these various required qualities the worthiness of those seeking entry. The question presents itself, therefore, as to whether the invalidating sanction of canon 542, 1°, not only extends to the deliberate perpetration of a fraud with regard to the formal impediments of the universal or particular law, but also to the case in which the admitting superior has been deliberately deceived concerning a notable deficiency in anyone of the qualities which are of importance to him in his judgment of the worthiness of candidates who apply for admission.

It seems that there is little room for doubt that the invalidating effects allotted to the perpetration of a fraud on entry into the novitiate likewise extend to the case in which one of these qualities is notably misrepresented or obscured so as to influence the superior's consent in the reception of a candidate.[39] First, it must be remembered that any notable error injected into the mind of an admitting superior through craft, cunning, or deceit is a fraudulent error, and as such its effects upon the consent of the institute or the acting superior must be judged according to the general principles governing the effects of fraud. Secondly, the impediment of fraud is not restricted only to the deliberate misrepresentation of the formal impediments found in the positive law, but it extends to any and all illicit representation through intrigue which may exercise a determining influence upon the consent of a superior in the reception of a candidate. Hence, the novitiate may be rendered invalid not only through the malicious concealment of a formal impediment enacted in the universal or particular law, but also through any grave and culpable deception concerning the physical, intellectual or moral qualities of a candidate so as to obtain his admission, which otherwise would have been denied.[40]

---

[39] Bidagor, "De dolo et eius effectibus in admissione ad novitiatum et professione religiosa," *Periodica,* XX (1931), 70*-71*. Although this author affirms this doctrine in the place cited, he seems to deny or qualify his view when stating his final conclusions. Cf. *ibidem,* p. 72*: "De ceteris [qualitatibus], vero, quamvis logice idem foret affirmandum, forsitan consequentia non congruerit cum mente legislatoris." This latter statement, however, could be understood as referring to the legitimacy of presuming that a superior is unwilling to receive a candidate who does not possess the qualities established by the constitutions. In either sense, however, it does not seem well sustained by the doctrine on fraud and the importance usually given to these qualities.

[40] Berutti, *Institutiones,* III, 139: "Dolo inductus, si illum recipiat quia circa ipsius qualitates physicas vel intellectuales aut morales de industria deceptus est, vel ab ipso candidato, vel a quopiam alio, etsi forte ab aliquo sodali eiusdem Religionis . . ."; Blat, *Commentarium,* lib. II, 594; Coronata

This gives rise to the practical problem of discerning under what circumstances fraud must generally be considered as determining when these qualities are the object of deception. As it was pointed out above, although the general doctrine on fraud postulated that the one affected by it suffer some grave injury to his rights before the nullifying saction of the law falls upon an act performed through its influence, there is involved here an act of consent the proper object of which is the worthiness of an individual for the religious life as it is lived in a particular institute. Hence, any grave defect of character, mind, or health which would notably prejudice an institute relative to the reception of a certain candidate must be judged, so it seems, in the absence of any clear indications to the contrary, as sufficient to qualify any deception concerning it as a determining fraud. At the same time it must be remembered that the importance given to these various qualities and the degree to which they must be realized will differ from community to community, depending upon its specific character and the nature of its mission. This is especially true with regard to the physical and intellectual qualities, since not all will demand the same robustness of health or the same degree of mental ability. Hence, it is not possible to establish an absolute norm that would cover every hypothetical case which might arise. One can, however, intimate certain general principles which one may use in judging the effects which fraudulent deception concerning these various qualities may have upon the consent of the institute in accepting candidates into its novitiate.

Although it is true that in the ultimate analysis, here as in the case of the formal impediments to licit entry, the validity of the novitiate of a candidate who has deliberately withheld or misrepresented information concerning his moral, intellectual, or physical qualities will repose in the mind of the superior who admits him, i.e., whether he considers a certain quality or lack of

---

Institutiones, I, 710; Mayer, *Benediktinisches Ordensrecht,* III, 38; Wernz-Vidal, *Ius Canonicum,* III, 200; Creusen, *Religious Men and Women in the Code,* p. 135; Cappello, *Summa Iuris Canonici,* II, 45-46; Brys, *Juris Canonici Compendium,* I, 534; Fransen, *Le dol dans la conclusion des actes juridiques,* p. 397; Oesterle, *Praelectiones Iuris Canonici,* I, 289; Larraona, "Commentarium Codicis," *CpRM,* XVII (1936), 17.

it as decisive in the formulation of his judgment,[41] this does not mean however that its invalidity is founded solely on this internal intellectual basis. For one must first know what the superior's will is before one can deliberately circumvent it. If the quality hidden or misrepresented is by its very nature commonly considered as grave matter, there would be a strong presumption that any deliberate withholding of information concerning it has been prompted through a fraudulent intent. But if its gravity is not immediately apparent, then, unless the superior has declared his mind on it or unless the community has a well known policy concerning it, one cannot immediately accuse the individual who is guilty of the material act of fraud as likewise guilty of a formal fraud. No one is to be judged guilty of fraud unless he is legitimately proved so. And under such circumstances, when the matter obscured cannot be considered grave in itself, at least according to the common estimation of men, one must not judge the individual as deliberately wishing to extort consent through its concealment. Hence, it is readily apparent that superiors must especially take care to see that candidates who seek entry into their various institutes are advised of the gravity of the various elements about which they are questioned orally or in writing.

Foremost among the various points which the constitutions usually charge the superiors to investigate diligently when admitting candidates are the moral character, the former life history, and the family background of the aspirant.[42] It is apparent that grave deception concerning any one of these three factors must be considered as having a determining influence upon the superior's judgment concerning the worthiness of the candidate. Hence, a candidate, or a third party who is questioned,[43] would be obliged, it seems, to reveal any notable externally manifest blemish on the candidate's moral character when it can prudently be suspected that such a blemish may lead to the candidate's exclusion. Among

[41] Bidagor, *ibidem*, p. 71*.

[42] *Constitutiones Ordinis Eremitarum S. Augustini*, n. 190; *Constitutiones Fratrum S. Ordinis Praedicatorum*, n. 84; *The Rule and General Constitutions of the Friars Minor*, n. 13; *Constitutiones Ordinis Recollectorum Sancti Augustini*, n. 215.

[43] Canon 544.

such facts one could list: protracted periods of excessive drinking, deliberate violation of the marriage laws of the Church through civil marriage or divorce, conviction for perjury before a civil court or an ecclesiastical tribunal, and any and all similar facts which may, in the superior's judgment, render a candidate notably less capable or less worthy of assuming the grave obligations of the religious state. It is to be noted that these examples are extreme cases, since they have been chosen as illustrative of those factors which will generally play an important rôle in determining the superior's consent in this act. Indeed, external vices of a much less grave nature may, and generally would, constitute a sufficient reason for the exclusion of a candidate. This obligation of revealing any grave moral blemishes, however, does not extend to the revelation of anything which, though sinful, does not pertain to the external forum.[44]

Besides personal defects of character, circumstances connected with the candidate may constitute sufficient grounds, under ordinary conditions, to exclude him. Among such circumstances one may list, it seems, facts about his former life, as, for example, the fact that he has served a prison sentence, that he has labored under *infamia facti* over a long period in the past or still labors under it in the present,[45] that he has led a dissolute life for many years in the past, that the Order will suffer hatred, infamy, or persecution through his reception. These facts must be generally considered as sufficient grounds for the assumption that superiors were disinclined to receive him. The same application may also extend, it seems, even to the case in which a candidate, in response to the questioning of the superior, were to hide the fact that he had been a former student in another seminary or a novice in another institute, since this fact is of grave importance to the superior in giving his consent, not only because the law requires him to obtain testimonial letters if such is true,[46] but also because he may be required to obtain permission of the Holy See before admitting

[44] Cappello, *Summa Iuris Canonici,* II, 46.
[45] Wernz-Vidal, *Ius Canonicum,* III, 187.
[46] Canon 544.

such a candidate to his institute.[47] In practice it will depend upon the disposition of the superiors with regard to the reception of such a candidate. Some constitutions prohibit the reception of candidates who have been dismissed from the novitiate of another institute.[48]

Deception concerning the family background may also be the source of a determining fraud. Authors concede that if a postulant concealed a family disgrace about which he had been questioned and which he knew or suspected would certainly have caused his exclusion, his admission would be generally invalid.[49] Such, for example, may be the case if he deliberately concealed the fact that he was the product of an illegitimate, nefarious, or sacrilegious union (if this fact were of importance to the community, and generally it will be), or that his parents and family were notorious apostates or heretics, or that there had been a number of suicides in his immediate family, or that his parents were living in public sin in flagrant violation of the Church's law on matrimony.[50] In fine, any grave moral deficiency in a candidate or his family which is externally manifest and which would certainly or most probably

[47] S. C. de Rel. et de Seminariis, decr. 25 iul. 1941—*Acta Apostolicae Sedis, Commentarium Officiale* (Romae, 1909-), XXXIII (1941), 371 (hereafter cited *AAS*). This decree in reality amounts to another impediment to licit entry into the religious state. Cf. Creusen, *Religious Men and Women in the Code,* p. 137.

[48] *Constitutiones Fratrum S. Ordinis Praedicatorum,* n. 75; *Constitutiones Ordinis Recollectorum Sancti Augustini,* n. 223.

[49] Creusen, *Religious Men and Women in the Code,* p. 135; Bouscaren-Ellis, *Canon Law, a Text and Commentary,* p. 260.

[50] It is to be noted that the candidate's family background is of grave importance especially when he is to be received as a candidate for the clerical state. Cf. S. C. de Rel., instr. 1 dec. 1931, n. 6: "Before they admit the clerical students to the novitiate, Superiors must obtain still fuller information regarding the candidates (cc. 544, 545), and must supplement the testimonial letters they have, which may be insufficient, by other careful investigations made by trustworthy persons. Nor should the Superiors neglect to get information about the moral qualities of the families from which the students come, and to learn whether their parents are free from such vices as easily reappear in the children."—*AAS,* XXIV (1932), 74. (Translation that of Bouscaren, *The Canon Law Digest* [2 vols. and Supplement through 1948, Milwaukee: Bruce, 1934, 1943, 1949], I, 476.)

have caused his rejection had it been known, must be revealed by the candidate or by third parties who have an obligation to do so.

Deception concerning the intellectual qualities of a candidate may be induced in regard to his mental capacity, his caliber as a student, or the actual degree to which he has advanced in his studies. The constitutions of most institutes generally make provisions for the rejection of any candidate who is not gifted with sufficient intelligence to carry on the duties of the religious state, at least according to the class of religious into which he is received. Mere lack of mental ability, however, unless the candidate were too dull for any occupation in the community, would not be sufficient to make his admission invalid, even though some deception may have been induced concerning it. The caliber of the candidate as a student will more often be the source of deception and, when it does occur, will more easily exercise a decisive influence upon the decision of a superior in receiving him. Most constitutions contain a phrase prohibiting superiors from receiving a candidate who has not shown sufficient ability in his lower studies to give solid hope that he will be able to acquire sufficient knowledge either to carry on the sacred ministry, if he be destined for the clerical state, or for the particular work in which the institute is engaged, whether it be lay or clerical.[51]

If any deception has occurred through manipulation of scholastic records or through cheating in an entrance examination, such deception must be judged by the general principle, i.e., whether or not the particular institute in question would have received the candidate had the truth about his scholastic record been known. The case may occur, for example, in which the institute has established a certain standard below which it is unwilling to receive any candidate, e.g., unless he possesses an average of 83% in his Latin and English courses. In such an eventuality, if a can-

[51] Cf., e.g., *Constitutiones Ordinis Eremitarum S. Augustini*, n. 192; *Constitutiones Fratrum S. Ordinis Praedicatorum*, n. 76; *The Rule and General Constitutions of the Friars Minor*, n. 19; *Constitutiones Ordinis Recollectorum Sancti Augustini*, n. 216: "Ad statum clericalem admittendi examinandi sunt, praeter vocationem, num bene didicerint litteras humaniores, praesertim linguam latinam, ita ut spes affulgeat eos sufficientem doctrinam fore assecuturos ad sacra ministeria rite obeunda."

didate were to manipulate his scholastic record deliberately, which was considerably below that mark, in order to circumvent this established standard, his novitiate would be certainly invalid. In the absence of an established standard, however, one must judge the influence which deception concerning the ability of the aspirant as a student may have had upon the decision of the superior to receive him by the general policy of the institute, the end towards which it is directed, and the mind of the acting superior. But, unless it can be established that, had the deception not been employed, the candidate would certainly have been rejected, one cannot declare his novitiate invalid in consequence of the employed deception.

Finally, the constitutions may demand that candidates who are admitted must have advanced to a certain degree in their course of studies, though these provisions in the constitutions, for grave reasons, usually allow for exceptions to the general rule.[52] Whenever the policy of the institute is such that it is generally unwilling to grant an exception to this general rule, and a candidate, in order to facilitate his entry, presents false diplomas or feigns possession of the required degree, his novitiate, it seems, is thereby rendered null and void.[53] Here, again, one must be certain that the lack of the required degree or diploma would have excluded him, although if the policy of the community is to exclude anyone who does not possess it, the presumption would stand that the superior is opposed to the reception of anyone who deliberately deceives him concerning this point.

Deception could likewise be employed for inducing a superior to receive a candidate by means of a malicious concealment or false representation of the general state of an aspirant's physical or mental health or the presence of a serious disease, or by means of a deliberate minimizing of the nature or seriousness of an ailment with which he may be afflicted. The factor of the physical

---

[52] *Constitutiones Ordinis Eremitarum S. Augustini,* nn. 192, 193; *Constitutiones Fratrum S. Ordinis Praedicatorum,* n. 76; *The Rule and General Constitutions of the Friars Minor,* n. 19.

[53] Fransen, *Le dol dans la conclusion des actes juridiques,* p. 397: "De la part du candidat: . . . prétendre posséder certaines qualités, certains diplômes qui faciliteraient son entrée." Cf. also Lefebvre, "Dol en droit canonique actuel," *DDC,* IV, col. 1950.

and mental health of the prospective candidates plays a major rôle in the decision of any superior when he passes on the qualifications of those who are to be admitted into the novitiate of his community. Not only does the spiritual well-being of the future religious himself depend to a great extent upon his ability to bear the strenuous duties and exercises of daily community life, but also his usefulness to the community in carrying on the particular mission to which it is dedicated. In some respects, at least legally considered, the factor of the candidate's health is even more serious than the considerations of his intellectual ability or moral qualifications. For, although the law grants superiors the right to dismiss religious, whenever mental debility or grave moral defects become apparent, even though they may have been admitted to simple profession,[54] or to prevent them from pronouncing solemn or perpetual vows at the expiration of temporary profession,[55] it forbids them to dismiss one whose physical or mental health has broken under the strain of community exercises or duties following his profession. Though the justice inherent in this provision of the law is quite manifest, its existence makes it doubly important that superiors should exercise judicious caution regarding the mental or physical soundness of applicants. Hence, any notable deception which is practiced concerning the general state or present condition of the candidate's physical or mental health must be considered, under ordinary circumstances, as exercising a decisive influence upon the superior's consent to admit him. And anyone who perpetrates or co-operates in such deception must be considered as having done a very real injustice to the community into which the candidate seeks entry.

The factor of health, however, like that of mental ability, must be not absolutely but relatively considered, that is to say, in the light of the peculiar character and particular end of the institute in question. By reason of canon 538 in the present Code, one of the prime requisites for licit entry into any institute in the Church is the fitness of the individual to bear the burdens of the religious

---

[54] Canon 647, § 2, 2°.

[55] Canon 637.

state. But, as authors well observe,[56] this provision must, in practice, be understood in a relative sense, since the basic minimum of physical or mental strength needed for fulfilling the duties assumed through the vows in the various institutes and for carrying on the work in which it is engaged will differ greatly from institute to institute. In evaluating the gravity of the defect obscured, whether of mental or of physical health, and the decisiveness of the concealment on the consent of the admitting superior, one must take into account the obligations, the austerities, and the labors to which the members of the institute bind themselves.

One can do little more than indicate certain general principles which may be used as a criterion for measuring the gravity of the influence which deception concerning health may have had upon a superior in accepting a candidate. Usually the constitutions of the various institutes direct the superior to make investigations concerning the health of those to be admitted and to exclude those: (a) who labor under a contagious or incurable disease; (b) who are habitually afflicted with some infirmity which may impede the perfect observance of the vows and precepts of the institute; (c) who do not possess sufficient physical or mental strength to bear the ordinary labors or studies which are demanded of members of the institute; and (d) who bear some notable bodily deformity from which derision could ensue.[57]

The various means by which these various factors concerning the health of the candidate must be verified are: examination by a competent physician deputed by or at least known to the community; questions directed to the candidate personally or to those associated with him; and the candidate's sworn testimony. In each case, however, the constitutions direct the superior to warn the candidate that any deception practiced, especially with regard to his physical or mental health, will render invalid not only his

---

[56] Cf., e.g., Berutti, *Institutiones,* III, 131; Schaefer, *De Religiosis,* p. 409; Wernz-Vidal, *Ius Canonicum,* III, 188.

[57] Cf., e.g., *Constitutiones Fratrum Discalceatorum Ordinis Sanctissimae Trinitatis* (Isola del Liri: Soc. Tip. A. Macioce et Pisani, 1933), nn. 573, 574; *Constitutiones Ordinis Eremitarum S. Augustini,* nn. 84, 184, 188; *Constitutiones Fratrum S. Ordinis Praedicatorum,* n. 84; *The Rule and General Constitutiones of the Friars Minor,* n. 16.

reception but his subsequent profession as well. Hence, the mind of the community and the accepting superior will generally be more easily demonstrated with regard to the various factors about which deception might occur concerning the prospective candidate's health than it will normally be with regard to the other qualities. At the same time, it must be noted that if these regulations in the constitutions are not faithfully carried out, the proof of fraudulent deception will be rendered most difficult.[58]

As noted above, of the three factors concerning the health of an individual which are of grave importance, the first is the general state of his physical or mental health. Thus, for example, the effect of deception upon a superior's consent must, it seems, be judged as decisive if a candidate, his parents, or family physician deliberately dissimulated or concealed the fact that he habitually labors under infirmities which hamper his normal activities; that he suffers such frail health that in the past he has frequently succumbed to complete nervous or physical breakdowns; that he tends to neurasthenia,[59] melancholia, mania, or morbidity of imagination; that he has an inherited weakness disposing him to tuberculosis; that he experiences constant and severe headaches, or that he nurses a heart condition which may readily lead to partial or complete disability. For no superior must be held to be of the mind and will to receive one whose physical or mental defects make him so great a risk. This list is by no means complete; it merely demonstrates those various factors about the general health of the prospective candidate which would indicate a lack of physical or mental fitness for the religious state, and as such would exclude him from entry into it and render invalid his admission if the admitting superior were deceived regarding them.

Secondly, deception could be practiced concerning the actual

---

[58] Larraona, "Commentarium Codicis," *CpRM*, XVII (1936), 17, note 182.

[59] The name for a group of symptoms resulting from some functional disorder of the nervous system, with severe depression of the vital forces. It is usually the result of prolonged and excessive expenditure of energy and is marked by a tendency to fatigue, lack of energy, loss of memory, insomnia, etc. It is very important to ascertain whether such a condition exists in a candidate, since it may easily lead to complete insanity under the strain of community life.

presence of a serious disease, curable or incurable, contagious or non-contagious. If the candidate dissimulates or hides the fact that he is affected with a contagious or an incurable malady which would be a constant annoyance to the institute, the decisive effect of the concealment upon the superior's consent is evident. The question could be raised concerning the effect of the concealment of a disease which though grave is curable. The classical canonists were of the opinion that if a candidate hid such a disease at his reception he could be repelled by the institute only if it did not respond to proper remedies within a year.[60] This opinion, of course, can no longer be sustained, for now one must judge deception concerning such an illness by the general principle of whether or not the candidate would have been rejected by the admitting superior had the truth concerning the illness been known to him when giving his consent. If the latter would certainly have repelled the former, the candidate's novitiate and subsequent profession would be rendered automatically null and void.[61]

Finally, although in speaking to the superior the candidate has made mention of the presence of the infirmity, he could fraudulently minimize the gravity of it in order to obtain admission. For example, the candidate could say that he is occasionally afflicted with slight attacks of rheumatism or pleurisy, but that he has been informed by a competent physician that this condition will not notably increase nor will it hamper him in his religious duties, whereas it was learned later that the physician had previously warned the candidate that the condition would steadily grow worse as he grew older and eventually would incapacitate him. Such deception, it seems, may likewise be considered under ordinary conditions as determining the consent of a superior and rendering it inefficacious, though its actual effect will depend upon the degree to which the illness was misrepresented.

In fine, one may sum up the whole doctrine concerning the fraudulent concealment or misrepresentation of one's physical or

---

[60] Cf. *supra*, p. 44.

[61] Creusen, *Religious Men and Women in the Code*, p. 135; Fransen, *loc. cit.;* Mayer, *Benediktinisches Ordensrecht,* III, 38; Vermeersch-Creusen, *Epitome Iuris Canonici,* I, 500; Wernz-Vidal, *Ius Canonicum,* III, 200; Berutti, *Institutiones,* III, 139; Cappello, *Summa Iuris Canonici,* II, 45; Lefebvre, *loc. cit.*

mental condition as follows: (1) the infirmity must be of such importance in its nature and extent that in and of itself it would furnish sufficient grounds upon which to reject the candidate; (2) the disease or condition must be truly existent at the time of the candidate's reception, so that, if it were known to the admitting superior, he would have undoubtedly considered it as sufficient to exclude the candidate; (3) knowledge of the disease must have been deliberately withheld or dissimulated with a view to producing an error concerning its presence or gravity so as to induce the superior's consent; (4) these three conditions must be verified with at least moral certainty as co-existent.[62] From this it is apparent that fraudulent deception concerning the state of the candidate's health is most difficult to demonstrate, unless a palpable fraud is present, as, for example, when there is evidence of a deliberate manipulation of medical documents, a sworn affidavit of the examining physician to the effect that the candidate had charged him to withhold certain facts about his health, or proof that the physician had warned the candidate of the true state of his health and told him not to enter the institute.

Since the validity of the subsequent profession, and indeed the value of the whole religious life of a candidate, is jeopardized through the perpetration of fraud in the act of entering the novitiate, the importance of warning candidates concerning it cannot be overemphasized. At the same time one must exercise judicious caution in declaring a novitiate without substance because of it, since, if due attention is given to all the various provisions enacted in the universal law concerning testimonials and to those of the particular law with regard to proper examinations, written and oral, then the probability of the perpetration of juridically relevant fraud affecting the novitiate will be rendered quite remote. However, once it has been proved beyond a reasonable doubt that fraud decisively affected the reason for which a candidate was received, nothing more need be demonstrated before his novitiate may be declared invalid.

---

[62] Toso, *Commentaria,* V, 230-231. This author develops this doctrine with regard to deception in the religious profession itself, such as would give rise to grounds for subsequent dismissal under canon 637. But the same principle may with equal force be applied to the act of entry into the novitiate.

CHAPTER XI

Superiors Competent to Admit Candidates to the Novitiate

In the preceding discussion of the principles which regulate the invalidating effects of force, fear, and fraud upon entry into the canonical novitiate it was ascertained that the use of these agencies to procure consent to this act results in its invalidity not only when they are employed against a candidate seeking entry into religion, but also when they are used for inducing the superior's consent to admit him as well. In this discussion specific reference was not made to the proper person, or combination of persons, in whom the competency of admitting candidates into the novitiate habitually resides. Since this factor may play an important rôle in determining the invalidity of the novitiate whenever duress or fraud is employed against the admitting superiors, it will be necessary to discuss in more detail the person, or persons, to whom this competency may be assigned either by the universal law or by the particular constitutions, the conditions upon which its licit and valid use may depend, and the consequent effects of duress or fraud upon the novitiate, whenever these agencies have been present in the consent given to the admission of a candidate.

In virtue of the general principle enunciated in canon 543,[1] the superior who is competent to admit candidates into the novitiate of any institute is the major religious superior, as the constitutions of each particular institute shall prescribe. The term major religious superior as used here must be understood in the sense of canon 488, 8°, that is, it embraces the abbot primate, the abbot superior of a monastic congregation, the abbot of an independent monastery even though it forms part of a monastic congregation, the superior general of the whole institute, the provincial superior, their vicars and all others who have powers equal to that of provincials. Among major superiors, therefore, one must also include the vicar general

[1] Canon 543. Ius admittendi ad novitiatum . . . pertinet ad Superiores maiores cum suffragio Consilii seu Capituli, secundum peculiares cuiusque religionis constitutiones.

of an institute, the vicars of religious men, the vice-provincial, as well as the superiors of nuns in independent monasteries like those of the Benedictines, Poor Clares, or Carmelites.[2] Although the Code restricts this right to those who hold the position of major superior in an institute, it does not designate specifically which of these various superiors shall have this right or whether any two of them shall hold it cumulatively. One must, therefore, check the constitutions of each particular community to ascertain this fact.

It is imperative to note that the term major superior must be understood here as embracing only those superiors who belong to the interior hierarchy of the institute itself, to the total exclusion of those under whom the institute may be placed in the external hierarchy of the Church,[3] with the exception of the Supreme Pontiff himself who, as the Supreme Moderator of all religious institutes, may admit novices into any order or congregation whatsoever.[4] In virtue of this fact, the local ordinary no longer enjoys the right of admitting novices into a diocesan congregation, as he did before the present Code.[5] Neither, it seems, can the constitutions grant him this right, since such a provision would be contrary to the universal law.[6] However, authors generally concede that, although the local ordinary cannot force a diocesan community to receive a certain candidate contrary to their wishes, he could nevertheless impede the entry of a certain candidate,[7] especially if there is a grave and objective cause for doing so and that cause is known to him officially.[8] These same observations seem to hold true with regard to nuns who are subject to the local ordinary or to a prelate of a regular institute. Larraona notes that this specific faculty is not uncommonly granted explicitly in the constitutions of these institutes.[9]

---

[2] Creusen, *Religious Men and Women in the Code,* p. 16; Larraona, "Commentarium Codicis," *CpR,* IV (1923), 41-44; cf. also Larraona, "Commentarium Codicis," *CpRM,* XVIII (1937), 325.

[3] Larraona, "Commentarium Codicis," *CpRM,* XVIII (1937), 321.

[4] Vermeersch-Creusen, *Epitome Iuris Canonici,* I, 509.

[5] Goyeneché, *De Religiosis,* p. 80; Vermeersch-Creusen, *loc. cit.*

[6] Larraona, *ibidem,* pp. 321-327.

[7] Vermeersch-Creusen, *loc. cit.*

[8] Larraona, *ibidem,* p. 322.

[9] Larraona, *ibidem,* p. 322, note 452.

Minor local religious superiors as such do not by reason of their office enjoy the competence of admitting candidates. Neither does the master of novices. Furthermore, it does not seem that the local religious superior may be habitually entrusted with this competence,[10] although inasmuch as this right pertains to the ordinary power of the major superior, the latter may delegate the local superior to perform this task in a particular case. If he does so, the delegation would, it seems, always be made ***propter industriam personae,*** and it would therefore be totally contrary to the mind of the Code that a subdelegation could be undertaken.[11]

Since the Code does not state that the council or chapter which the major superior must consult or whose consent he must obtain is to be his own, it is left to the particular law of the institute to designate whether the vote of the local, provincial, or general chapter or council is required for this act.[12] The precise nature of this vote, whether it is merely consultative or deliberative, is for its ultimate determination and specification likewise left to the particular law of each order or congregation.[13]

If the constitutions require merely a consultative vote of the council or chapter, then, once the superior has obtained this vote, he is free to follow it in his decision or to act contrary to it.[14] Whether or not he acts validly in receiving a candidate without asking this advice of the council or chapter when such is required by the law is a disputed question, since authors do not agree on the interpretation of canon 105, 1°, on this point. Vermeersch maintained that such a consultation is not essential to the valid action of the superior when the particular law does not specifically state so.[15] Goyeneché, on the contrary, holds that the novitiate would be invalid under such circumstances were the superior to receive the candidate without calling for a consultative vote of the

---

[10] Berutti, *Institutiones,* III, 151.

[11] Larraona, *ibidem,* pp. 325-326; Goyeneché, *De Religiosis,* p. 81.

[12] Schaefer, *De Religiosis,* p. 449.

[13] Goyeneché, *De Religiosis,* p. 80; Schaefer, *ibidem,* n. 821; Vermeersch-Creusen, *Epitome Iuris Canonici,* I, 509; Fanfani, *De Iure Religiosorum,* n. 194.

[14] Canon 105, 1°.

[15] *Epitome Iuris Canonici,* I, 208-209; Michiels, *Principia Generalia,* p. 417.

council or chapter as specified in the constitutions.[16] Until the present doubt of law on canon 105, 1°, is dispelled, it seems safe to say that though the entry of a novice under such conditions would be illicit, it would not be invalid.[17]

Whenever the deliberative vote of the council or chapter is required by the constitutions, the major superior cannot admit a candidate unless he obtains a favorable majority of the votes cast. It is disputed, however, whether or not he is obliged to accept a candidate once the chapter or council has given a favorable vote for him. Vermeersch and Creusen maintain that the superior may not reject the candidate once the council decides in favor of him.[18] Coronata and others argue, on the contrary, that a favorable vote by the chapter or council does not oblige the superior to accept the candidate, but that the superior is at all times free to reject the candidate if he sees fit to do so.[19] They argue that the rôle of the chapter in this act is solely one of assistance, having been established as a protective norm against the acceptance of undesirable characters, while the actual right of admitting them lies in the major superior himself. This latter opinion seems solidly probable in view of the fact that canon 543 specifically confers the right of accepting candidates upon the superior, and not on the chapter. Furthermore, some constitutions make explicit mention of this right of the provincial.[20] Hence, it seems that, though the major superior must have the deliberative approval of the chapter or council in such circumstances, he does not need to follow their decision approving of a candidate but he retains the liberty of rejecting such an approved candidate if he deems it wise to do so.[21]

---

[16] "Consultationes," *CpR,* III (1922), 265; cf. also "Consultationes," *CpR,* IV (1923), 120; Goyeneché, *De Religiosis,* p. 81; Creusen, *Religious Men and Women in the Code,* p. 139; Coronata, *Institutiones,* I, 716.

[17] Beste, *Introductio in Codicem,* p. 163; Regatillo, *Institutiones,* I, 133.

[18] Vermeersch, "Annotationes," *Periodica,* XI (1922), 28; Creusen, *Religious Men and Women in the Code,* n. 181, p. 139.

[19] Coronata, *Institutiones,* I, n. 572, p. 717; Beste, *Introductio in Codicem,* p. 368.

[20] Cf., e.g., *Constitutiones Fratrum S. Ordinis Praedicatorum,* n. 89: "Provincialis admissionem vel reiectionem candidati decernat, ita tamen ut adspirantes a Consilio vel Capitulo reiectos admittere nequeat, admissos vero reiicere valeat."

[21] Cf. Larraona, "Consultationes," *CpR,* I (1920), 368, note 10; Goyeneché, "Consultationes," *CpR,* III (1922), 53 sq.

Finally, the constitutions of a particular institute may decree that the right of admitting members into it is to reside in the chapter as such, as is the case in the Order of St. Benedict.[22] In such an eventuality the chapter together with the major superior would constitute a collegiate moral person, and the superior would not be free to act contrary to the majority opinion. Even though he may personally judge a candidate as undesirable, he would not be free to reject him except in case of a tie vote, at which time the law concedes him the right to break such a tie by casting another vote.[23]

In view of these various hypotheses, the term superior in canon 542, 1°, on forced entry into the novitiate must be understood as referring to the physical or moral person, or those collectively, to whom the competence of admitting novices exclusively pertains according to the constitutions of each individual institute. Three possible combinations may be realized: (a) this right may be granted to the major superior with the advice of the chapter or the council; (b) the major superior may be competent only after a decisive vote of the council or the chapter; (c) the major superior may form a moral person with the council or the chapter in performing this act. For a theoretical treatment of the possible effects of duress or fraud upon the admission of a candidate under any one of these three combinations, it makes no appreciable difference whether the council or the chapter designated for this duty is that of the local house, of the province, or of the whole institute. For, in ultimate analysis, the determining factor of whether or not force, fear, or fraud actually vitiated consent given in the admission of a candidate will rest solely upon the nature of the rôle played by the superior, or the chapter or council, who are affected by it when admitting him.[24]

In the first possible hypothesis, that is, when the major religious superior is competent to admit candidates with the advice of the council or the chapter, the rôle of the chapter is merely consultative, and as such it does not have a determining influence upon the legal efficacy of the consent given by the major superior. Hence, in such an eventuality, even though the members of the council or

[22] Augustine, *A Commentary on the New Code of Canon Law,* III, 215.
[23] Canon 101, 1°.
[24] Larraona, "Commentarium Codicis," *CpRM,* XVII (1936), 18.

the chapter may be led to cast their vote under the determining influence of duress or fraud, as long as the superior himself is unaffected by these agencies his consent given to the admission of a candidate is legally as well as psychologically unimpaired. Conversely, whenever the superior himself acts under duress or through deceit in such an arrangement, his consent would be nullified automatically if these agencies represented the inspiring cause for which he admits a candidate, even though the chapter was totally unaffected by it. The reason for these observations lies in the fact that under such an arrangement the superior himself is the principal agent; the chapter or the council merely aids his judgment.[25]

In the second hypothesis presented, that is, when the major superior is competent to admit candidates, but only with the deliberative vote of the council or the chapter, the chapter plays a decisive rôle in determining the juridical sufficiency of the consent of the superior, so much so, in fact, that were he to consent without first obtaining a favorable majority, his action would lack the juridic force needed to produce any legal effect. Hence, under such circumstances, whenever the members of the chapter are forced through duress or induced through fraud to cast a favorable vote for a particular candidate, his novitiate would be rendered automatically null and void thereby. This may be the case either when the majority of the votes cast are vitiated through such unjust interference with the chapter, or when those votes which in reality produce the majority are so affected.[26]

Whenever such a case does occur, even though the superior who has received a favorable vote under such conditions later receives the candidate knowingly and willingly, unaffected by any of these agencies, the novitiate is rendered without juridical substance, because the legal effectiveness of his consent hinges upon the valid action of the council or chapter supporting it. On the other hand, if the chapter gives a favorable vote unhampered by unjust interference, but the superior who must ultimately admit the candidate is coerced or deluded into receiving him (though he was disposed not to receive him in spite of the favorable vote of the chapter), the

---

[25] Schaefer, *De Religiosis,* p. 431.

[26] Canon 169, § 1, 1°; canon 101, § 1, 1°.

novitiate would likewise be invalid, according to the opinion presented above to the effect that the superior is free to admit or reject a candidate in spite of the favorable vote of the chapter. For in reality, in this latter case the superior's consent is that which plays the determining rôle in the ultimate reception of the candidate. And hence, if he is efficaciously moved to receive a candidate through unjust duress or fraud, the novitiate would thereby be automatically rendered null and void.[27]

Finally, if the council or the chapter itself forms one moral person in the admission of novices, the same principles apply as were outlined in the foregoing case concerning the decisive vote of the chapter. Hence, whenever the majority of the votes cast for a candidate, or those which go to make up a majority, represent the product of unjust duress or fraud, the novitiate of the candidate in question would be rendered null and void.

It is important here to point out again that it makes no difference, as far as the legal effects are concerned, whether the duress or fraud brought to bear upon a superior proceeds from the candidate himself or from a third party.[28] Thus, for example, if a wealthy relative of the candidate in question held the mortgage to a large portion of the property of the institute, and threatened foreclosure if the superior or chapter refused to admit the candidate into the novitiate, the novitiate would be invalid even though the candidate had no knowledge of such action and in reality would have disapproved of it had he known. The same holds true with regard to the element of fraud. Thus, if one of those individuals who is to grant testimonial letters by reason of canon 544 were to misrepresent some grave moral or physical defect deliberately, which he knew or suspected would keep the candidate from being accepted, the novitiate would be rendered invalid if the consent of the superior admitting the candidate did in fact hinge upon the hidden fact, even though the candidate himself was unwilling that such deception be employed in his favor.

A point which requires special emphasis whenever the superior himself is the principal agent in the reception of candidates is that

[27] Larraona, *art. cit.*

[28] Vermeersch-Creusen, *Epitome Iuris Canonici,* I, 500; Cappello, *Summa Iuris Canonici,* II, 48.

the agencies of duress or fraud, in order to have an invalidating effect upon the admission of a candidate, must continue up to the very moment of and exist at the time of his actual admission or reception into the canonical novitiate. Hence, in the eventuality that the duress or fraud which was perpetrated for securing the admission of a novice exerted a determining influence upon the formal approbation of the candidate, but ceased either to exist or to play a decisive rôle at the time of his formal acceptance, the novitiate would not thereby be rendered invalid. Once fear is inflicted, however, it is considered to persevere unless there are positive signs of its retraction.[29]

Finally, it should here be noted that whenever fraud has been used to induce the consent of a council or chapter, even though its rôle is merely consultative, as a general rule the same fraud which affects the members of the chapter will likewise affect the admitting superior, although the opposite may be the case more easily when the agency of duress is employed. For, usually whenever the members of a council or a chapter recommend a candidate with their consultative vote, the superior will follow their opinion on receiving him. And, if they acted through fraud, he will generally act, at least indirectly, through that same fraud. When, however, it can be ascertained that it did not affect him, then its effect must be assessed accordingly.

---

[29] Larraona, "Commentarium Codicis," *CpRM,* XVII (1936), 18, note 184; Wernz-Vidal, *Ius Canonicum,* III, 200; Badii, "Il dolo nel Codice di Diritto Canonico," *Il Diritto Ecclesiastico,* XL (1929), 313.

CHAPTER XII

The Penal Sanction Affecting Forced Entry Into the Novitiate

Canon 2352. Excommunicatione nemini reservata ipso facto plectuntur omnes, qualibet etiam dignitate fulgentes, qui quoquo modo cogant . . . virum aut mulierem ad religionem ingrediendam. . . .

The constant and grave solicitude of the Church for the perfect liberty of those who are about to take the most serious step of embracing the religious state is reflected in the present legislation not only in the fact that automatic invalidity is decreed to fall upon a novitiate which is entered upon through the unjustly exerted influence of another, but likewise in the fact that the law has directed the most severe penal sanction of automatic excommunication against anyone who, in any way whatsoever, unjustly coerces another to seek entry into the religious state. Hence, a study of the effects of force, fear, and fraud upon entry into the canonical novitiate would not be complete without a consideration of this penalty inflicted upon those who deliberately employ these agencies to bring about consent to this act.

The penal sanction of automatic excommunication, as it is found in canon 2352 of the present Code, is not new in ecclesiastical law; the present law is but a restatement of the former discipline on this point, which was formulated in the twenty-fifth session of the Council of Trent,[1] and which is extended on some points while restricted in scope on others. By reason of the Tridentine legislation formerly in effect, excommunication was visited upon anyone who dared to coerce a *woman* into the religious state against her will. This penal sanction of the Council of Trent in no way pertained to the forced entry of a young man into an institute of

[1] Conc. Trident., sess. XXV, *de regularibus*, c. 18.

men. As Suarez pointed out,[2] the Council, through its censure, was attempting to prevent that which was considered as a common danger, and since coercion was more apt to occur in influencing a young woman to enter a convent than in the case of a young man entering a monastery, it restricted the delict which was the basis of its censure to the use of coercion against young women. The present law, however, has eliminated this distinction between the forced entry of men and women, and now extends the scope of the delict thus censured to embrace the forced entry of the former as well as the latter.

On the other hand, the present law restricts the Tridentine legislation on two other points. The first of these is to be found in the restrictive clause which the Council added to its canon to the effect that it was permitted, under certain conditions then recognized in the law, to force a woman into the cloister, even against her will.[3] Since the present legislation has dropped all reference to this reservation, one must now, in virtue of canon 6, 5°, consider the reservation abrogated and hence the present law in effect has made all coercion, regardless of its medium, its purpose, or its end, illicit and liable to the penal sanction by the very fact that it is used for influencing the consent of one embracing the religious state.

The second point upon which the present law has revised that of the Council of Trent is to be found in the provision of the Council whereby not only those who forced another into religion fell under its censure, but also all those who should "in any way and without a just cause impede the holy wish of virgins or other women to take the veil or pronounce vows." Hence, the Council invoked a sanction against unjust coercion not only when the latter was used for inducing another to enter religion, but also when it was used for forcing another to desist from doing so. Although this provision is no longer in effect and one would not therefore fall under censure by hindering another from embracing

---

[2] Suarez, tr. VII, *De religione,* lib. 5, c. 9, nn. 3, 4—*Opera Omnia,* XV, 335-336.

[3] Cf. *supra,* p. 37.

the religious state, yet unless one had a just cause for doing so one would sin grievously if one deliberately employed these agencies to this purpose.[4] For, as St. Thomas declared,[5] in one's choice of one's state in life one must enjoy complete freedom in one's selection. Hence, whenever an individual is guilty of exerting undue influence to divert another from embracing the religious state, he sins, even though perhaps he is not liable to penal sanction.

Both the present Code, as well as the Tridentine law, indicate explicitly that all, no matter with what dignity invested, are subject to this particular censure whenever they are guilty of this specific delict. The phrase *qualibet dignitate fulgentes,* which appears in both laws, was formerly interpreted as referring only to those vested with ecclesiastical dignities, to the exclusion of those who held offices in the state. And hence authors were wont to exclude the highest authority in the state from incurring automatic excommunication whenever he was guilty of forcing a woman into the religious state.[6] Today, however, canonists understand this phrase in canon 2352 as referring not only to those vested with ecclesiastical dignities, but also to civil magistrates, not excluding the supreme heads of state.[7] Hence, all those subject to ecclesiastical law, not exclusive of the parents or relatives of the person coerced, whether lay or cleric, whether inferior or superior, not exclusive of major religious superiors or even bishops, with whatever dignity vested, whether ecclesiastical or civil, inclusive also of the supreme head of state, are liable to automatic excommunication whenever they are guilty of forcing another into the religious state. Cardinals alone are not included under this penalty, since they are not expressly mentioned here.[8] Whenever anyone, however, acts through ignorance, even though vincible, either of

---

[4] Blat, *Commentarium,* lib. V, 256-257.

[5] *Summa Theologica,* II-II, q. 104, a. 5, in c.

[6] Cf. Coronata, *Institutiones,* IV, 496.

[7] Vermeersch-Creusen, *Epitome Iuris Canonici,* III, 348; Blat, *Commentarium,* lib. V, 256; Cocchi, *Commentarium,* VIII, 310; Farrugia, *Commentarium in Censuras Latae Sententiae Codicis Juris Canonici* (Militae, 1921), p. 21 (hereafter cited *Commentarium in Censuras*).

[8] Canon 2227, § 2.

the prohibition of the law or of the existence of this censure, he may be held not to incur it.[9]

The Council of Trent explicitly declared that not only those who were the principal agents of duress were liable to excommunication, but also all those who in any way gave advice, aid or encouragement to such action, as well as those who, while knowing that a particular individual did not assume the religious habit voluntarily, in any way whatsoever took part in this coerced entry either through their presence, consent, or authority.[10]

Although the present Code has dropped all explicit reference to co-operators in this delict, by reason of the general principle of canon 2231, which is operative with regard to every penal canon in the Code, not only those who play the principal rôle, or those who are co-agents in the perpetration of this delict are liable to the penalty attached to it in the law, but also all those who must be considered as effective co-operators incur it in the same manner as the principal author himself. In order, however, to be qualified as an effective co-operator, one's contribution to the eventuation of the crime must be such that, had one not taken part in it, it *could not have been committed.*[11] One may not, therefore, be considered as an effective co-operator in the delict of forcing another into the religious state whenever one merely facilitates his forced entry procured by another. If, however, one places an action without which the forced entry of a candidate could not have been obtained, one is then guilty of the delict in the same manner as the principal agent himself and therefore liable to the penalty of automatic excommunication involved in the committed delict.

By reason of this doctrine, authors interpret canon 2352 as extending not only to those who deliberately set to work to force a

---

[9] Cerato, *Censurae Vigentes Ipso Facto a Codice Iuris Canonici Excerptae* (2. ed., Patavii: Typis Seminarii, 1921), p. 81 (hereafter cited *Censurae Vigentes*).

[10] Cf. *supra*, pp. 36-37.

[11] Canon 2209, § 3; Michiels, *De Delictis et Poenis*, Vol. I, *De Delictis* (Lublin: Universitas Catholica, 1934), pp. 322, 323; Eltz, *Cooperation in Crime*, The Catholic University of America Canon Law Studies, n. 156 (Washington, D. C.: The Catholic University of America Press, 1942), pp. 117-120.

candidate into the novitiate, but also the admitting superior, if the sole right of admitting novices resides in him, or the council or chapter, if it has a deliberative vote in this matter, whenever they have certain knowledge that a particular candidate is entering because of unjust coercion, and, nevertheless, admit him. This conclusion is derived from the principle: if they had not cooperated, the delict could not have been committed.[12] It would not affect the council or the chapter, however, if the members had merely a consultative vote in the admission of novices.

Before the censure can take effect, the delict must have been realized perfectly according to the proper signification of the terms of the law.[13] Although, as Coronata points out,[14] the text of this canon seems to indicate that the delict is realized whenever one exerts undue influence upon an individual to receive orders, to enter the novitiate, or to pronounce vows, even though the individual may in fact not do so, authors generally attach a restricted interpretation to the words used in the text of the canon and hold one liable to this penalty only if the effect of the coercion has in fact followed.[15] Hence, the observation of Augustine that, if a chaplain of Sisters preaches to an academy of girls that their only salvation is in the convent, he is certainly not far from incurring this censure, must be regarded, it seems, as an overstatement. For, although coercion such as is here outlawed under penal sanction could possibly be exerted through such a medium, the probability of its taking effect must be considered generally as quite remote.[16] One must agree with this author, however, that if a chaplain per-

---

[12] Cocchi, *Commentarium,* VIII, 310; Beste, *Introductio in Codicem,* p. 979; Vermeersch-Creusen, *Epitome Iuris Canonici,* III, 348; Jombart, "Des Délits et des Peines," *Traité de Droit Canonique publié sous la direction de Raoul Naz* (4 voll., Vol. IV, Parisiis: Letouzey et Ané, 1948), IV, 757.

[13] Canon 2228.

[14] *Institutiones,* IV, 496.

[15] Sole, *De Delictis et Poenis* (Romae: Pustet, 1920), p. 328; Cappello, *De Censuris* (Augustae Taurinorum, 1919), p. 136; Cipollini, *De Censuris Latae Sententiae iuxta Codicem Iuris Canonici* (Taurini, 1925), p. 190 (hereafter cited *De Censuris*); Pistocchi, *I Canoni Penali del Codice Ecclesiastico* (Torino-Roma, 1925), p. 184 (hereafter cited *I Canoni Penali*); Cerato, *Censurae Vigentes,* p. 82; Coronata, *loc. cit.;* Cocchi, *loc. cit.*

[16] Augustine, *A Commentary on the New Code of Canon Law,* VIII, 407.

sists in such a practice he should certainly be removed from his position.

The phraseology employed in canon 2352 has given rise to a divergency of opinion among canonists as to the precise nature and extent of the delict which falls under this penal sanction. The dispute centers around the phrase *quoquo modo cogant,* through which the lawgiver designates the precise delict which is here subject to censure. Some authors seem to be of the opinion that the term *cogant* must be restricted to moral coercion only, or fear, and hence the qualifying phrase *quoquo modo* must be understood as referring merely to the various means through which fear may be engendered for the purpose of extorting consent to entry into the religious state, i.e., by threats, blows, beatings, importunate and oft-repeated entreaties, and so forth.[17] But, as Roberti points out,[18] although this opinion is true as far as it goes, it is insufficient to explain the text of the canon. For, if it were the mind of the legislator to censure only moral coercion in this act, the word *cogant* would have been sufficient of itself and there would have been no need to add the phrase *quoquo modo,* since once fear is unjustly employed for the extorting of consent, then juridically it does not matter what concrete means may have been used for this end. Hence the addition of this phrase to the canon seems to indicate that the lawgiver had more in mind than punishing moral coercion only.

Another group of canonists interpret this phrase as embracing not only moral coercion, but physical force and fraud as well.[19]

---

[17] Vermeersch-Creusen, *Epitome Iuris Canonici,* III, 347-348. Although it is true that these authors do not explicitly exclude another interpretation, the foregoing one is the only one they offer.

[18] Roberti, "De s. ordinatione ex metu suscepta et de poenis in eos qui quoquo modo coegerint(concordia canonum 214, § 1 et 2352)," *Apollinaris,* I (1928), 49.

[19] Wernz-Vidal, *Ius Canonicum,* VII, 529; Toso, *Commentaria,* II, 92; Cocchi, *Commentarium,* VIII, 309; Beste, *Introductio in Codicem,* p. 979; Jombart, *ibidem,* p. 756; Cerato, *Censurae Vigentes,* p. 81; Cipollini, *De Censuris,* p. 190; Pistocchi, *I Canoni Penali,* pp. 182-183; Sole, *De Delictis et Poenis,* p. 326; Salucci, *Il Diritto Penale secundo il Codice di Diritto Canonico* (2 voll., Subiaco: Tipografia del Monasteri, 1926-1930), II, 239

They reason that the purpose of this censure is to penalize all those who efficaciously interfere with the liberty of any individual when giving consent to any one of the three acts mentioned in canon 2352. One must not therefore understand the phrase *quoquo modo cogant* as restricting the delictual foundation for the censure merely to the agencies of fear or physical force, but rather one must interpret these words as extending this penal sanction to all types of coercion whatsoever which may be used for inducing or restricting the consent of anyone placing one of these three acts. Hence, not only those who make use of force or fear to extort consent to entry into the novitiate are liable to censure, but also those who deliberately employ fraud to procure this same effect fall under automatic excommunication. For, they argue, it appears to involve an inexplicable antinomy in the law of the Code for it to declare the novitiate as well as the profession without juridic substance whenever consent is given to these acts because of force, fear, *or fraud,* and at the same time to declare that those who use force or fear to induce consent to these acts are liable to censure, but not those who use fraud.

Opposed to this view, however, stands another group of canonists, of equal weight and number, who argue that although the wording of this canon could be extended to embrace the interpretation given to it by the second group, strictly in view of the fact that one is here dealing with a penalty and thus must adhere to a strict interpretation,[20] one must adhere closely to the words of canon 2352, which do not include the element of fraud.[21] They

(hereafter cited *Il Diritto Penale*); Larraona, "Commentarium Codicis," *CpRM,* XVII (1936), 18; Cappello, *De Censuris,* pp. 135-136; Noldin-Schönegger, *De Poenis Ecclesiasticis* (13. ed., C. I. C. adaptata secunda, Oeniponte, 1922), p. 93.

[20] Canon 19.

[21] Blat, *Commentarium,* lib. V, 256; Augustine, *A Commentary on the New Code of Canon Law,* VIII, 407; Cappello, *Summa Iuris Canonici,* III, 568; Coronata, *Institutiones,* IV, 495; Farrugia, *Commentarium in Censuras,* p. 22; Ayrinhac-Lydon, *Penal Legislation in the New Code of Canon Law* (New York: Benziger Brothers, 1936), p. 246; Cervia, *De Professione Religiosa,* p. 175; Chelodi-Ciprotti, *Ius Canonicum de Delictis et Poenis* (Trento: Libreria Moderna Editrice, 1943), p. 114; Roberti, *ibidem,* p. 52; Pellé *Le Droit Pénal de l'Eglise* (Parisiis: P. Lethielleux, 1939), p. 385.

argue that, although a systematic ordination may seem to demand that fraud be likewise included under this censure, and the words *quoquo modo* may be construed to extend somewhat the meaning of *cogant,* since this phraseology could likewise be understood (and even more correctly without extending the accepted meaning of *cogant*) as referring to the medium through which fear is inflicted or to the persons employed for this purpose, directly or indirectly, strictly taken these words do not necessarily embrace the element of fraud.[22]

This conclusion is further borne out, they argue, by the fact that whenever, in other parallel places in the Code, the law means to include fraud as well as fear, it accurately and clearly distinguishes between them[23] or at least uses such phraseology as can be applied to both fear and fraud.[24] Hence, if the legislator had meant to include the perpetration of fraud under this canon, he could have easily intimated his mind of doing so either by clearly distinguishing between these two agencies or by using a term which is of itself applicable to both. As the canon stands in the Code one cannot consider fraud as included in its terminology except analogously. But, since one is here treating of a penalty, it is forbidden to extend the law analogously.[25] Therefore, until the legislator declares otherwise, it seems evident that the perpetration of fraud with the aim of inducing one to embrace the religious life does not render one liable to this penal sanction.

The opinion of these authors seems to the writer to be sound theoretically and safe in practice, in spite of the fact that one could argue, as indeed those who hold the second opinion do argue, that the purpose of the law is to penalize all coercion as

---

[22] Roberti, *loc. cit.*

[23] Cf., e.g., Canon 1684, § 1. Si quis motus metu gravi . . . vel *dolo circumventus* . . .; Canons 1685, § 1, and 1686 . . . metum intulit aut *dolum patravit* . . . (italics are the writer's).

[24] Cf., e.g., canon 103, § 2. Actus *positi* ex metu gravi . . . vel ex dolo . . .; Canon 185. Renuntiatio ex metu gravi . . . dolo aut errore *facta* . . . (italics supplied).

[25] Cf. canon 20; canon 2219, § 3. Non licet poenam de persona ad personam vel de casu ad casum producere, quamvis par adsit ratio, imo gravior, salvo tamen praescripto can. 2231.

long as it represents the medium through which consent is unjustly extorted. If the here delineated divergency of opinion serves any purpose, it is to demonstrate that the wording of the law is not clear. Furthermore, this interpretation is more consonant with the rules of canons 19 and 2219, § 1, *in poenis benignior est interpretatio facienda,* since it is the mild and more restrictive interpretation of a penal law. While, therefore, both views regarding the interpretation of the phrase *quoquo modo cogant* are theoretically tenable, nevertheless, in practice, the more benign may safely be followed.

In accordance with this solution, therefore, one incurs this censure whenever one forces another into religion in any manner whatsoever, whether by force or fear, whether these agencies are exerted directly or indirectly, personally or through another, as long as the used coercion, whatever its form or medium, represents the efficacious cause for which one is moved to assume the habit of a religious institute. The inflicting of a qualified reverential fear certainly suffices for the incurring of this penalty,[26] as does the unjust use of one's authority to this effect.[27] One does not incur it, on the contrary, when one counsels another to enter the religious state or exhorts one who is deliberating on taking this step, or even if one exerts some slight pressure on one who, though deliberating, is hesitant.[28]

Pellé advances the opinion that when fear is inspired for a just and serious motive, though in a blameworthy manner, there is not furnished a sufficient basis for the incurring of the censure of automatic excommunication.[29] But, as Jombart points out,[30] this opinion does not seem to have any solid foundation in the law, since all fear used for the procuring of consent to entry into religion must be branded as basically unjust. Furthermore, the canons in which invalidity is decreed to fall upon the three acts mentioned in canon 2352 use universal terminology, thus making

[26] Farrugia, *Commentarium in Censuras,* p. 22.

[27] Cipollini, *De Censuris,* p. 190.

[28] Cerato, *Censurae Vigentes,* p. 82-83; Jombart, *loc. cit.*

[29] *Le Droit Pénal de l'Eglise,* p. 385.

[30] *Loc. cit.*

all coercion exerted against an individual performing them illicit by the very fact that it is used.

According to the precise wording of canon 2352, excommunication is automatically incurred by anyone forcing another to enter *religion.* In this the present law has restricted the Tridentine law, which also included forced entry into a monastery as distinct from entry into religion.[31] By entry into religion, as here understood, according to the universal opinion of the authors,[32] the canon means entry into the canonical novitiate of a legitimately erected religious institute.[33] The reason for this is clear; one does not properly enter a religious institute until one assumes the habit of the institute. But since the habit is not assumed until one enters the novitiate itself, one cannot be said to be forced into religion until one enters the novitiate.[34] A postulant may be considered as one who is postulated as an apt candidate for admission, but who is not yet admitted.[35] He is in reality nothing more than a qualified guest, who does not enjoy the privileges and favors of the religious state.[36] Hence, even though one may force another to enter the postulancy of an institute, as long as the coercion is withdrawn at the time he is admitted into the novitiate, the delict is not complete and the consequent censure is therefore not incurred. At the same time, however, if the coercion continues to exercise at least a virtual influence upon the act of entering the canonical novitiate, the delict is present, and the censure incurred.[37]

Finally, it must be noted that canon 2352 declares that one incurs excommunication automatically only if one forces another

---

[31] Cf. *supra,* p. 37.

[32] Blat (*Commentarium,* lib. V, 256) is the only author who likewise extends this censure to forced entry into the postulancy. He draws this conclusion from the fact that the postulancy is treated under Title XI of the Code, which bears the superscription: *De admissione in religionem.* This conclusion, however, does not seem well-founded, as the arguments in the text indicate.

[33] Cf., e.g., Larraona, "Commentarium Codicis," *CpRM,* XVII (1936), 19, note 430; Schaefer, *De Religiosis,* p. 430; Coronata, *Institutiones,* IV, 496.

[34] Sole, *De Delictis et Poenis,* p. 327.

[35] Cipollini, *De Censuris,* p. 191.

[36] Regatillo, *Institutiones,* II, 419.

[37] Vermeersch-Creusen, *Epitome Iuris Canonici,* III, 348.

into *religion.* The term religion must be understood in the strict sense of this word according to canon 488, 1°, i.e., as only those societies which have been *approved* by a legitimate ecclesiastical authority, the members of which tend to evangelical perfection according to the laws proper to their society, by the profession of *public vows,* whether perpetual or temporary, the latter renewable after the lapse of a fixed time. Hence, all the various types of institutes listed under canon 488, 2°, would fall within the ambit of this censure, including religious congregations of diocesan approval. The censure, on the contrary, is not incurred by one who forces another to enter a society in which, though the common life is observed, public vows are not taken,[38] as, for example, the Congregation of the Missions or the Society of St. Philip Neri.[39] Neither is it incurred by one who forces another to enter a society which is not legitimately erected at least by the local ordinary, or which, though it was once legitimately erected, has later been suppressed.[40]

[38] Coronata, *Institutiones,* IV, 496; Blat, *Commentarium,* lib. V, 256; Cocchi, *Commentarium,* VIII, 309-310.

[39] Cocchi, *loc. cit.*

[40] Cerato, *Censurae Vigentes,* pp. 82-83.

CHAPTER XIII

Sanation and Computation of a Novitiate Affected by Fraud or Duress

As long as a candidate seeking entry into the canonical novitiate, or the superior designated to receive him, remains under the decisive influence of force, fear, or fraud, both the one and the other are juridically incapable of placing a valid act of consent for the concession or the assumption of the juridic status of the novitiate. It matters not whether either is conscious of this invalidating effect or not; ignorance of invalidating and disqualifying laws does not excuse from them, nor does it impede their effect.[1]

Since, however, these agencies, as invalidating obstacles to the inception of the canonical novitiate, are transient by their very nature, it follows that the moment they cease to impair the consent of the candidate or superior affected by them they likewise cease to be diriment impediments to this act. The question arises therefore as to whether one must consider the entire novitiate as vitiated by the very fact that these agencies have been used to influence the initial consent given to it, either on the part of the candidate or on the part of the superior, or whether one may consider the novitiate status as beginning to run with juridical effect from the moment they cease to obstruct valid consent, and the one affected by them makes a free and spontaneous choice in accepting or conceding the novitiate status. Or, more precisely, what procedure must be followed whenever it is discovered either in the course of the novitiate or after the pronouncement of religious vows that, although the initial act of consent given by a candidate or the superior at the inception of the novitiate was juridically defective in consequence of the influence of fraud or duress, these agencies either ceased entirely or at least ceased to exert a determining influence upon the consent of the one affected by them at some time during the course of the novitiate? Likewise, must the solemnities through

[1] Canon 16, § 1.

which the beginning of the novitiate year is generally signalized be repeated before the time required for the novitiate may be considered to run with legal effect? Two distinct theories are upheld among present day canonists concerning the juridical effects and the computation of the novitiate whenever it is entered upon under the decisive influence of duress or deceit.

The first of these is that advanced by Goyeneché,[2] Larraona,[3] and Berutti.[4] These authors maintain that, although the novitiate remains invalid as long as any one of the diriment impediments enumerated in the Code obstructs its legal effect, whenever it is a case of one of those impediments which may cease either through the mere passage of time or upon a simple act of spontaneous consent, the novitiate begins to run juridically from the moment it can be ascertained with moral certainty that the impediment has ceased, provided that the consent of the admitting superior was given in a valid manner in the original act of admitting the candidate, and that it indubitably perseveres. This opinion is built upon two fundamental arguments.

In the first place, so these authors argue, the act of legitimate admission into the novitiate is as a general rule entirely independent of the moment in which the novitiate status begins to run. In fact, it may be placed before the candidate is even qualified to begin the novitiate, as long as his disqualification or the impediment by which he is bound will certainly cease either through the simple passage of time or through the placing of an act of consent. This manner of arguing, they say, is perfectly legitimate, for the act of the superior in admitting a candidate is not directed so much to his qualifications at the time at which it is placed as it is to that time at which the novitiate status begins to run with legal effect. Once, therefore, the superior has done all that is necessary on his

---

[2] "Consultationes," *CpR,* IV (1923), 222-224; "Consultationes," *CpRM,* XXII (1941), 80-81.

[3] "Commentarium Codicis," *CpRM,* XVII (1936), 9; "Commentarium Codicis," *CpRM,* XXII (1941), 121, 122, 126.

[4] *Institutiones,* III, 149. This opinion is likewise advanced by Vidal, Schaefer, and Cocchi, but these authors confine their observations to the impediment of nonage. Cf. Wernz-Vidal, *Ius Canonicum,* III, 197; Schaefer, *De Religiosis,* p. 427; Cocchi, *Commentarium,* IV, 120.

part for the valid admission of a candidate, and his consent is not revoked before the time at which the candidate becomes qualified to assume the novitiate status validly, the superior's consent obtains its full effect from the moment the candidate becomes qualified, apart from every necessity for the superior to place a new act of consent or to ratify the one already placed. For once the superior performs all that is required by the law for the valid inception of the novitiate, his will to effectuate it must be considered as persevering at least virtually during the entire time the candidate remains in the novitiate, unless there are positive indications to the contrary.[5]

In the second place, so they argue, according to the present law neither the investiture ceremony itself nor any other solemnity through which the inception of the canonical novitiate is usually signalized is required for its validity. Although it is true that canon 553 states: "Novitiatus incipit susceptione habitus, vel alio modo in constitutionibus praescripto," this canon does not contain any clause which is either explicitly or implicitly invalidating in effect.[6] Hence, even though these solemnities are not complied with in a certain instance, neither the inception nor the prosecution of the novitiate would be vitiated thereby. All that is required to effect the novitiate status validly is that the superior freely concede it on the one hand, and that the candidate freely accept it on the other.[7]

---

[5] Goyeneché, "Consultationes," *CpRM,* XXII (1941), 80.

[6] Canon 11.

[7] Approved authors before the present Code disputed the point as to whether the reception of the habit or other solemnities prescribed by the constitutions or by custom were necessary for the validity of the inception of the novitiate. Suarez (tr. VII, *De religione,* lib. 5, c. 13, n. 6—*Opera Omnia,* XV, 359), Pirhing (*Jus Canonicum,* lib. III, tit. 31, n. 29), and Wernz (*Ius Decretalium,* III, 305) defended the view that the solemnities which usually signalized the beginning of the novitiate were only accidental to its validity, and that nothing more was required than that the superior admit the candidate on the one hand, and that the candidate place himself in those circumstances in which the novitiate was to be made and freely give his consent to it, on the other hand. Reiffenstuel (*Ius Canonicum,* lib. III, tit. 31, n. 92) and Schmalzgrueber (*Ius Ecclesiasticum,* lib. III, tit. 31, nn. 56, 57, 58) favored the view that the reception of the habit or the other solemnities

Now, once the superior has intimated his intention of receiving a candidate by placing the formal act through which his consent is externally made manifest, whether or not the candidate places his consent simultaneously or at a later time seems not to make any essential difference as far as the legal requirements for valid entry into the novitiate are concerned. As long as the superior's consent is validly intimated, and at least virtually perseveres, it seems that the novitiate must be considered as running validly from the moment the impediment obstructing the novice's consent disappears and he gives his consent freely. For once he has done so, all that is required for the valid inception of the novitiate has been realized.

Since the solemnities indicating the beginning of the novitiate are only accidental in nature, nothing more need be proved, it seems, beyond the fact that the candidate did give deliberate and spontaneous consent at some moment, and the novitiate may be computed from that time. The effect of the diriment impediments which have been established in the Code is therefore like to that of a *conditio sine qua non* which is placed in a contract; the moment the condition is verified, the contract takes effect.[8] Hence, as soon as the impediment ceases, by that very fact the subsequent portion of the novitiate begins to run validly. Whenever, therefore, one is admitted into the canonical novitiate invalidly as a result of the influences of grave duress or deceit, the moment one gives consent freely to this act the noviceship may be considered as running validly, provided the will of the superior may be presumed to persevere at least virtually.[9]

---

mentioned in the constitutions were necessary for the valid inception of the novitiate. They based their opinion upon the declaration of the Council of Trent (Conc. Trident., sess. XXV, *de regularibus,* c. 15) to the effect that the novitiate began with the reception of the habit. But as Larraona points out, the Council of Trent did not state that the reception of the habit was required for valid entry into the novitiate, and today it is commonly held that these solemnities are not required for the valid inception of this status. Cf. Larraona, "Commentarium Codicis," *CpRM,* XXII (1941), 121, note 871.

[8] Goyeneché, *ibidem,* pp. 80-81; Larraona, *ibidem,* p. 126.

[9] Berutti, *Institutiones,* III, 149.

The second opinion is that advanced by Coronata,[10] Oesterle,[11] and Blat,[12] who maintain that the novitiate status cannot be considered as having been juridically conceded as long as the novice is hindered from entering upon it because of a diriment impediment, and that therefore the time for the novitiate cannot be computed unless there is another clear manifestation of consent in the external forum according to the prescribed formula, after the impediment has ceased or a dispensation from it has been granted. Coronata argues that, whenever a diriment impediment is present at the time a novice is admitted into the novitiate, not only the beginning but the entire novitiate as well as the subsequent profession is rendered invalid, since that which is invalid from the beginning does not become valid through the mere passage of time. Hence, if it is discovered during the course of the novitiate, or after the profession of vows, that one of the invalidating impediments was present at the beginning of the novitiate, though it ceased at a later time, the entire novitiate must be begun over and the solemnities signifying its inception must again be placed before it may be considered as running with juridical effect. He argues against the opinion of Larraona and Goyeneche by saying that one cannot appeal to the interpretative will of the superior by maintaining that he certainly wished to fulfill all that was required by the law of the Church in giving his consent to the admission of a candidate; this presumption must yield to the truth, and the truth remains, namely that in admitting a candidate contrary to the law of the Church the superior has placed an act which is without juridic effect, regardless of whether he was in good faith or bad.[13]

Oesterle concurs with this opinion of Coronata and argues that the manner of conceding the juridic status of the novitiate is not left to the superior to decide, but that the novitiate must be considered as beginning to run with legal effect only when the habit is in fact imposed, or the other formalities of the constitutions are placed. Hence, if these formalities are lacking, the novitiate does

---

[10] *Institutiones,* I, 713.

[11] *Praelectiones Iuris Canonici,* I, 304.

[12] *Commentarium,* lib. II, partes II et III, 327-328.

[13] Coronata, *loc. cit.*

not begin to run with legal effect, and since that which is not valid from the beginning cannot become valid except through revalidation or sanation by the Roman Pontiff himself, the entire novitiate must be considered without juridic effect. Whenever, therefore, a superior admits a candidate who is bound by a diriment impediment that is transient in nature, one cannot consider the former reception as becoming effective from the moment the impediment ceases, but a new reception is required before the novitiate becomes valid before the law.[14] In support of this argument he appeals to a decree given by the Sacred Congregation of the Council, issued on May 17, 1919,[15] concerning the invalidity of legal transactions performed in opposition to canon 1532 with regard to the alienation of ecclesiastical property. In this decree it is indicated that whenever one of the solemnities required for the validity of a transaction is lacking, it cannot be revalidated except through a new act of consent legitimately manifested.

This opinion of Oesterle and Coronata would certainly be true if the formalities which usually accompany the inception of the novitiate were required for its validity. Canon 1680 explicitly declares that an act is to be considered without juridic substance whenever either the essential constituent elements of the act are wanting, or the solemnities required by the law under pain of invalidity are not complied with. But it must be noted that according to the common opinion among canonists today the law does not require any particular solemnities as essential to the valid inception of the novitiate over and beyond the simple manifestation of consent on the part of the superior and the candidate. Hence it seems that the opinion advanced by Goyeneché, Larraona, and Berutti is solidly probable and may acceptably be used in practice until the Holy See definitely decides the matter otherwise. Since no special solemnity other than the agreement of the superior and the candidate is required for beginning the novitiate validly, it is not unreasonable to assume that the time of the noviceship may be computed validly from the moment consent is given freely by both of them. Only when a formal investiture with the religious garb

---

[14] Oesterle, *loc. cit.*

[15] S. C. C., decr. *Albiganen. et Aliarum, Sanationis Alienationum,* 17 maii 1919—*AAS,* XI (1919), 382-387.

is required by the particular constitutions for the valid inception of the novitiate would this position be untenable.[16] And Larraona observes that it is the practice of the Holy See not to permit the constitutions to require this act for the validity of the novitiate.[17]

This opinion would have special application whenever it is ascertained near the completion of the canonical novitiate that the novice did in fact give valid consent after he had spent some time in the novitiate. It would be of value especially in those institutes in which a second, or constitutional, year of novitiate is required by the particular constitutions. Thus if one would allow the canonical year to run from the day valid consent is given, there would never be any question about the validity of the novitiate in the case in which the second, or constitutional, year is required only as a prerequisite for the licitness of the profession. But if both years are required by the constitutions for the validity of the profession, it is obvious that any overlapping of the two periods would require a corresponding postponement of the profession, under peril of invalidating the profession. Even in the case in which the second, or constitutional, year is not required for the validity of profession, the novice who is delayed because of the invalidity of the first portion of his novitiate cannot be lawfully professed with the other members of his class without a dispensation. His profession, however, would be validly made were no such a dispensation obtained.

Whenever the invalidity of the novitiate is discovered only after the pronouncement of religious vows, or whenever serious doubts arise concerning its validity, the norms of canon 586 then become operative. Since the lack of validity in the canonical novitiate constitutes an external impediment to the valid profession of vows, a simple renovation of vows, whether juridic or devotional, would not suffice in itself to convalidate the original act of profession, even though perhaps the person may have spent a long period of time in the religious state in good faith. For here it is entirely proper to apply the rule of law to the effect that that which is invalid from the beginning does not become valid through the mere passage of time,[18] since the validity of the canonical novitiate is an

---

[16] Blat, *Commentarium,* lib. II, partes II et III, 327.

[17] "Commentarium Codicis," *CpRM,* XXII (1941), 122.

[18] Reg. 18, R. J., in VI°.

essential element to the validity of the religious profession.[19] The juridic renovation of the profession effects a convalidation only when the superior and the candidate know of the impediment and remove it or have it sanated beforehand. This renovation, however, must not only be an act of simple confirmation of the previous profession, but it must be a totally new act diverse from the former profession, and its effects arise as of the time at which it is made, and not from the time of the former profession.[20]

Whenever the profession is rendered null and void for the fact that force, fear, or fraud vitiated a portion of the novitiate, but did not affect the profession itself, one may have recourse to the Holy See for a sanation of the original act of admission, or for a dispensation from the complete performance of the novitiate and a sanation of the profession. This petition may be sent either by the religious himself or by the institute. If the institute foresees that knowledge of the invalidity of the profession may unduly disturb the religious in question, then, as long as from all appearances his consent continues, one may petition a sanation even unknown to him.[21] Unless a *sanatio in radice* is obtained, however, both the profession and the entire novitiate must be repeated.[22]

Whenever an individual is certain that his profession is invalid, but he cannot prove its invalidity in the external forum, some authors are of the opinion that he is not bound either to renew his profession or to petition a sanation *in radice*.[23] Bidagor, however, is of the opinion that one must petition the Sacred Penitentiary under such circumstances to obtain a sanation in the internal forum.[24] In practice it seems that this opinion is the better one to follow, lest subjective conviction of the invalidity of the profession give rise to scruples.

Whenever the profession is dubiously valid for the reason that there are grave arguments against the validity of the novitiate, the

---

[19] Coronata, *Institutiones,* I, 767.

[20] Schaefer, *De Religiosis,* p. 585.

[21] Schaefer, *De Religiosis,* p. 586.

[22] Wernz-Vidal, *Ius Canonicum,* III, 287.

[23] Schaefer, *De Religiosis,* p. 587; Coronata, *Institutiones,* I, 769.

[24] "De dolo et eius effectibus in admissione ad novitiatum et professione religiosa," *Periodica,* XX (1931), 73*.

Code orders the religious in question either to repeat the novitiate and the profession, or at least to obtain a sanation from the Holy See *ad cautelam.* If, however, he refuses to repeat the novitiate and the profession or to seek a sanation *ad cautelam,* the case must be referred to the Holy See for its examination and decision.[25] Merely subjective doubts, however, must be disregarded; only when objective and probable doubts arise may one attack the validity of the profession, since its validity must be presumed until its invalidity is proved with certainty. Whenever there arises the case of a dubious profession as the result of a novitiate which itself was of dubious value, and the religious refuses to petition a sanation or to repeat his profession, the institute cannot petition a sanation unknown to him, and it would in fact be invalid if it were petitioned without his consent, or at least if he did not accept it after it had been petitioned for him.[26]

The reception of a public status in the Church through the pronouncement of public vows demands that there be a declaration by a public authority to the effect that the status was not validly assumed, whenever such is the case.[27] Hence, before an individual may leave the religious institute, a formal juridical declaration concerning the invalidity of his profession must be made. This declaration may be made by the major religious superior, if the institute in question is an exempt clerical institute, or by the local ordinary, if it is not an exempt institute. The nullity of the profession need not be established judicially; it suffices that moral certainty be obtained in any manner whatsoever, v.g., through a simple consideration of the facts of the case.[28] Although one may, in the case of a controversy, institute a process that is patterned on that which is used for establishing the invalidity of the marriage bond, authors generally recommend that one simply refer the case to the Holy See for its consideration and subsequent decision.[29]

---

[25] Canon 586, § 3.

[26] Coronata, *Institutiones,* I, 768; Schaefer, *De Religiosis,* p. 587.

[27] Wernz-Vidal, *Ius Canonicum,* III, 286.

[28] Coronata, *loc. cit.;* Schaefer, *loc. cit.;* Vermeersch-Creusen, *Epitome Iuris Canonici,* I, 552; Wernz-Vidal, *Ius Canonicum,* III, 285; Goyeneché, "Consultationes," *CpR,* VI (1925), 88-90.

[29] Cappello, *Summa Iuris Canonici,* II, 69; Wernz-Vidal, *ibidem,* pp. 287-291; Goyeneché, *ibidem,* p. 90.

CONCLUSIONS

The following conclusions are offered as justified by the present study:

1. The historical evolution of the impediment of force, fear, and fraud, establishes the fact that the fundamental reasons for which the Church legislates against coerced entry into religion are: (a) to protect the full liberty of the individual who assumes the grave obligations of this state, and (b) to preclude the unhappy effects which are usually consequent upon coerced acceptance of these obligations.

2. Otherwise than with relation to the act of religious profession, the nullifying effects of duress and deceit upon the act of entering the canonical novitiate are derived solely from the positive ecclesiastical law.

3. The novitiate is rendered invalid through force, fear, or fraud not only when these agencies are used by a superior or a candidate one against the other, but likewise whenever they are employed by an extraneous person against either one or both of them, unknown to, or even contrary to, the will of the one benefited by their use.

4. Only that fear which is inflicted by another human agent is of any juridical consequence. Hence, fear inspired by any other cause than a free human agent does not invalidate the canonical novitiate.

5. The judicial and juridical doctrine concerning the element of gravity in juridically relevant fear with relation to the nullity of the marriage contract is applicable with equal scope and effect to the nullity of the act of entering the religious state.

6. Although the law postulates that fear represents an unjust violation of the rights of the individual seeking entry into religion before it invalidates his action, it has in effect declared all fear used for influencing consent to this act as essentially unjust.

7. It is probable that the novitiate is rendered invalid not only when consent given to it, either by a candidate or the admitting superior, represents the product of direct coercion, but likewise

whenever it is the indirect result of fear, i.e., when the aggressor inspiring the fear has no intention of forcing the individual to choose this particular act.

8. In order that a juridic act may be considered as automatically invalid, or as liable to rescission, on the count of fraud, one must conclusively prove through moral arguments based upon conjectures and presumptions that the act was in fact the result of an erroneous judgment which was fraudulently created by the intentional maneuvers of another.

9. Whenever a candidate is led to seek entry into religion while under the influence of substantial deception concerning the nature of the novitiate or the religious state, his novitiate is rendered automatically invalid not only by reason of the positive law, but by reason of the natural law as well.

10. Fraud is substantial whenever it affects the general principles of the religious state, such as its essential means, its primary purpose, its fundamental obligations, its permanence, or its necessity.

11. The novitiate is rendered automatically invalid not only when a candidate enters upon it while under the substantial deception, but also whenever he is led to seek entry into the novitiate under the preponderant influence of accidental fraud. Fraudulent error is the decisive reason for consent whenever the candidate is of the mind and will at the time of his entry that, were the error dispelled or the truth known, he would certainly not have entered.

12. Whenever the admitting superior is induced to receive a candidate through substantial deception, the novitiate is null and void not only by reason of the positive law, but also by reason of the natural law. Fraudulent deception is substantial on the part of the superior if it results in an error concerning the person admitted, or concerning some substantial quality which redounds to an error concerning the person, or if he is induced into error concerning the class of religious into which the candidate was received.

13. The canonical novitiate is rendered automatically invalid by reason of canon 542, 1°, not only when a superior acts through substantial deception, but also whenever fraudulent accidental error is the antecedent reason for which he is induced to receive a candidate whom he otherwise would have rejected.

14. In the absence of any positive declaration to the contrary, one must generally presume that a superior, in receiving candidates into the novitiate, is of the mind and will not to receive them whenever they are impeded by reason either of the positive law or of the particular constitutions, unless a dispensation has previously been obtained from these impediments.

15. It seems certain that the invalidating effects of fraud extend to the case in which one of the impediments or irregularities barring the reception of orders is deliberately concealed with the aim of obtaining admission into a clerical institute as a candidate for orders.

16. It seems certain that the invalidating effects of fraud extend likewise to the case in which qualities of morals, intellect, or health which are demanded by the institute of those who seek entry into it are notably misrepresented or obscured.

17. The opinion of those authors who hold that the terminology of canon 2352 does not include the element of fraud is solidly probable. Therefore, one does not incur automatic excommunication whenever he has used fraud to induce another to enter the religious state.

18. Although the novitiate remains invalid so long as force, fear, or fraud continues to affect the consent of a candidate or the superior, it is probable that it begins to run with legal effect from the moment these agencies cease entirely, or at least cease to exert a determining influence, and the one affected by them places an act of free and spontaneous consent.

19. Whenever the novitiate is rendered invalid through the presence of an invalidating impediment, it is not necessary, after the impediment has ceased or a dispensation from it has been granted, to repeat the solemnities through which its inception is usually signalized, unless these solemnities are required for the validity of the novitiate by the particular constitutions of the institute.

BIBLIOGRAPHY

Sources

Acta Apostolicae Sedis, Commentarium Officiale, Romae, 1909-

Bruns, H. T., *Canones Apostolorum et Conciliorum Saeculorum IV-VII,* 2 voll., Berolini, 1839.

Codicis Iuris Canonici Fontes, cura Emi Petri Card. Gasparri editi, 9 voll., Romae (postea Civitate Vaticana) : Typis Polyglottis Vaticanis, 1923-1939. (Voll. VII-IX, ed. cura et studio Emi Iustiniani Card. Serédi).

Collectanea S. Congregationis de Propaganda Fide, 2 voll., Romae: Typographia Polyglotta Vaticana, 1907.

Concilii Tridentini Diariorum, Actorum, Epistularum, Tractatuum, Nova Collectio, 13 voll., Friburgi Brisgoviae: Herder, 1901-, Vol. IX, *Pars Sexta Actorum,* collegit, illustravit, edidit Stephanus Ehses, 1924.

Constitutiones Fratrum, Discalceatorum Ordinis Sanctissimae Trinitatis, Isola del Liri: Soc. Tip. A. Macioce et Pisani, 1933.

Constitutiones Fratrum S. Ordinis Praedicatorum, Romae: apud Domum Generalitiam, 1932.

Constitutiones Ordinis Eremitarum S. Augustini, Romae: Typis Polyglottis Vaticanis, 1926.

Constitutiones Ordinis Recollectorum Sancti Augustini, Romae: Typographia Augustiniana, 1937.

Corpus Iuris Canonici, editio Lipsiensis secunda post Aemilii Ludovici Richter curas . . . instruxit Aemilius Friedberg, 2 voll., Lipsiae, 1879-1881. Editio anastatice repetita, Lipsiae: Tauchnitz, 1928.

Jaffé, Philippus, *Regesta Pontificum Romanorum ab condita Ecclesia ad annum post Christum natum MCXCVIII,* 2. ed., correctam et auctam auspiciis Gulielmi Wattenbach curaverunt S. Loewenfeld, F. Kaltenbrunner, P. Ewald, 2 voll., Lipsiae, 1885-1888.

Mansi, J. D., *Sacrorum Conciliorum Nova et Amplissima Collectio,* 53 voll. in 60, Parisiis, Leipzig, Arnhem, 1901-1927.

Monumenta Germaniae Historica, Legum Sectio II, Capitularia Regum Francorum, 2 toms in 5 voll., ed. A. Boretius et V. Krause, Hannoverae, 1883-1897.

———, *Legum Sectio III, Concilia,* 2 voll. in 4, ed. F. Maassen, A. Werminghoff, H. Bastgen, Hannoverae-Lipsiae, 1893-1924.

Potthast, Augustus, *Regesta Pontificum Romanorum inde ab anno Post Christum Natum MCXCVIII ad annum MCCCIV,* 2 voll., Berolini, 1874-1875.

Rule and General Constitutions of the Friars Minor, The, Paterson, New Jersey: St. Anthony Guild Press, 1936.

Sacrae Romanae Rotae Decisiones seu Sententiae, quae iuxta Legem Propriam et Constitutionem "Sapienti Consilio" Pii PP. X prodierunt, cura eiusdem S. Tribunalis editae, Romae, 1912-

Schroeder, H. J., *Canons and Decrees of the Council of Trent, Text, Translation and Commentary,* St. Louis-London: B. Herder and Co., 1941.

Reference Works

Andreae, Joannes, *In Sex Decretalium Libros Novella Commentaria,* 6 voll. in 5, Venetiis, 1581.

Augustine, Charles, *A Commentary on the New Code of Canon Law,* 8 vols., Vols. II and III, 1. ed., Vol. VIII, 2. ed., St. Louis: B. Herder, 1919-1924.

Ayrinhac, H. A.-Lydon, P. J., *Penal Legislation in the New Code of Canon Law,* New York: Benziger Brothers, 1936.

Azo, *Summa Codicis,* Venetiis, 1530.

Barbosa, A., *Collectanea Doctorum tam Veterum quam Recentiorum in Jus Pontificium Universum,* 6 voll. in 3, Lugduni, 1637.

Bastien, Pierre, *Directoire Canonique à l'Usage des Congrégations à Voeux Simples,* 3. ed., Bruges: Beyaert, 1923.

Benedictus XIV, *De Synodo Dioecesana,* 4 voll., Mechliniae, 1842.

Berutti, Christophorus, *Institutiones Iuris Canonici,* 6 voll., Voll. II, III et VI, Taurini-Romae: Marietti, 1936-1943.

Beste, Udalricus, *Introductio in Codicem,* 3. ed., Collegeville: St. John's Abbey Press, 1946.

Biederlack, J.-Führich, M., *De Religiosis,* Oeniponte, 1919.

Blat, Albertus, *Commentarium Textus Codicis Iuris Canonici,* 5 voll. in 7, Romae: apud "Angelicum," 1921-1938. Lib. I, 1921; lib. II, ed. altera, 1921; lib. II, partes II et III, 3. ed., 1938; lib. III, pars I, 2. ed. aucta et emendata, 1924; lib. III, partes II-VI, 2. ed., 1934; lib. IV, 1927; lib. V, 1924.

Bouix, Dominicus, *Tractatus de Jure Regularium,* 5 tom. in 2 voll., Parisiis, 1857.

Bouquillon, T., *Theologica Moralis Fundamentalis,* Brugis, 1890.

Bouscaren, T. L.-Ellis, Adam C., *Canon Law, a Text and Commentary,* Milwaukee: Bruce Publishing Co., 1949.

Bouscaren, T. L., *The Canon Law Digest,* 2 vols. and Supplement through 1948, Milwaukee: Bruce Publishing Co., 1934, 1943, 1949.

Brys, J., *Juris Canonici Compendium,* 10. ed., 2 voll., Brugis: Desclée, De Brouwer et Sii., 1947-1949.

Butler, Cuthbert, *Benedictine Monachism,* London: Longmans, Green and Co., 1919.

Butler, E. C., *Sancti Benedicti Regula Monasteriorum,* 2. ed., Friburgi Brisgoviae: Herder, 1927.

Cappello, Felix M., *De Censuris,* Augustae Taurinorum, 1919.

———, *Summa Iuris Canonici,* 3 voll., Voll. I et II, 4. ed., Vol. III, 3. ed., Romae: apud Aedes Universitatis Gregorianae, 1945-1948.

———, *Tractatus Canonico-Moralis de Sacramentis,* 3 voll. in 5, Vol. III, 3. ed., Augustae Taurinorum-Romae: Marietti, 1933.

Cerato, Prosdocimus, *Censurae Vigentes Ipso Facto a Codice Iuris Canonici Excerptae,* 2. ed., Patavii: Typis Seminarii, 1921.

Cervia, Eugenius, *De Professione Religiosa,* Faventiae: apud Societatem Thypographicam Faventinam, 1938.

Chelodi, J.-Ciprotti, P., *Ius Canonicum de Delictis et Poenis,* Trento: Libreria Moderna Editrice, 1943.

———, *Ius Canonicum de Matrimonio,* 5. ed., Vicenza: Societa Anonima Tipografica Editrice, 1947.

———, *Ius Canonicum de Personis,* 3. ed., Vicenza-Trento: Libreria Moderna Editrice, 1942.

Cipollini, A., *De Censuris Latae Sententiae iuxta Codicem Iuris Canonici,* Taurini, 1925.

Cocchi, Guidus, *Commentarium in Codicem Iuris Canonici,* 8 voll. in 5, Voll. II, III, IV et VIII, 4. ed., Vol. VII, 3. ed., Augustae Taurinorum: Marietti, 1937-1947.

Coronata, P. Matthaeus Conte a, *Institutiones Iuris Canonici,* 5 voll., Voll. I, II, III et IV, 2. ed., Taurini: Marietti, 1936-1945.

Creusen, J., *Religieux et Religieuses d'après le Droit Ecclésiastique,* 3. ed., Bruxelles-Parisiis: Beauchesne, 1924.

———, *Religious Men and Women in the Code,* translated by Edward Garasché, 4. Eng. ed. by Adam Ellis, Milwaukee: Bruce Publishing Co., 1942.

Davis, H., *Moral and Pastoral Theology,* 4 vols., New York: Sheed and Ward, 1935.

Delatte, P., *A Commentary on the Rule of St. Benedict,* New York: Benziger, 1921.

De Lugo, Joannes, *Opera Omnia,* 7 voll., editio summo studio et diligentia mendis expurgata, Tom. I, *De Justitia et Jure,* Venetiis, 1718.

De Meester, A., *Juris Canonici et Juris Canonico-civilis Compendium,* 3 voll. in 4, Vol. II, editio nova, Brugis: Desclée et Sii., 1923.

Deroux, M., *Les Origines de l'Oblature Bénédictine,* Vienne, 1927.

Dictionnaire d'Archéologie Chrétienne et de Liturgie, Parisiis: Letouzey et Ané, 1907-

Dictionnaire de Droit Canonique, publié sous la direction de R. Naz, 10 voll. ou 60 fascicules, Parisiis: Letouzey et Ané, 1924-

Eltz, Anthony, *Cooperation in Crime,* The Catholic University of America Canon Law Studies, n. 156, Washington, D. C.: The Catholic University of America Press, 1942.

Fagnanus, Prosper, *Commentaria in Quinque Libros Decretalium,* 4 voll., Venetiis, 1692.

Fanfani, Ludovicus, *De Iure Religiosorum ad Normam Iuris Canonici,* 2. ed., Taurini-Romae: Marietti, 1925.

Farrugia, Nicholaus, *Commentarium in Censuras Latae Sententiae Codicis Juris Canonici,* Militae, 1921.

Fransen, Gerard, *Le dol dans la conclusion des actes juridiques,* dissertationes ad gradum magistri in Facultate Theologica vel in Facultate Juris Canonici consequendum conscriptae, series II, n. 37, Gembloux: Duculot, 1946.

Gasparri, Petri Card., *Schema Codicis Iuris Canonici,* 4 toms in 2 voll., Romae: Typis Polyglottis Vaticanis, 1913.

———, *Tractatus Canonicus de Matrimonio,* 2 voll., editio nova, Romae: Typis Polyglottis Vaticanis, 1932.

Giacchi, Orio, *La violenza nel negozio giuridico canonico,* Milano: Dott. A. Giuffrè, 1937.

Gonzalez-Tellez, Manuel, *Commentaria Perpetua in Singulos Textus Quinque Librorum Decretalium,* 5 voll. in 4, Venetiis, 1699.

Goyeneche, S., *Iuris Canonici Summa Principia de Religiosis,* Romae: Tip. Pol. "Cuore di Maria," 1938.

Guido de Baysio, *Rosarium seu in Decretorum Volumen Commentaria,* Venetiis, 1577.

Hess, Bede, *Manuale de Regula et Constitutionibus Ordinis Fratrum Minorum Conventualium,* Romae: Typis Polyglottis Vaticanis, 1943.

Hostiensis [Henricus de Segusio], *Commentaria in Quinque Libros Decretalium,* 5 voll. in 3, Venetiis, 1581.

———, *Summa Aurea,* Venetiis, 1570.

Innocent IV, *Commentaria in Quinque Libros Decretalium et in Decretales Suas,* Augustae Taurinorum, 1581.

Jardí, Antonio de la C., *El Derecho de las Religiosas,* 2. ed., Vich: Editorial Seráfica, 1927.

Kirchenlexikon, 2. ed., 12 voll., et Index, Freiburg im Breisgau: Herder, 1882-1903.

Kuttner, Stephan, *Kanonistische Schuldlehre von Gratian bis auf die Dekretalen Gregors IX, Studi e Testi,* n. 64, Città del Vaticano: Biblioteca Apostolica Vaticana, 1935.

Marc, C., *Institutiones Morales Alphonsionae,* 18. ed., 2 voll., Lugduni, 1927.

Maroto, Philippus, *Institutiones Iuris Canonici,* 2 voll., Vol. I, 3. ed., Romae: apud "Commentarium pro Religiosis," 1921.

Mayer, Heinrich, *Benediktinisches Ordensrecht in der Beuroner Kongregation,* 3 voll., Beuron: Kunstverlag Hohenzollern, 1929-1936.

McLaughlin, Terence, *Le très ancien droit monastique de l'Occident,* Vienne-Parisiis: A. Picard, 1935.

Merkelbach, Benedictus H., *Summa Theologiae Moralis,* 3. ed., 3 voll., Parisiis, 1938.

Michiels, Gommarus, *De Delictis et Poenis,* Vol. I, *De Delictis,* Lublin: Universitas Catholica, 1934.

———, *Normae Generales Juris Canonici,* 2. ed., 2 voll., Parisiis-Tornaci-Romae: Desclée et Socii, 1949.

———, *Principia Generalia de Personis in Ecclesia,* Lublin, Polonia: Universitas Catholica, 1932.

Migne, J. P., *Patrologiae Cursus Completus, Series Latina* (*MPL*), 221 voll., Parisiis, 1844-1864; *Series Graeca* (*MPG*), 161 voll., Parisiis, 1857-1866.

Noldin, H., *Summa Theologiae Moralis,* 5. ed., 3 voll., Ratisbonae, Romae, et Neo Eboraci, 1904.

Noldin, H.-Schönegger, A., *De Poenis Ecclesiasticis,* 13. ed. (C. I. C. adaptata secunda), Oeniponte, 1922.

Noval, J., *Commentarium Codicis Iuris Canonici,* Liber IV, *De Processibus,* 2 voll., Vol. I, Augustae Taurinorum-Romae: Marietti, 1920.

Oesterle, Gerardus, *Praelectiones Iuris Canonici,* Vol. I, Romae: apud Collegium S. Anselmi, 1931.

Ojetti, B., *Commentarium in Codicem Iuris Canonici,* 4 voll., Vol. II, Romae: apud Aedes Universitatis Gregorianae, 1928.

———, *Synopsis Rerum Moralium et Juris Pontificii,* 4 voll., Romae: 1909-1914.

Panormitanus [Nicolaus de Tudeschis], *Commentaria in Quinque Libros Decretalium,* 5 voll. in 7, Venetiis, 1588.

Payen, G., *De Matrimonio in Missionibus,* 3 voll., Vol. II, 2. ed., Zi-Ka-Wei: Typographia T'ou-se-we, 1936.

Pejška, Joseph, *Jus Canonicum Religiosorum,* 3. ed., Friburgi Brisgoviae: Herder, 1927.

Pellé, Abbe P., *Le Droit Pénal de l'Eglise,* Parisiis: P. Lethielleux, 1939.

Pennafort, S. Raymundus, *Summa Juris Canonici,* Veronae, 1744.

Petrovits, J. J. C., *The New Church Law on Matrimony,* Philadelphia: John J. McVey, 1919.

Piatus, Montensis, *Praelectiones Juris Regularis ad Usum Fratrum Minorum Ordinis S. Francisci Capuccinorum,* 3 voll., Parisiis, 1888-1891.

Pirhing, Ernricus, *Jus Canonicum Nova Methodo Explicatum, Omnibus Capitulis Titulorum,* 4 voll., Dilingae, 1722.

Pistocchi, M., *I Canoni Penali del Codice Ecclesiastico,* Torino-Roma, 1925.

Prümmer, Dominicus, *Manuale Iuris Canonici,* 4. ed., Friburgi Brisgoviae: Herder and Co., 1927.

Regatillo, Edwardus, *Institutiones Iuris Canonici,* 2 voll., Vol. I, 2. ed., Vol. II, 1. ed., Santander: Sal Terrae, 1942-1946.

———, *Ius Sacramentarium,* 2 voll., Santander: Sal Terrae, 1945-1946.

Reiffenstuel, Anacletus, *Ius Canonicum Universum,* 5 voll. in 7, Parisiis, 1864-1870.

Roberti, Franciscus, *De Processibus,* 2 voll., Vol. I, 2. ed., Romae: apud Custodiam Librariam Pontificii Instituti Utriusque Iuris, 1941.

Rufinus, *Die Summa Decretorum,* ed. H. Singer, Paterborn, 1902.

Salucci, Raffael, *Il Diritto Penale secundo Il Codice di Diritto Canonico,* 2 voll., Subiaco: Tipografia del Monasteri, 1926-1930.

Sanchez, Thomas, *Disputatio de Sancto Matrimonii Sacramento,* 3 voll., Antverpiae, 1607.

Schaefer, Timotheus, *De Religiosis ad Normam Codicis Iuris Canonici,* 4. ed., Città del Vaticano: Typis Polyglottis Vaticanis, 1947.

Schmalzgrueber, Franciscus, *Ius Ecclesiasticum Universum,* 5 voll. in 12, Romae, 1843-1845.

Schroll, M. Alfred, Sr., *Benedictine Monasticism as Reflected in the Warnefrid-Hildemar Commentaries on the Rule,* New York: Columbia University Press, 1941.

Sole, Iacobus, *De Delictis et Poenis,* Romae: Pustet, 1920.

Suarez, Franciscus, *Opera Omnia,* ed. nova a Carolo Berton, 28 voll., Parisiis, 1856-1878.

Thomae, S., Aquinatis Doctoris Angelici Opera Omnia iussu impensaque Leonis XIII, P. M. edita, Romae, 1882-; *Summa Theologica,* Romae, 1888-1906.

Thomassinus, Ludovicus, *Vetus et Nova Ecclesiae Disciplina circa Beneficia et Beneficiarios,* ed. postrema, cum Parisiensi accuratissime collata, 10 voll., Magontiaci, 1787.

Toso, Albertus, *Ad Codicem Iuris Canonici Commentaria Minora,* 5 voll., Voll. II et V, Romae: apud "Jus Pontificium," 1922-1927.

Van Hove, A., *Commentarium Lovaniense in Codicem Iuris Canonici,* Vol. I, Tom. I, *Prolegomena ad Codicis Iuris Canonici,* 2. ed., Mechliniae-Romae: H. Dessain, 1945; Tom. IV, *De Rescriptis,* Mechliniae-Romae: H. Dessain, 1936.

Vermeersch, A.-Creusen, J., *Epitome Iuris Canonici,* 3 voll., Voll. II et III, 6. ed., Vol. I, 7. ed., Mechliniae-Romae: H. Dessain, 1940-1949.

Victorius ab Appeltern, *Compendium Praelectionum Juris Regularis,* editio altera et emendata, Parisiis-Tornaci, 1913.

Vlaming, T. M., *Praelectiones Iuris Matrimonii,* 2 voll., Vol. II, 3. ed., Bussum in Hollandia: Paulus Brand, 1921.

Wernz, Franciscus, *Ius Decretalium ad Usum Praelectionum in Scholis Textus Canonici sive Iuris Decretalium,* 6 voll., in 10, Romae-Prati, 1898-1914.

Wernz, F.-Vidal, P., *Ius Canonicum ad Codicis Normam Exactum,* 7 voll. in 8, Voll. III et VII, 1. ed., Vol. VI, 2. ed., Voll. II et V, 3. ed., Romae: apud Aedes Universitatis Gregorianae, 1933-1949.

Articles

Allers, Rudolph, "Some medico-psychological remarks on canons 1068, 1081, and 1087," *The Jurist,* IV (1944), 351-380.

(Anonymous), "Consultationes," *Jus Pontificium,* III (1923), 150.

Badii, Caesare, "Il dolo nel Codice di Diritto Canonico," *Il Diritto Ecclesiastico,* XL (1929), 305-326.

Bidagor, R., "De dolo et eius effectibus in admissione ad novitiatum et professione religiosa," *Periodica,* XX (1931), 60*-73*.

Bieter, Francis, "The Canon Law on Deceit," *The Ecclesiastical Review,* XLVI (1922), 42-51.

Claeys Bouuaert, F., "De metus influxu," *Jus Pontificium,* VI (1926), 105-111.

Gillet, P., "De actione rescissoria ob dolum (can. 103)," *Jus Pontificium,* IX (1939), 323-324.

Goyeneche, S., "Consultationes," *Commentarium pro Religiosis,* III (1922), 263-272.

———, "Consultationes," *Commentarium pro Religiosis,* IV (1923), 120-122.

———, "Consultationes," *Commentarium pro Religiosis,* VI (1925), 86-92.

———, "Consultationes," *Commentarium pro Religiosis et Missionariis,* XVI (1935), 233-241; 313-320.

———, "Consultationes," *Commentarium pro Religiosis et Missionariis,* XXII (1941), 78-82.

Huonder, A., "Oblati-Oblatae," *Kirchenlexikon,* IX, 619-626.

Jombart, E., "De ingressu ex metu," *Periodica,* XII (1923), (55)-(56).

———, "Des Délits et des Peines," *Traité de Droit Canonique publié sous la direction de Raoul Naz,* 4 voll., Vol. IV, Parisiis: Letouzey et Ané, 1948.

Larraona, A., "Commentarium Codicis," *Commentarium pro Religiosis,* IV (1923), 39-46.

———, "Commentarium Codicis," *Commentarium pro Religiosis,* XV (1934), 359-367.

———, "Commentarium Codicis," *Commentarium pro Religiosis et Missionariis,* XVII (1936), 8-19.

———, "Commentarium Codicis," *Commentarium pro Religiosis et Missionariis,* XVIII (1937), 227-237.

———, "Commentarium Codicis," *Commentarium pro Religiosis et Missionariis,* XXII (1941), 119-126.

———, "Consultationes," *Commentarium pro Religiosis,* I (1920), 365-374.

Leclercq, "Oblat," *Dictionnaire d'Archéologie Chrétienne et de Liturgie,* XII, 1857-1877.

Lefebvre, Ch., "Dol en droit canonique actuel," *Dictionnaire de Droit Canonique,* IV, coll. 1347-1357.

Lemosse, Max., "Dolus (Evolution historique de la theorie du)," *Dictionnaire de Droit Canonique,* IV, coll. 1357-1372.

Oesterle, Gerardus, "De relatione inter metum gravem et invaliditatem novitiatus et professionis," *Commentarium pro Religiosis,* XV (1934), 386-411.

Peinador, Antonius, "De ingressu in statum religiosum, iure naturali invalido," *Commentarium pro Religiosis,* XV (1934), 142-151, 281-290; *Commentarium pro Religiosis et Missionariis,* XVI (1935), 388-395; 444-452.

Roberti, F., "De actione rescissoria ob dolum," *Apollinaris,* III (1930), 143-145.

———, "De metu indirecto quoad negotia iuridica praesertim matrimonium," *Apollinaris,* XI (1938), 557-561.

———, "De s. ordinatione ex metu suscepta et de poenis in eos qui quoque modo coegerint (concordia canonum 214, § 1 et 2352)," *Apollinaris,* I (1928), 48-52.

Salsmans, J., "Circa vitia consensus," *Jus Pontificium,* X (1930), 104-108.

Vermeersch, A., "Annotationes," *Periodica,* XI (1922), 28-31.

———, "Canon 542, 2°, et dispensatio ab irregularitate," *Periodica,* XX (1931), 136*-137*.

———, "De metu qui, saltem ex lege positiva, excusat ab obligationibus vitiato consensu susceptis, praecipue de metu ab intrinseco vel extrinseco," *Periodica,* XVII (1928), 141*-143*.

Wyszynski, M., "Utrum metus indirecte incussus dirimere possit matrimonium," *Jus Pontificium,* X (1930), 193-200; XI (1931), 42-51; XII (1932), 43-52; XIII (1935), 52-63.

Periodicals

Apollinaris, Romae, 1928-

Commentarium pro Religiosis, Romae, 1920-1934; ab anno 1935: *Commentarium pro Religiosis et Missionariis.*

Ecclesiastical Review, The (originally *The American Ecclesiastical Review,* Philadelphia, 1889-1943), Washington, D. C., 1944-

Il Diritto Ecclesiastico, Romae, 1890-

Jurist, The, Washington, D. C., 1941-

Jus Pontificium, Romae, 1921-1940.

Periodica de Religiosis et Missionariis, 8 voll., Brugis, 1905-1919 (Vol. I: 1905, 2. ed., 1911; II et III: 1907, 2. ed., 1911; IV: 1909, 2. ed., 1913; V: 1911, 2. ed., 1913; VI: 1912; VII: 1912-1914; VIII: 1919); ab anno 1920: *Periodica de Re Canonica et Morali utilia praesertim Religiosis et Missionariis,* 7 voll., Brugis, 1920-1927 (Vol. IX: 1920; X et XI: 1922-1923; XII: 1923-1924; XIII: 1924-1925; XIV: 1925-1926; XV: 1926-1927); ab anno 1927: *Periodica et Re Morali, Canonica, Liturgica,* Brugis (1927-1936) et Romae (1937-), Vol. XVI, 1927-

ABBREVIATIONS

AAS—Acta Apostolicae Sedis.
Bruns—*Canones Apostolorum et Conciliorum IV-VII.*
CpR—Commentarium pro Religiosis.
CpRM—Commentarium pro Religiosis et Missionariis.
DDC—Dictionnaire de Droit Canonique.
ER—Ecclesiastical Review, The.
Fontes—Codicis Iuris Canonici Fontes, cura . . . Gaspari editi.
Jaffé—*Regesta Pontificium Romanorum,* etc.
Mansi—*Sacrorum Conciliorum Nova et Amplissima Collectio.*
MGH—Monumenta Germaniae Historica.
MPG—Migne, *Patrologia, Series Graeca.*
MPL—Migne, *Patrologia, Series Latina.*
Periodica—Periodica de Re Canonica et Morali utilia praesertim Religiosis et Missionariis.
Potthast—*Regesta Pontificum Romanorum,* etc.
S. C. C.—Sacra Congregatio Concilii.
S. C. de Pròp. Fide—Sacra Congregatio de Propaganda Fide.
S. C. de Rel.—Sacra Congregatio de Religiosis.

BIOGRAPHICAL NOTE

James Victor Brown, O.R.S.A., was born on June 8, 1921, in Snyder, Nebraska. After completing his elementary education at St. Leo's Parochial School, he attended Snyder Public High School, from which he was graduated in May, 1938. In the fall of the same year he entered the novitiate of the Order of the Recollects of Saint Augustine in Kansas City, Kansas, where he made his religious profession on September 9, 1939. After the completion of his philosophical and theological courses at St. Augustine's Mission Seminary, Kansas City, Kansas, he was ordained to the priesthood at Saint Benedict's Abbey, Atchison, Kansas, on May 25, 1946. Following his ordination, he for one year attended Rockhurst College, Kansas City, Missouri, where he had been enrolled in the summer sessions during his seminary career. In September, 1947, he entered the School of Canon Law at the Catholic University of America, and received the degree of Bachelor in Canon Law in June, 1948, and the degree of Licentiate in Canon Law in June, 1949.

ALPHABETICAL INDEX

CANON LAW STUDIES*

306. WATERS, REV. JOSEPH L., S.S.J., J.C.L., The Probation in Societies of Quasi-Religious.
307. REGAN, REV. MICHAEL J., J.C.L., Canon 16.
308. BYRNE, REV. HARRY J., J.C.L., Investment of Church Funds.
309. GALLAGHER, REV. THOMAS V., J.C.L., The Rejection of Judicial Witnesses and Testimony.
310. CHATHAM, REV. JOSIAH G., Ph.D., S.T.L., J.C.L., Force and Fear as Invalidating Marriage: The Element of Injustice.
311. BROWN, REV. JAMES VICTOR, O.R.S.A., J.C.L., The Invalidating Effects of Force, Fear, and Fraud upon the Canonical Novitiate.
312. DUERR, REV. CHARLES J., B.A., J.C.L., The Judicial Notary.
313. GONZALEZ, REV. FRANCISCO J., O.S.A., J.C.L., De Parocho Religioso Eiusque Superiore Locali.
314. HANNON, REV. JAMES J., J.C.L., Holy Viaticum.
315. SADLOWSKI, REV. ERWIN L., J.C.L., The Sacred Furnishings of Churches.
316. SEGO, REV. ARTHUR A., J.C.L., Dispensation from the Interpellations.
317. WATERHOUSE, REV. JOHN M., J.C.L., The Power of the Local Ordinary to Impose a Matrimonial Ban.
318. FREIN, REV. EUGENE B., J.C.L., The Discretionary Power of the Defender of the Matrimonial Bond.
319. CARTON, REV. GEORGE A., J.C.L., The Time Factor in the Gaining of Indulgences.
320. WALSH, REV. JOHN J., C.C.Sp., J.C.L., The Jurisdiction of the Interritual Confessor in the United States and Canada.
321. UNTERKOEFLER, REV. ERNST L., S.T.L., J.C.L., The Presiding Judge in Matrimonial Causes of First Instance.

---

*A complete list of the available numbers in the series will be found in earlier studies. Send orders to The Catholic University of America Press, 620 Michigan Avenue, N.E., Washington 17, D. C.

www.ingramcontent.com/pod-product-compliance
Lightning Source LLC
LaVergne TN
LVHW050249080826
844660LV00012B/614

* 9 7 8 0 8 1 3 2 2 4 8 6 2 *